Muslims in the Margin: Political Responses to the Presence of Islam in Western Europe

W.A.R. SHADID AND
P.S. VAN KONINGSVELD (EDS.)

MUSLIMS IN THE MARGIN: POLITICAL RESPONSES TO THE PRESENCE OF ISLAM IN WESTERN EUROPE

KOK PHAROS PUBLISHING HOUSE

CIP-Gegevens Koninklijke Bibliotheek, Den Haag

© 1996, Kok Pharos Publishing House,
Kampen, the Netherlands
Cover Design by Rob Lucas
ISBN 90 390 0520 6
NUGI 651/631

Contents

Preface

This book is the first of two volumes in which the edited version is published of the proceedings of the congress on Islam, Hinduism, and Politics in Western Europe held in Leiden from the 7th through the 9th of September, 1995, under the auspices of the Dutch Organisation for Scientific Research (N.W.O.). This congress marked the completion of the national research-project "Religion of Ethnic Groups in the Netherlands" sponsored by the Foundation for Research in Philosophy and Theology (S.F.T.), in which scholars and research-assistants from the Free University of Amsterdam, the Catholic University of Nijmegen, and Leiden University have participated. The aim of this concluding conference was to create a platform for Dutch researchers to communicate directly with their colleagues active in the same field of research from other Western European countries.

The contributions of the conference have been divided into two volumes, each dealing with distinct issues. In the present volume, *Muslims in the Margin: Political Responses to the Presence of Islam in Western Europe*, the subject is treated from the perspective of the countries of immigration at large. The second volume will more specifically stress the perspective of the Muslims vis-à-vis their new societies.

Apart from an introductory chapter, the present book contains fourteen contributions by specialists from various European countries (Belgium, Denmark, France, Germany, Italy, the Netherlands, Spain, Switzerland, and the United Kingdom) in which the following issues are examined: the political impact of dominant representations of Islam, views on Islam of Western European political parties, and negotiations between Muslims and governments on national and local levels. A general bibliography is provided, in which the materials pertaining to the individual contributions have been integrated.

Leiden, January 15, 1996
W.A.R. Shadid and P.S. van Koningsveld

Politics and Islam in Western Europe:

An Introduction

Wasif Shadid & Sjoerd van Koningsveld

Since the fifties of the present century there has been a significant increase of inhabitants with an Islamic background in the countries of the European Community. Their number is estimated at this moment between 7 and 10 million. Their juridical status, which is influenced by a great number of national and international political factors, varies from citizenship of a European member state to that of foreigners. Concerning the right of foreigners to participate politically in one way or another, many discussions have taken place, both at the European and national levels. In Sweden and the Netherlands, for example, foreigners have been given the right to participate, both actively and passively, in local elections. Those who possess the citizenship of a European member state, on the other hand, are, of course, already fully entitled to participate politically. They indeed do participate, to some extent and in various manners, in European political life.

The involvement of minorities in politics has been the subject of a considerable number of studies. However, these studies are rarely concerned with the political role in Western Europe, of both Islam as a mobilising factor, and the Muslims as a religious group comparable with other confessional groups creating political parties.

As the result of these developments an increase in political organization and participation, both from the side of individual persons with an Islamic background and of Islamic organizations, can be observed within the European scene. In some countries initiatives have been taken to create Islamic political parties, while in these and many other countries the established political parties often nominate members with an Islamic background among their candidates. Furthermore, many discussions have taken place about the feasibility of the integration of Islam within the European social and political systems. Cabinet ministers, established political parties and their representatives, in reaction to national and international events, have developed views about the nature of Islam, which are being crystallized in the policies of the national governments. Central issues in these discussions are, for instance, the compatibility of Islam and parliamentary democracy and human rights, the fear of religious fundamentalism and fanaticism, as well as the oppression of women by Islam.

At the occasion of many national events involving Islam in one way or another, governments or Islamic organizations have attempted to initiate a dialogue. The same holds true for the implication of various aspects of national and local policies with regard to social and juridical space available for the observance of Islamic religious prescriptions. Examples of such attempted contacts concerned the founding of mosques and Islamic cemeteries, the observance of Islamic dressing and dietary rules, as well as the subsidizing of religious education and Islamic schools. In most countries, however, Muslims have not succeeded in creating a representative platform which can, with authority, negotiate with the government bodies concerned.

Nevertheless, one observes at the same time a growing number of political measures affecting Islamic religious life. These measures are usually based on consultations with certain diplomatic bodies, groups, or experts, who have not been invested formally with any representative quality from the side of Muslims or their organizations. Exceptions notwithstanding, little attention has thus far been paid to the processes of consultation and negotiation between governments and Muslims, as they do actually take place. Knowledge of these processes, however, is a necessary prerequisite in order to understand the tendencies of the official policies of these various government bodies.

Representations of Islam

The representation of Islam is a factor of great political and social significance, as is born out by all contributions to the present volume. It influences, among others, the analysis of the causes responsible for the prevailing position of deprivation of Muslim minorities in Europe. It also lies at the root of identifying ways to overcome the present antagonism between majorities and minorities. In his contribution *Ballard* discusses three options to resolve what he calls the intensifying process of polarization in which we are currently enmeshed. First of all he is of the opinion that any attempt to resolve the problem by further excluding Muslims is doomed to failure, since such policies actually constitute an open invitation to minority communities to close ranks to reinforce their distinctiveness.

The second option which Ballard discusses is that, if European Muslims would adopt less alien modes of behaviour, they would encounter much less hostility and much greater acceptance. However, the Islamic tradition as a whole is much less aggressive and, above all, far more intellectually sophisticated than most Europeans have ever been able to acknowledge. Therefore, the suggestion that Muslims can earn greater respect by acting in a less challenging way wholly misses the point. Current Muslim aggressiveness is best understood as a strategic vehicle which is currently being deployed as a means of challenging exclusion and devaluation.

The third option offers the suggestion that Europeans should make a much greater effort to inform themselves about Islam. Yet, even though Ballard regards such a commitment as welcome, he believes that even if it were implemented there is still good reason to doubt that the availability of more accurate information about Islam would have any significant impact in its own right on current attitudes. After all, Europe has had the Islamic world as its neighbour for more than a millennium, but it has never succeeded either to acknowledge it as an equal, or to take its cultural or religious traditions seriously.

In conclusion, Ballard is of the opinion that the most urgent priority for Europe is to acquire a better understanding of itself and its own history.

The same issue of the representation of Islam is discussed for France, from a more practical angle, by *Wihtol de Wenden*. She draws attention to the prevailing negative image of Islam as a religion of colonised, of poor people, of obscurantism, unable to adapt itself to French values. Although the new generation of young Muslims in France convey a different image of Islam, using it as an instrument of communitarist expression, the public opinion associates these new forms of identitary expression almost exclusively with integrism and political terrorism. She discusses the problem of the interpretation of the Islamic revival among the younger generation in France. Is it only a matter of identitary development, related to specific age-groups (especially adolescents), or is it caused by more far-reaching factors in the social and political sphere? In the first case, it may regarded as a temporary issue of minor importance only. In the second case, however, it may be interpreted as a sign expressing the desire for a separate social and juridical status for French Muslims in the future. Such a communitarist development would contradict the French model of secularism, which is based on the equality of all citizens, regardless of their religious preference.

In his contribution, *Herbert* adds another dimension to the problem of the representation of minorities, focusing his attention on the image given to them in British research. In the research which Herbert examines, the concepts of race and ethnicity occupy a dominant place. In particular, it is assumed that colour is the principal determinant of discrimination to the extent that other factors, for instance, religion, which is disregarded a priori, can be neglected. A second feature of these research results, criticized by the author, is that most emphasis is placed on the oppression of the minority by the majority, thus leaving possible responses of the minority groups undiscussed. The result is that, when the possibility to explain discrimination on the basis of colour is absent, the discrimination is blamed on an ascribed poverty of the minority cultures. In contra-distinction to this prevailing representation, Herbert pleads for more attention to the differential nature of discrimination, which may imply that Muslims are also discriminated against as a group on the basis of their religion, which is deemed by some to be in contradiction with the basic values of British society. The methods followed in the various studies scrutinized by the author do not permit this type of differentiality to be identified.

Political views on the position of Islam

Concerning the political response to the presence of Muslims in Spain, *Abumalham* distinguishes the so-called 'major' and 'minor' policies. Under the major policy she includes the attention political parties pay in their electoral programs to immigration and immigrants, the implementation of specific legislation, the administrative difficulties which the implementation brings about, and the European communitarian policy concerning immigration. In this regard she asserts that the State government has invested a great deal of attention in the issue by developing a whole legal corpus concerning the position of immigrants in Spain. Regarding the implementation of the established legal texts Abumalham points out three obstacles: (1) the existence of a clear interference between the competencies of the concerned ministries; (2) a clash between the regulations of the European Community and the Spanish reality; and (3) instead of resolving existing problems, the creation of new problems which are caused by the complexity of the norms regulating the acquisition of permits and other rights.

The 'minor policy', on the other hand, includes the activities or responses of local and regional administrations who manage matters such as education, health, and housing. Abumalham states that the ideology of the political parties affects the performance of the minor policy. In this regard left-wing parties seem to pay greater attention to advocate a clear option as regards integration and inter-culturality. However, the conservative national parties on the regional level stress the same matters, and their social programs are more progressive than those developed by the state-lead socialist party. Abumalham states that this interest is mainly caused by the search of these Spanish communities for their national identity, the defense of their own language (Catalan, Basque, Galician), and the claiming of their particular idiosyncrasy.

A more or less comparable difference in the responses of left-wing and right-wing political parties to the presence of Muslims in the Netherlands is also emphasized by *Shadid and Van Koningsveld*. The authors show that the views of political parties in the Netherlands on the multicultural society are more diverse and vary considerably in relation to three issues: immigration, socio-economic emancipation, and the preservation of cultural identity. In this regard they discern the perspectives of rejection, discouragement, as well as selective, corporate, and liberal pluralism.

As to immigration and remigration, a continuum can be drawn which varies from 'the country is full', on the one hand, to 'the country is not full', on the other, as defended by the rejectionists and liberal pluralists respectively. In between, one can find those who stress that the Nether-

6 *Wasif Shadid & Sjoerd van Koningsveld*

lands 'is not an immigration country', and those who are of the opinion that de facto it 'became an immigration country' as defended by the discouragers and by supporters of the selective and corporate pluralists, respectively. However, except for the liberal pluralists, each of the distinctive perspectives stresses the importance of reducing immigration to the number stipulated by international treaties and national regulations. In other words, these perspectives do not differ fundamentally, but gradually, on the issue of immigration: immigration to the Netherlands should be restricted, but the manner in which this should be brought about differs.

As regards the desirability of pluralism and the outcome of cultural contact, there exists hardly any difference between the various perspectives. Except for the corporative pluralists who prefer a cultural mosaic, they factually strive towards a monocultural society model.

A similar consensus can also be found concerning their ideas on improving the weak socio-economic position of minorities. It is interesting to mention that, except for the liberal pluralists, all other perspectives have elements of 'blaming the victim', in which the causes of the situation are essentially explained from within the groups themselves, i.e., by their culture and by their lack of conditions necessary for their emancipation, such as insufficient education and schooling. Only the liberal pluralists 'blame the system' and stress that deprivation is mainly due to direct and indirect forms of discrimination against the groups concerned.

In regard to the emancipation of immigrants in the Netherlands *Gowricharn and Mungra* discuss the integration through the historical phenomenon of pillarization, and through markets. They conclude that, although the immigrant communities are loosely organized and do not exhibit all features of the traditional pillar system, there are tendencies towards forms of an 'immigrant's pillar'. In this connection they refer to the numerous companies, mosques and temples, sport organizations, and schools and to the inroad which they made to political parties, the media, and trade unions. Furthermore, they are of the opinion that the pillar-model of integration does not contradict the desire of the Dutch government to integrate immigrants through markets. On the contrary, due to the expansion of the 'immigrant-pillar' the number of jobs increases. Therefore, they expect that the encouragement of pillarization will expand the labour market and improve the position of immigrants.

Negotiations between Muslims and Governments

It is widely recognised that the integration of Islam within the social, political, and cultural contexts of Western European states and societies cannot be brought about satisfactorily without democratic processes of negotiation between the government authorities at various levels, on the one hand, and recognized representative bodies of Islam, on the other hand. However, both the prevailing legal traditions and the dominant political convictions concerning the contents and goals of these negotiations differ widely from one country to another, and even between different municipalities or different social sectors within one country. The same holds true for the conditions to be fulfilled by bodies that can be accepted as a negotiating partner on behalf of Islam on the basis of its representativity. Various aspects of the complexities of these processes of negotiation are illustrated by contributions to this volume.

First of all, at the European level the primordial question may be posed whether Islam should be integrated within the secular context of the western nation-states on the basis of its recognition as a religious community with its own legal statute. Should some form of communitarianism be adopted, including the eventual recognition of (some aspects of) Islamic personal law, or should integration take place on the basis of the acquisition of European citizenship, including the effect of secular civil law? In his contribution, *Tibi* discusses the possible relevance of the situation in India, where Muslims, within an officially secular context, enjoy recognition as a community in the legal sense, including the right of application of Islamic family law. He draws attention to the negative influence this system is exercising on the rise of Hindu anti-Islamic fundamentalism and warns against the risks of applying it within the Western context. According to him, this might ultimately lead to the creation of Muslim ghettos and to the further growth of anti-Islamic xenophobia. He therefore argues for political integration on the basis of European citizenship, which should be distinguished from assimilation in the cultural and religious sense.

In discussing the vicissitudes of Muslims in Switzerland, *Waarden-burg*, on the other hand, stresses the positive influence that may be exercised on the integration-process by the creation of Muslim associations that are addressing Swiss society by appealing explicitly to two of its prominent values: the right to be different and the right to cultural autonomy. In doing so he follows the sociological distinction between the Islamic institutions created during the first phase of the provisional presence of immigrants, on the one hand, and those which spring up during a second phase, viz. when the immigrants are becoming aware of the long-term nature of their settlement in the new host-country on the other. The former are described as passive, traditional, and conservative in their aim not to lose the cultural and religious background of their countries of origin. The latter are characterised by an active self-awareness, directing themselves to the society of which they are a part, with cultural demands using an Islamic discourse. This Islamic discourse obtains an ideological dimension by offering a theoretical explanation of the difference between minority and majority. Western observers may have great difficulty in appreciating this discourse. Nevertheless, Waardenburg stresses, it helps these immigrants to identify themselves as Muslim and fosters a new kind of communal togetherness. Through this discourse, Muslim associations look for an interaction with society and with the authorities in order to obtain a legitimate and recognized place. According to the author, this also presupposes a certain degree of integration and may strengthen integration further. From this perspective, Muslim associations of the new type may be seen as agents of integration and emancipation. However, notwithstanding this great value attached to Islamic associations and communities, Waardenburg also stresses that the emancipation of Muslims in Europe is basically a social and political issue requiring the acquisition of full political, economic, and social rights. Negotiations between Muslim associations and other interested parties should take place on a democratic basis; these should be pursued pragmatically, with an open attitude to requests that are justifiable and without ideological hang ups. In the long term, everyone concerned will be called to engage in a common struggle, step by step and without utopian blueprints, against current forms of injustice which Muslims and non-Muslims alike recognize. In this domain, both groups can arrive at common action, political and otherwise through dialogue, furthering much-needed emancipation.

On a less theoretical level, however, one must take into account the practical problems to be overcome by Muslims and governments in order to meet each other at the negotiating table. Perhaps the most illustrative example in this volume of the manifold obstacles to be overcome in order to start a negotiating process at the national level, which aims at translating the possibilities of the law into concrete facilities, is offered by *Leman and Renaerts*. In their contribution they offer a detailed historical survey of twenty years of dialogues at different institutional levels between authorities and Muslims in Belgium. Notwithstanding the fact that Islam was officially recognized in 1974 by the Belgian public authorities, many potential facilities, offered by the law, still remain unexploited. This holds true, for instance, for the salaries of imams and for other important forms of financial support granted by the Belgian State to the recognized religious communities. Important factors hampering the acquisition of equal rights by Belgium's Muslims are the influence of foreign governments (sometimes with contradictory political interests), the ethnical, theological and political division of the Muslims, and the anti-Islamic xenophobia spread by several political circles. The concrete data provided for Belgium tend to mitigate or relativate the feasibility of the creation of one "Islamic community" in the countries of Western Europe, let alone the role attributed to a system of Islamic communitarianism within the Western secular context.

Given that Islamic religion instruction began to be given in official education immediately after the recognition of the Islamic religion, the debate on the representativity of the Islamic interlocutors has concerned, above all, competence relating to the appointment of Islamic religious teachers. Attention focused entirely on this question, with the result that other problems (for example, mosques, or the appointment and remuneration of imams) remained somewhat in the shade. On the other hand, the permanent desire to respect the principle of equality with other recognized religions, and the dominant position of the Catholic Church in this context, has had the effect that the debate on the representativity was long reduced to seeking a moral and spiritual authority to represent all Islamic communities, leading to constant dead-ends. The authors state that a pragmatic dialogue has finally been realized in Belgium. It appears that a turning point was reached recently when, in 1994, the idea of entrusting full powers to a spiritual authority was abandoned, and a more pragmatic

formula was adopted, which consisted of uniting around a table representatives of Islamic tendencies who did not claim to be spiritual leaders, but
simply acceptable, credible "technicians" who wished to ensure fulfilment
by the Belgian authorities of a number of consequences and implications
arising from the recognition of the Islamic religion. Furthermore, they
state that the pragmatization of relationships between the Belgian authorities and Islamic communities, as well as the presence of political leaders
of Islamic origin in the various traditional parties in Belgium should
normally mark a turning point constituting a counter-balance to the
permanent interest of certain embassies and great foreign mosques of
Islamic fundamentalist leanings in all the affairs of the Belgian Islamic
community.

The rare and recent experiences of Muslims and Government in Italy in
taking steps toward the negotiating table show features very similar to the
Belgian case. In his contribution, *Allievi* provides, first of all, the basic
sociographic data concerning the Muslims and Islamic institutions in Italy,
which so far were available in Italian only. He then pays special attention
to the attempts of Muslims to secure an agreement with the Italian government which will eventually allow more facilities provided by the law to be
exploited for the building up of an Islamic infrastructure. In remarkable
similarity to the process in Belgium -especially during the initial stages of
the process- two groups from the Muslim side are competing with each
other to acquire the recognition of the Italian State as the official interlocutor on behalf of the Muslims: one group, which is attached to the
Islamic Cultural Centre of Italy in Rome, is dominated by the official
representatives of Muslim countries of origin, and the other group is the
Union of Communities and Islamic Organizations in Italy, created by
Muslims in Italy themselves. One of the problems which remains to be
solved is that an "agreement" (intesa) between the Italian State and
religious groups has always concerned, at least in the past, Italian citizens
of a different religion, and not foreign nationals, nor, as in the case of the
Islamic Cultural Centre of Italy, even foreign countries. As the process in
Italy is still in its initial stage, Italian state officials and politicians might
want to learn from the longer experiences of several other countries.

Another detailed discussion of the political context of Islam at the
practical level is provided by *Pedersen* for Denmark. The author concen-

trates on the discourse of public authorities and institutions in relation to Islamic religious life, which obviously has wider social implications and significance. He stresses that, due to the specific social processes involved, the issue of religious freedom has, in this perspective, risen to become a question about democracy. This point is further brought into focus by the fact that Muslims who have been in Denmark for 25 years, whether still holding foreign citizenship or having already acquired Danish citizenship, still do not have the same opportunities or access to a well functioning religious infrastructure which the majority of the Danish population have. This is especially obvious for the obtaining of immigration permits for new imams, facilities in relation to the tax system, differences in ascribed authority concerning the registration of births and deaths, as well as the establishment of suitable burial conditions. The author further points to various forms of discrimination of Muslim pupils in public schools (among others as the result of prevailing prejudices about Islam) and the lack of adequate facilities for Islamic religious practice in hospitals, prisons, and the labour market (including the trade unions). In adopting a philosophical terminology, the author concludes that the Danish "system world" provides insufficient space for the special dynamic of an Islamic "life world" which could underpin a social structure for Muslims on an equal footing with non-Muslims in Danish society. In discussing these ideas, the author does not refer to special demands of an Islamic community to acquire a statute differing from society at large, but, on the contrary, to the lack of realization of rights guaranteed by the Danish Constitution to be applicable for all residents, regardless of their religious convictions.

That the question of democracy and equal rights is put at stake in the issue of religious freedom is further illustrated by the comparative study of *Dwyer and Meyer* of the establishment of Islamic schools in the Netherlands, the United Kingdom, and Belgium. Political debates in the three countries about the desirability of Islamic schools reveal identical trends and concepts. Those who are in favour of these schools defend them by stressing that the freedom of education and the principle of equality are at stake. Central to the debates in the three countries is, moreover, the complex question of integration. Opponents have argued that Islamic schools will hinder integration. Supporters of Islamic schools, however, offer a different understanding of the influence of these schools and stress that they might promote integration, especially because of their positive impact on the development of the identity of Muslim pupils. Parallels are often drawn with the experiences of other minority religious groups who have used confessional schools as a means of integration and emancipation. It seems that the main reason for the pioneering position of the Netherlands, with its 29 Islamic schools, as compared to Belgium and the United Kingdom lies in the strong juridical and financial position Christian schools enjoy as a result of intra-Dutch historical developments unrelated to Islam. With regard to Britain, the authors stress the importance of a piece-meal challenging of existing legislation, since Muslims do not have recognised rights within the British state as a religious group. Furthermore, the existence of an established Church is seen as important ideological force which can be evoked in debates about the recognition of minority religious groups within the UK. In Belgium, recognition of Islam made Islamic religious education in state schools possible. The fact that this education has been realised on a large scale seems not only to make the call for Islamic schools less strong than in the UK and the Netherlands, it also influences the political climate. The dominant political view in Belgium is that the religious needs of Muslims are sufficiently met by the Islamic religious education organised in state schools and so the establishment of Islamic schools is 'unnecessary'.

Negotiations between Muslims and Local Governments

In the light of the preceding data concerning negotiations between Muslims and public institutions at national levels, negotiations between Muslims and local governments reveal additional complicating factors hampering the emancipation of Muslims which are specific for local and regional politics.

In their contribution on the reaction between local authorities and Islamic organizations, *Rath and Feirabend* draw a comparison between two major Dutch cities. They explain that a wide range of Islamic institutions has been established, prompting intervention by the state and others to regulate the space for such institutions. At the same time, however, they stress that the process of making space for Islam is not self-evident.

Although the state has to conform to the prevailing laws and regulations, thereby applying the constitutional principle of equality, the legal framework does not necessarily determine the outcome: the law is not always strict and clear, but can be abstract, broad, or ambiguous, while the purpose behind such rules may not be sufficiently clear. Furthermore, due to the national policy of decentralization, local authorities can have a greater say in the implementation of general rules. This leaves room for political and ideological struggle. Civil servants and politicians involved in practical politics can then use their discretionary powers to 'colour' their decisions.

This explains why the processes of making space for Islam in local politics in the cities of Rotterdam and Utrecht have such different outcomes. The local authorities of Rotterdam have encouraged and supported the inclusion of Islamic associations in politics, while the authorities of Utrecht have adopted a more exclusionary attitude. Initially, the local authorities of Rotterdam and Utrecht did share a similar ideological representation of Islam and its adherents. This representation revolves around negatively evaluated notions of Islamic collectivism and traditional leadership, and around fears regarding the interference of foreign powers, the absence of democracy, the influence of political extremism, and the undermining of the separation of Church and State. The provision of space for Islamic associations in Rotterdam was a political action coupled with changes in the ideological domain in the sense that characteristics associated with Islam were gradually put aside, and that socio- or ethno-cultural characteristics of immigrants came to the fore. The principle of equality was now applied to immigrant ethnic minority groups rather than to religious groups, and was placed within the political framework of the local ethnic minorities policy which aimed at the integration and upward social mobility of immigrant ethnic minorities. Ever since, Islamic associations have been given the opportunity to participate in local politics, if only as ethnic minority associations, which means that Islamic associations have not been granted a 'natural' position outside the field of the ethnic minority policy.

In his comparative study of three small Dutch cities, *Beck* concludes, first of all, that due to the lack of fixed standards of judgement, minority policy, like many other aspects of local politics, is based on the personal preference of the alderman involved. This holds even true in the case of the existence of a municipal advisory committee that deals with minorities affairs. Secondly, local policy makers appeared unaware, or did not wish to be aware, of the importance and function of Islam in the day-to-day life of a great number in the Netherlands, nor did they seem to be cognizant of the role of religion in its emancipating effect on social and cultural aspects of identity and self-image. In the third place, Beck concludes that requests of subsidies for stimulating religious activities were only complied on the basis of their social-cultural nature. Nevertheless, in some cases, where municipal authorities were willing to assist religious organizations in building up their infrastructure, the existing internal division between competing groups proved to hinder these initiatives.

1

Islam and the Construction
of Europe

Roger Ballard

Just where and what is Europe? And what are the consequences of that construction? It should come as no surprise that such questions are rarely asked. Although the assumption that Europe is a clearly demarcated geographical space, and that its inhabitants (together with their large global diaspora) share a wide range of social, cultural and biological characteristics which mark them off from non-Europeans is a routine — and possibly a defining — feature the contemporary world, Europeans are by no means exceptional in taking the basic parameters of their conceptual order almost wholly for granted. Yet just who *are* Europeans? What makes them such? Why are the boundaries of Europe, and hence of Europeanness, located where they are? In what ways do Europeans differ from non-Europeans? Just how and why did this disjunction, whatever its foundations, gain its current salience?

Once broached, the importance and significance of these questions is self-apparent. To address them we must begin by exploring the issues empirically, in order to establish just where the borders of Europe and Europeanness are located, and how they are conceptualised by those involved. But this exercise also leads directly on to a second, for if these borders are socially constructed rather than self-evident facts of nature — as is invariably the case with man-made boundaries — we are also faced with a further set of questions: just *why* has Europe been so constructed, and what are its consequences?

Where and what is Europe?

The physical boundaries of Europe as conventionally understood are relatively easy to identify: like millions of other schoolchildren, I learnt from my geography teacher that Europe is the landmass lying to the north of the Mediterranean, the Black Sea, the mountains of the Caucasus and the Caspian, and although the precise location of the disjunction between Europe and Asia was a little uncertain, this could be resolved by drawing a line from the Arctic ocean down through the Ural mountains to the Caspian. So that was that: we had been provided, or so we thought, with an unambiguous definition of Europe's spatial character.

Yet our conceptualization of Europe involved much more than an ability to mark off and label the northwestern corner of the much larger Afro-Asiatic landmass. In common, I suspect, with millions of others, we also took it for granted that the indigenous inhabitants of this area (a group to which I and my classfellows manifestly belonged) also shared certain common characteristics, and on the basis of which Europeans could therefore be differentiated from non-Europeans. But just what were those characteristics? As I recall, our teachers offered us a much less specific account of Europe's social identity, but even so our lessons, further supplemented by what we learned from films, comics, adventure stories and so forth provided us with plentiful material from which to draw our own conclusions. Hence despite the very obvious differences between Europe's various national components, we took it for granted that all Europeans shared, by definition, a number of common cultural characteristics — even if we would have been hard-pressed to specify just what these were. We also took if for granted that although North America and Australia might be far removed from Europe in spatial terms, those parts of their population which were of European descent were 'like us'. As such they stood in sharp contrast to the indigenous peoples of these colonised territories, and indeed to the indigenous inhabitants of Asia and Africa, whom we perceived as standing quite outside — and indeed as being alien to — the European civilization to which we ourselves belonged. To be sure we might often have been most unclear about the actual content of these differences, but our education and socialization nevertheless generated a mindset which indicated that the disjunction between Europeans and non-Europeans was both profound and far reaching.

Nor was this perception restricted solely to the cultural sphere. European languages such as French, German, Russian, Spanish, Italian were those which we might expect to learn as a normal part of our education — even if our very English agenda led us to make little more than a feeble effort to do so, on the grounds that it was more reasonable to expect for 'foreigners' to learn English than for us to learn another language. But there were foreigners and foreigners. Beyond the immediate arena of at least potentially learnable European languages lay a wide variety of much more exotic tongues, such as Arabic, Chinese, Hindi and Turkish, and to which only the most serious academic scholars could ever hope to gain access.[1]

Over and above all this there is also the question of biological difference — or at least of differences in physical appearance. Although I cannot recall being offered an explicitly biological explanation of European distinctiveness during the course of my schooling, it is not without significance that I and my contemporaries grew up in the post-holocaust era. If for no other reason our experience was almost certainly very different from that of our predecessors, given that biological understandings of 'race' and racial difference were a routine component of the intellectual and educational environment throughout the first half of the twentieth century. But even if the post-holocaust generation of Europeans was not formally exposed to biological theories of human difference, I am very conscious that it was only when I took an undergraduate course in Physical Anthropology that I was explicitly introduced to the scientific evidence and arguments with which to demonstrate the falsity of such a perspective.

However very few undergraduates attended such courses, then or now. Instead the educational system's preferred approach to the issue was (and is) simply to exclude biological theories of 'race' from the intellectual agenda. Such a strategy can easily be shown to be grossly inadequate, for in the absence of an explicit challenge to popular ideas, expectations and perceptions, they can only be expected to persist — and certainly did so in our case. Hence even if our formal education offered no explicit support for such perceptions, we nevertheless took it for granted that 'European' was amongst other things a *biological* category, such that all Europeans shared a distinctive biological heritage. Once again we would have been hard-pressed to identify just what these differences were, except in one sphere: skin colour and physical appearance. Europeans, we took it for granted, were 'white', such that all non-Europeans could be expected to have a significantly darker skin colour than our own.

While the arguments above reflect my own experience of primary and grammar schooling in southern England in the immediate post-war period, and although perceptions and experiences will inevitably vary a good deal by age, class and social context, I suspect that the mind-set into which I and my peers were socialised were far from unique. Although local variations are bound to exist, I nevertheless suspect that such perceptions and self-identifications are characteristic not just of an English experience such as my own, but are also shared across the length and breadth of Europe. If so it becomes even more important to explore how and why such ideas came into existence, why they are so structured, how and why they have been perpetuated, and most significantly of all, what purpose their existence serves.

The arbitrary character of the European construct

One of the most important obstacles to an exploration of the genesis of taken for granted constructs is that the ideas and differentiations in which they are grounded appear to be so obvious and inevitable that their arbitrary foundations are comprehensively obscured. Hence at the risk of stating the obvious, it is worth setting out the evidence that Europe's conventional boundaries have indeed been arbitrarily constructed — at least in the sense that it would be perfectly possible to erect alternative disjunctions by utilising a differing combination of linguistic, cultural, geographical and biological criteria.

While the identification of the huge promontory lying to the north of the western Mediterranean and the Black Sea as a distinctive territorial unit — whether we label it Europe or West Asia is immaterial — might seem at first sight to be a sensible act of classificatory geography, a moment's reflection reveals that there is no reason why this physical space should of necessity be of any great social, political or economic importance. To our contemporary imagination the Mediterranean appears to be an obvious setter-apart of differing worlds, but it was not always so: until a few centuries ago an inland sea offered a relatively safe and certainly much speedier means of travel and transportation than did the land, and few other civilizations were more united-by-sea than that which grew up around the Mediterranean. And while road, rail and air transport may recently have undermined the long-standing superiority of maritime communication, it is striking that although the straits of Gibraltar and the Bosphorous now mark an exceptionally wide conceptual gulf, the straits of Dover and Denmark — although physically wider — mark much less significant conceptual disjunctions.

Why should this be so? Why should the boundaries of what we identify as Europe lie where they do and be so strongly marked? One possibility is that the intrinsic biological characteristics of the residents of this territory are sufficiently distinctive to support this disjunction as a fact of nature. Certainly most Europeans assume that this is so, and in crude terms one can see why they should hold this belief: on the mean, the indigenous inhabitants of the West Asian peninsula have markedly paler skin colouration than that found amongst the remainder of the species. Moreover this excessive paleness does have clear biological foundations. As a result of generations of selective adaptation the level of melanin found in the skins of the indigenous population of the northwesterly corner of the Euro/Afro/Asian landmass *is* significantly lower than the mean for *homo sapiens* as a whole. Moreover this genetic deficiency can be relatively straightforwardly explained as an adaptive response to the limited UV exposure experienced during generations of residence in a cool, cloudy, and relatively northerly territory by a population with a largely vegetarian diet containing low levels of vitamin D (Loomis, 1967). Yet although population genetics does at least partially affirm the notion of European distinctiveness, what it most emphatically does not confirm is the popular assumption that Europeans can be unhesitatingly identified as a clearly demarcated population in biological terms. Quite the contrary. Population genetics leads to quite the opposite conclusion, for what it reveals is not clear-cut categorical boundaries but rather multiple clinal variations in gene frequencies, few of which are congruent with each other. Hence even if one of the few distinctive genetic features of Europe's population arises from their local adaptation to UV deficiency, the clinal character of this genetic trait means that it is no way restricted to a clearly bounded population. Hence for a human geneticist it comes as no surprise that the skin colour differential between populations living on either side of the straits of Gibraltar or the Dardanelles is virtually non-existent. In other words population genetics offers no explanation for the conventional location of Europe's boundaries, or indeed for the erection of any other categorical (and hence 'racial') boundaries within the species *homo sapiens* (Cavalli-Sforza, 1995).

Yet if the biological basis of European distinctiveness is a myth (albeit as a classic example of a charter for an institution in the Malinowskian sense) the claim may well turn out be more soundly grounded in social, cultural and linguistic terms, not least because a belief that such commonalities do indeed exist is no less central to the myth of Europe than is the claim to a common biological heritage. However close examination demonstrates once again that this expectation has relatively little substance. Firstly Europe exhibits a high degree of internal social, cultural and linguistic variation — as for example, between Scotland and Greece, or between Russia and Spain. Secondly when it comes to marking off its boundaries, we encounter just the same phenomena as we did with the genetic arguments: despite a strong conceptual commitment to the presence of radical cultural disjunctions between Greeks and Turks, Spaniards and Moroccans, and Georgians and Azeris, close examination soon reveals that the continuities — especially in terms of popular traditions of music, poetry, cuisine and dress — across these so-called boundaries are far more extensive than chauvinist defenders of deep-rooted difference are normally willing to admit.

Europe, Christianity and Islam

How, then, is the manifest vigour and stability of the idea of Europe to be explained? My own view is that the one possibility that I have overlooked so far — that Europe's distinctiveness is best understood in *religious* terms, on the grounds that its contemporary boundaries are largely congruent with the disjunction between Christianity and Islam — deserves the closest possible examination. Of course some reservations about this definition still need to be borne in mind. As current developments in Bosnia remind us, Europe's wholly indigenous population also includes communities with a long-standing commitment to Islam; moreover Europe's population now includes some ten million Muslims whose presence derives from post-war labour migration. Likewise it is by no means the case — whatever popular European imagination may assume — that the territories to its south and east are wholly populated by Muslims. Islam may have been politically dominant in the Middle East and North Africa for well over a millennium, but Iraq, Syria, the Lebanon, Palestine and above all Egypt[2] the local population has always contained a small (but often very significant) Christian and Jewish presence. Hence apart from these caveats, there seems little doubt that at least in conceptual terms, if not so emphatically in empirical terms, the variable most closely congruent with Europe's current spatial boundary is a religious one: between popular commitment Christianity on the one hand, and to Islamic political dominance on the other.

This in turn sets the agenda for the remainder of this paper, which is devoted firstly to an exploration of the historical emergence of the idea of Europe, and secondly to an examination of the way in which the conceptual disjunction between Christendom and its inhabitants and their perceived Islamic alter has been developed and utilised over the centuries. I would argue that without an awareness of the history of these developments, it is quite impossible to understand why the boundaries of Europe and Europeannesss should have been erected at their current location, or to appreciate why those boundaries are still defended with such vigour, despite the fact that popular commitment to the more spiritual dimensions of the Christian tradition is in steep decline almost everywhere.[3]

The Crusades and the foundation of the European enterprise

Although it is undoubtedly the case that the idea of Europe has a long history, the way in which it was construed in ancient times shows very little congruence with modern usage;[4] and since one of the most obvious correlates of Europe's boundaries as currently conceptualised is the disjunction between Christendom and Islam, there is good reason to expect that an examination of the dynamics of the initial encounter between proto-Europe and its Islamic counterpart will provide a particularly useful analytical starting point. However in so doing I should emphasise that this is not to suggest that the Crusaders were therefore engaged in a European enterprise in a contemporary sense. Quite the contrary: the Crusaders perceived themselves not as Europeans but as warriors for Christ, and as conducting righteous war against the evil followers of a false prophet who had illegitimately occupied the holy land. Yet despite the apparently distant agenda of these medieval defenders of Christendom, many aspects of the Crusader's enterprise, and most especially of the conceptual vision in terms of which they legitimated their activities, prove to be remarkably congruent with contemporary European images, values and assumptions.

With this in mind I do not intend to pay any attention to the social and political tensions within the Church, or amongst the feudal aristocracy of the Frankish region where the Crusader's extraordinary military adventures were hatched: such a discussion is way beyond the scope of this Chapter. My aim, by contrast, is to explore the *ideas* in terms of which the Crusaders justified their adventure, and also the way in which they conceptualised the disjunction between the values which they saw themselves as fighting for, as opposed to those which they attributed to their enemies — the inhabitants of the territories over which they gained (or at least sought to gain) control.

In carrying out this exercise it soon becomes apparent not only that the Crusaders were remarkably ill-informed about the values and capabilities of their opponents, but also that in some senses this was not at all surprising. It was not just that Islam had become politically dominant in much of the territory formerly controlled by the Byzantine and Persian Empires; by the tenth century C.E. its population was a great deal more prosperous than the proto-European territories to the north and west, whose mean level of education, literacy, and intellectual awareness was also dramatically lower than in these Islamic lands. Yet if the Frankish Crusaders were consequently far less sophisticated than their oriental opponents, there is also a strong sense in which their ignorance was quite deliberate. As Daniel (1975) demonstrates in devastating detail, the intruders made almost no effort to gain a positive understanding of the Islamic world, preferring instead to view their new-found enemies through the highly restrictive prisms of their own limited and inevitably self-justifying understandings.

So just what was the vision of themselves and their opponents which was thus produced? From their own pious standpoint, any deviation from established Christian orthodoxy was by definition a dangerous heresy; but this was a heresy of the severest possible kind, since it went far beyond disputes about the precise relationship of Jesus with the other components of the Christian Godhead which then racked the Church. Islam went much further, for this was a tradition which denied Jesus' messianic status (although not his prophethood) in favour of what assumed to be an alternative Messiah. In the light of the strong tendency towards dualistic thinking embedded within Latin Christianity — and whose roots I shall explore later — it is hardly surprising Muslims soon came to be viewed not just as infidels and idolaters, but also but as a manifestation of the deep-rooted conflict between the forces of goodness and evil. It was on this basis that early medieval Christians convinced themselves that Muslims must be followers of the anti-Christ, and that Islam's central objective was to attempt to undermine the project for human redemption which Jesus Christ had set in train.

Setting the theological arguments aside for a moment, it is not hard to identify mundane reasons why those who joined the Crusades might have found this vision attractive. Over and above the opportunity which it offered to the organisers of the Crusades to persuade their followers that the pursuit of distant injustices — or what could be so perceived — was of far greater importance than finding remedies to more local difficulties, in the eleventh century Islam's very success did indeed seem both perplexing and deeply threatening to many of the inhabitants of this poor and peripheral region. With the rise of Islam, almost all the most important centres of wealth, power and scholarship in the circum-Mediterranean region were incorporated into the new order, and in 732 an Islamic army marched as far north as Poitiers before retreating to consolidate its hold over the Iberian peninsula. From the Crusaders' perspective Islam was not just the epitome of threatening otherness, but appeared to be successfully swallowing the entire known world: it was therefore an ideal target against which to direct unrequited hostility.

Christendom versus Islam

Yet just how was this Islamic other conceptualised? Not surprisingly the Prophet Muhammad himself was a central focus of attention, most particularly by contrast with Jesus of Nazareth. In so doing the Christians would have no truck with the Islamic view of Jesus (as well as all the Jewish prophets) as one of a number of prophetic messengers, to which the revelation vouchsafed to Muhammad revelation was the final seal. Then as now so little interest was taken in the actual content of Islamic theology that this possibility was not just ignored, but actively resisted. Hence instead of being viewed as a participant in the same tradition as Jesus Christ, the Prophet Muhammad (whose name was often deliberately misspelt as Mahound) was routinely perceived as representing its very inverse. Some aspects of that inversion have already been noted, such that Muhammad was viewed as the anti-Christ and the personification of evil. But the trope went much further: Jesus' chasteness was unfavourably contrasted with Muhammad's alleged licentiousness, on the grounds that Muhammad not only married a multiplicity of wives but had also enjoyed an active sex-life; Jesus' avoidance of violence was also unfavourably compared with Muhammad's alleged passion for war, given Muhammad's role as an active and indeed successful military leader; likewise Jesus' simplicity, honesty and straightforwardness was unfavourably compared with Muhammad's alleged deviousness and duplicity, on the grounds that the precise details of the revelations which the Prophet had received from Allah (and which the Christians in any case always dismissed as mere delusions) developed and changed during the course of his career. And if Christianity, and indeed Jesus himself, was the epitome of purity, then this rival tradition was by definition its inverse — evil and impure. Hence Muhammad was not only perceived as a licentious, vicious, violent and duplicitous personification of the evil anti-Christ, but also as comprehensively black.[5]

How best can we analyze these perceptions? While this construction (as well as its many successors) is manifestly profoundly misinformed about the teachings of Islam and its Prophet, to put a great deal of analytical effort into demonstrating its untruth is surely to miss the point. By contrast an exploration of how and why it is that the users of these images were so determined to misguide themselves, and indeed why their successors have continued so to do for the best part of a millennium is far more illuminating. Hence I would argue that instead of highlighting the mistaken character of these images (deeply and insultingly mistaken though they are) they are much better understood as the consequence of boundary construction, and most especially one in which those within the boundary have sought to establish and validate their own (ideal) characteristics by attributing a wholly inverse set of attributes to the alien others who stand immediately outside it. In logical terms this amounts to the use of the formula {*p* is what *not-p* is not}, a procedure which not only serves to underline the arbitrary and above all non-essential basis of most processes of boundary construction, but also to illuminate the underlying structural logic of Crusader's vision of the nature of the disjunction between themselves and their opponents.

Jesus	:	Mahound
Christ	:	Anti-Christ
Chaste	:	Licentious
Subject of violence	:	Initiator of violence
Merciful	:	Vicious
Honest	:	Duplicitous
Inspired	:	Mad
Righteous	:	Sinful
Pure	:	Impure
Light	:	Darkness

If this analysis is sound, it follows that the ascription of such a catalogue of inadequacy to Islam and its Prophet was of immense convenience to the Crusaders since it allowed them to comprehensively differentiate themselves from their opponents whilst also underlining the inherent justice of their cause. It also follows that such constructions reveal nothing of value about the real character of the *alter* from which they chose to differentiate themselves, for the central function of the attributes in the right hand column is to throw those in the left hand column into the clearest possible relief.

The Crusades, Islam and the construction of Europe

Given their use of such a frame of reference, the quite outrageous way in which the Crusaders behaved towards all those whom they encountered once they had crossed the Bosphorous and entered Muslim-controlled territory becomes more explicable — although in no sense more justifiable. From within the confines of this taken for granted mind set the entire population of the territories they entered appeared to be equally alien, with the result that the Crusaders treated local Christian and Jewish communities with almost as much hostility as Muslims: all were viewed as equally 'other', and hence their very presence in the Holy Land was antithetical to the righteous objectives of the defenders of the True Cross.[6] Justification for the Crusaders' many bloody outrages was therefore immediately available.

Yet despite their initial success in carving out a precarious toe-hold for themselves in Palestine, the Crusaders were unable to sustain that presence for long. Having captured Jerusalem in 1099 C.E., they were expelled from the city by Salah-ad-din in 1187,[7] and lost control of their last bastion in Acre just over a century later in 1291. Once mobilised, the Muslims soon overwhelmed the Frankish incursion. What is most striking, however, is that although these trans-Mediterranean adventures gave the intruders first-hand experience of the Islamic world, this had remarkably little impact on attitudes and opinions — whether popular or scholarly — back home. Hence despite the immense (but still largely unacknowledged) impact of Islamic learning on the Latin world, little or no interest was taken in either the religion or civilization which had produced it. Instead the vision of Islam as the antithesis of Christianity was eagerly reinforced, as was the equation between 'Saracens', 'Moors' and all kinds of oriental others.

It was in this sense that the Crusades can usefully be regarded as a mould-setting development. In the face of the emergence of an overwhelmingly powerful Islamic order to its south and east, a sense of collective identity began to crystallise amongst the population of the territory which was subsequently to identify itself as Europe — and most especially as western Europe. However the banner under which collective mobilization began to be organised was that of Christendom, while the other at whom this nascent power was directed was perceived as being Muslim, oriental and black. The foundations around which contemporary conceptualizations of Europe were to be constructed were now in place.

The Re-conquest of Spain and the logic of the Inquisition

Nevertheless it took some time before the idea of Europe expanded to fill its current conceptual space, not least because the greater part of the Iberian peninsula was incorporated into the Islamic world in 718 C.E. Under the Ummayad Khalifas, who ruled in great splendour until 1031 C.E., Al-Andalus became increasingly prosperous; and although the region's military strength declined under their successors, it remained an intellectual and cultural powerhouse for several centuries thereafter. Indeed it was not until 1492 C.E. that the last Muslim foothold in Iberia, the kingdom of Granada, finally surrendered to the forces of the Christian reconquest. What is worth noting, however, is the sharp contrast in the character of inter-religious relationships in Christian as opposed to Islamic Spain.

While the initial Islamic irruption from North Africa undoubtedly took the form of a military conquest, by no means all Spanish Muslims were immigrants from elsewhere. While the ancestral origins of many members of the ruling elite may — like the Ummayads themselves — have lain elsewhere in the Islamic world, many members of the region's indigenous population were also willing converts to Islam. And if only to counter pernicious mythology, it is worth emphasising that it is *not* the case that Spain's Muslim rulers made great efforts to force their subjects to convert, or that non-converts were placed in a position of severe social and economic disadvantage. Quite the contrary: Islamic Spain contained thriving Jewish and Christian populations, and although ultimate political dominance may have been in Muslim hands, members of all three traditions treated each other with considerable mutual respect — as was generally the case throughout the Islamic world.[8]

However the Christian reconquest which gradually forced its way out of the barren highlands of Castile into the more prosperous south brought with it a much more narrow minded set of attitudes, largely grounded in the proto-European assumptions which had been developed during the course of the Crusades. As far as the Conquistadors were concerned, the Christian tradition allowed no space for pluralistic compromises. Hence the reconquest not only entailed a reassertion of political control, but also a comprehensive process of re-christianization, since Islam and Judaism were regarded as wholly alien to, and indeed as wholly unacceptable within, a Christian context. Spanish Jews and Muslims were therefore offered a stark choice: either they could convert, or leave on pain of death. Despite a considerable amount of emigration, many Jews and Muslims avoided expulsion by adopting Christianity, although this by no means brought their troubles to an end. On the contrary the 'new Christians' — known as Marranos if of Jewish origin, and Moriscos when of Muslim descent — remained the objects of intense suspicion. The slightest of evidence that their lifestyles included so-called 'un-christian' practices was held strongly against them, whilst their hereditary origins were for long afterwards held to throw doubts on the genuineness of their religious commitment.

Thus despite Christianity's formal commitment to proselytization and the prospect of conversion, being a Christian was perceived as involving much more than belief and religious practice: the precise details of one's personal lifestyle, and indeed of one's descent came to be regarded as just as important. And it was precisely because of continuing suspicions about the reality of the new Christians' commitment to their adopted faith that the Inquisition took such vigorous shape in Spain, since the most important heresies which it's investigators sought to root out were those which might potentially be harboured by the Moriscos and Marranos. Hence in sharp contrast to the expectations of Al-Andalus, not only was religious pluralism rendered unacceptable, but religious commitment — whether to Christianity, Judaism or Islam — came to be seen as a matter of heredity.

These developments had some very important consequences for the evolution of the idea of Europe. In the first place what we might now describe as process of ethnic cleansing, in which Jewish and Islamic practice was eliminated from the Iberian peninsula, powerfully reinforced the expectation that (Christian) religious homogeneity was an essential foundation of the social order; the extension of this homogeneity right through to the straits of Gibraltar established another of contemporary Europe's boundary markers; and last but not least the inquisition further entrenched the view that Judaism and Islam were intrinsically alien to Christendom/proto-Europe, full membership of which was also identified as hereditarily determined. Once equipped with this mindset, it also followed that the immense intellectual and architectural achievements Al-Andalus could only be perceived as a Moorish, alien, and un-European — and thus of no account. Nor was this just true of Spain: the extent of the Islamic contribution to the development of European civilization is still largely overlooked to this day, while the long standing Muslim presence in Bosnia, Albania, Bulgaria, Russia and the Ukraine was rendered equally invisible. Given Europe's vision of itself, the prospect that Europe might have, or ever have had, and Islamic dimension became such a contradiction in terms that it became quite literally unthinkable.[9]

The legitimation of global imperialism

Yet if Europe's vision of itself was initially laid down in pre-modern times, and thus in response to the then prevailing socio-political context, the global economic and political order has since been radically transformed, above all by the subsequent process of European Imperial expansion. But although our central concerns here are with processes of ideological construction rather than of political and economic change, there can be little doubt that this pre-modern ideological vision not only served to legitimate the Imperial process, but was itself profoundly affected by the enthusiasm with which it was deployed in these new circumstances.

Within that wider conspectus, it is worth noting the central role of Spain in the initial development of the new global order, symbolised by the spectacular coincidence between the fall of Granada, Islam's last stronghold in Spain, and Christopher Columbus' departure for the 'New World' in 1492 C.E.. Since the subsequent global process of discovery, conquest, colonization and exploitation was initiated in the immediate aftermath of the reconquest, it is hardly surprising that those involved continued to deploy exactly the same ideological framework to legitimise their activities. Hence the new global imperialists not only justified their activities in Christian terms — or at least in terms of the expansion of Christendom — but also took it for granted that while the idolatrous heathens whom they encountered were ripe for conversion, they were also by definition inherently inferior and untrustworthy, and could therefore never be their colonizers' social or political equals. Similarly while the various sets of adventurers who sought to gain access to the honey-pot were soon engaged in vicious mutual competition, all were nevertheless agreed on one point: however great their mutual conflicts, they were all Christians. Hence their mutual differences were as nothing as compared to those between themselves and the black barbarians whose territories and persons they sought to exploit and overrun.

It was on this basis that the trope which I have already outlined was elaborated still further, but this time with specific respect to tropical Africa. Unfortunately I have insufficient space to explore these developments in detail, other than to suggest that the pattern of oppositions which I set out below are already present in Shakespeare's Tempest, and that they can be found in full flower in (for example) Burrough's novel *Tarzan of the Apes*, as well in Hollywood's many screen adaptations of the story.

European	:	African
White	:	Black
Civilization	:	Jungle
Intellect	:	Physical strength
Sexual restraint	:	Sexual abandonment
Reason	:	Passion
Responsive to law	:	Responsive to violence
Religion	:	Superstition
Culture	:	Nature

Once entrenched within the European psyche, this conceptual framework began to be globally applied, not least because it provided the process of Imperial expansion with ideological foundations which were both comprehensive and apparently secure.

Imperial expansion not only brought Europeans into contact with a much wider range of others than those of which they had previously been aware, but also precipitated a dramatic change in the balance of power across that disjunction. In sharp contrast to the experience of the Crusaders, the well-armed adventurers who advanced the frontiers of Empire to encompass the Americas, tropical Africa and Indonesia encountered opponents who were for the most part much weaker than themselves, most especially in military terms.[10] Political subordination was so easily imposed that it was widely assumed to be permanent.

As a result of these global Imperial adventures the balance of power across the Mediterranean also begun to change: Europe and Europeans grew steadily wealthier, while the formerly prosperous regions to their south and east entered a period of steady decline,[11] so much so that they too were eventually subjected to Imperial domination. French colonization in North Africa began in 1834, and by 1848 was sufficiently well-entrenched for Algeria to be declared an integral — but of course subordinate — part of France; in 1883 Britain effectively took control of Egypt, even if the country was never formally colonised; and when the Ottoman Empire collapsed in the aftermath of the first world war, Britain, France and Italy encompassed its remnants as their 'Protectorates'. Needless to say the ideological vision of the intrinsic superiority of all things European reached new heights during this period.

Judaism and the construction of Europe

Tempting though it might be to run straight on with an examination of the role which European visions of its external *alter*s played in this process, we must nevertheless pause for a moment to consider the impact of another crucial component in the construction of Europe, namely reactions to its principal internal *alter*: Judaism. While Islam rather than Judaism was the primary focus of the reconquest and thus the inquisition, the subsequent relative decline in the economic and political power of the Islamic world rendered it a much less useful *alter* around which to construct a sense of a collective European identity. Islam was just not threatening enough to fill such a role. Yet if Imperial success made European hegemony apparently unchallengeable without, a new paranoia emerged with respect to its internal integrity: that represented by the perceived threat of a Jewish presence.

Although the size of the Jewish population was everywhere relatively small, its members heavy concentration in commerce, and especially in banking, gave the community a particularly salient public profile. Yet while bankers rarely attract much popular affection — most especially amongst those indebted to them — the intensity of the anti-semitic attitudes which erupted in early modern Europe cannot be explained on these grounds alone. After all the vast majority of Jews were *not* financiers. Instead the foundations of anti-semitism were similar to (and indeed were initially generated in the same period as) the Crusaders' anti-Islamism. Jews, like Muslims, were perceived as embodying the antithesis of Christian values; and if anti-Islamism was largely organised around a critique of the Prophet Muhammad, anti-Jewish hostility also had theological groundings, although in this case focusing primarily on the Jews' alleged responsibility for the crucifixion. Despite the privilege of their direct exposure to Jesus' teaching, the Jews were perceived as having deliberately and perversely rejected Christ's message, and indeed to have killed him — an act for which they must and should be held eternally to blame.

Once again popular understandings of Jews and Jewishness were in no way grounded in an awareness of the actual content of Jewish belief and behaviour. Just as with the Muslims — although with even less excuse given their immediate spatial proximity, as well as the biblical foundations of Jewish law and practices — Christian commentators remained (and were once again determined to remain) profoundly ignorant about such matters. Instead they preferred to assume that their Jewish neighbours' lifestyles and religious practices must by definition be the inverse of their own.

Hence if Christians lived by honest toil, Jews were perceived as making a living through gratuitous, mean-minded and exploitative financial manipulation; and if upright Christians worshipped the one true God, Jews were not only perceived as having perversely rejected the revelation which they had been privileged enough to witness, but also as organising their worship around rituals which were an even more perverse simulacrum of Christian practice. Hence it was widely believed that in the secrecy of their own tight-knit and clannish communities Jews celebrated a devilish version of the Eucharist, where they deliberately consumed the blood of specially sacrificed Christian infants. Using the same analytical approach as that which we deployed earlier, the following patterns can be seen to emerge in a Jewish/Christian context:

Christians	: Jews
Workers	: Usurers
Honest	: Dishonest bloodsuckers
Generous	: Mean
Open	: Closed and clannish
Straightforward	: Devious
Human	: Inhuman
Inspired by God	: Inspired by the devil
Pure	: Polluted

As before, these oppositions tell us nothing of any reliability about Judaism, for the Jews' alleged characteristics were constructed once again as the inverse of the qualities which their Christian excluders believed to be characteristic of themselves.

Aryanism, Anti-semitism, and the articulation of German nationalism

Although elaborated in a particularly dramatic way during the course of the Reformation,[12] these ideological constructions were by no means confined to the religious sphere, as became dramatically apparent in the context of the explosive growth of German nationalism during the eighteenth and nineteenth century. As the German-speaking peoples of central Europe grew acutely conscious of their condition of political disunity, particularly in comparison to their great rivals, the French, the elaboration of an ideology of German-ness around which to construct a new sense of national unity became an urgent priority. This task was far from straightforward, however, not least because the Germans were well aware that their rivals to the west had long dismissed them as backward and uncivilised. How, then, could they construct a vision of themselves as a civilised people when the normal means of doing so — through an assertion of roots in an ancient Roman heritage — was bound to confirm the higher status of the French, whose Latin connections were manifestly much closer than their own?

It was in this context that the discovery of the remarkably close correspondence between the grammatical and lexical structure of Sanskrit and a number of European languages — and most particularly (or so it was believed) with German — came as a godsend. As Poliakov (1974) shows, this at long last provided German nationalists with a means of confirming that their civilization had ancient roots, not so much in what they could now dismiss as degenerate Rome, but rather in the even more ancient (and therefore more 'classical') traditions of Indo-European civilization. While this had the disadvantage (as some might see it) of offering at least one group of non-Europeans ideological equality with Europeans, this was of little concern to the Germans: unlike the French, the Portuguese and above all the British they had no imperial presence in India. Moreover the great advantage of the theory of Aryanism from a German nationalist perspective was that it allowed them to construct a claim to distinctiveness which not only marginalised the French, but also enabled them to exclude their eastern rivals the Slavs even more firmly on the grounds that their heritage was non-Aryan. Hence nineteenth century German romanticism enjoyed immense success as it constructed a new and highly influential myth about the allegedly Aryan roots of European civilization in general, of the Germans in particular.

Yet however vacuous these Aryan fantasies may have been, they were far from harmless, not least because the occupants of the territory which nationalist sentiment now claimed as its natural heritage was far from homogeneous. While the Slavs were the most numerous of the allegedly alien non-Aryan groups resident in this territory, at an ideological level a much smaller group was perceived as offering a far greater threat to national integrity: that long-standing target of Christian chauvinism, the Jews. Hence the Jews' symbolic role as a convenient *alter* around which Germany — and beyond that Europe — might construct a sense of its religious and social integrity was powerfully reinforced.

Nor was that all. Not only did Aryan theory further legitimate hereditarian explanations of all aspects of social, cultural and religious distinctiveness, whilst also suggesting that any admixture of alien blood was necessarily a threat to the integrity of the superior Aryan *zeitgeist*, but this outlook was seen as being readily compatible with one of the most significant (and certainly one of the most intellectually influential) developments in nineteenth century science — Charles Darwin's theory of natural selection. And while Darwin himself was a great deal more careful than the enthusiastic 'Darwinism' which his discoveries inspired, the hereditarian, hierarchical and essentialist perspective espoused his followers was soon the intellectual rage across the length and breadth of Europe. As a result thinkers within a wide range of disciplines began to put an immense amount of effort into showing how all forms of human differentiation, whether social, cultural, religious or biological, within such an evolutionary schema. Of course virtually all of this 'science' has since been comprehensively discredited, but this did not occur before an immense amount of damage had been done. By the end of the nineteenth century the process of racialization (Miles 1989) was in full swing, such that ethnic and national disjunctions of all kinds were routinely represented as being biologically grounded.

This had far-reaching implications. Firstly the arbitrary character of all such disjunctions was comprehensively obscured by the assumption that they were naturally grounded, and therefore inevitable; secondly given the taken for granted assumptions of social Darwinism, it followed that all social, cultural and religious practices of all kinds could be arranged across a hierarchical spectrum from the more fit to the less; thirdly these ideas were immediately used not only to suggest that the social disjunctions to which these gave rise were biologically innate, but also to legitimize all forms of social inequality across them. It seemed so simple. Surely it was only right and proper that the more fit and more advanced should hold sway over those whose primitive characteristics rendered them less fit, less advanced and therefore less civilized?

Having penetrated virtually all areas of nineteenth century thought, such assumptions were swiftly applied in every conceivable context. It is not hard to see why. On the one hand they offered a ready means of legitimising the dramatically widening inequalities between metropolitan Europe and the global sweep of its Imperial possessions, and on the other of explaining away Europe's many internal inequalities, whether of class, ethnicity or religion. All could now be seen as equally 'natural'. No-where was this tendency more salient, or more significant, than with respect to Europe's Jewish population. Scientific racism powerfully reinforced the long-standing view that Judaism was the antithesis of Christianity, for the Jews' semitic heritage was now confirmed not only as being different from and inferior to that of Europeans, but also as a threat to their *biological* integrity, and especially to the purity and vitality of their unique Aryan heritage.

As Poliakov (1982) demonstrates in his masterly overview, these ideas — albeit in various local guises — found a ready reception in all parts of Europe. Yet against this background Germany nevertheless emerges as a special case, since German nationalist's long-standing use of Jews and Jewishness as its central *alter* meant that nowhere was this mode of thinking embraced more enthusiastically than in Germany. One hardly needs to emphasise its horrific consequences: in an effort to cull out the biologically backward elements from the population, whether they were physically or mentally handicapped, Gypsies or Jews, six million souls were herded into gas chambers.

Indeed so outrageous was this episode in European history that once highlighted by the victors of 1945, it wholly transformed the way in which ethnic differentiation would be conceptualised, at least for the immediate future: since then the overt biologization of ethnic difference has been wholly discredited, at least in polite circles, and 'race' has therefore had to be placed between inverted commas. Yet before moving on to explore the subsequent developments, two points are worth making. Firstly that even though the holocaust was the ultimate apotheosis of the Aryan (and in a narrow sense German) fantasy, it must not be forgotten that the remainder of Europe's population offered little serious resistance to this process of ethnic cleansing — and thereby implicitly acquiesced in it.[13] Secondly, and consequently, the ideas which underpinned the holocaust cannot be seen as unique to Germany; they had become (and in all probability still remain) a pan-European phenomenon.

Europe and Islam in the late twentieth century

Although it would be idle to suggest that anti-semitic attitudes, or indeed more general support for theories of biological racism, have been entirely eclipsed in the aftermath of the holocaust, it is indisputable that the public expression of such views did become profoundly unfashionable, such that they now play a much more attenuated role in the construction of Europe than they did half a century ago. Instead other means — and most especially a renewed emphasis on culture rather biology as an essential source of difference, and above all though a resurgence of anti-Islamic paranoia — have been used to achieve just the same ends. So it is that as we approach the millennium long-dormant ideas about and attitudes about the 'Islamic threat' have sprung suddenly back into fashion, to provide a powerful new dynamic in the way in which Europe makes sense of itself. To appreciate the logic of this development we must briefly consider the radical shifts which have taken place in the pattern of political and economic relations between Europe and the Islamic lands to its south and east during the course of past half century.

Firstly Europe's previously minuscule Muslim population has increased dramatically in size, largely as a result of the arrival of long-distance labour migrants in the midst of the post-war industrial boom. Although the migrants' national origins were extremely diverse, and by no means all were Muslim, the scale of Europe's Islamic population increased dramatically. It is now at least ten million strong, and rising fast. Secondly the steep rise in the price of oil during the nineteen seventies and eighties not only emphasised the extent to which Europe had come to rely on the Muslim world as a source of energy, but also highlighted the scale of the consequent outflow of wealth, even if the benefits of this new-found affluence was in fact largely confined to tiny ruling elites in Saudi Arabia, the Gulf Emirates and (although slightly less dramatically) the Maghreb. Thirdly since rapid economic growth in Europe has been accompanied by continued stagnation in the Arab world (for very little of the new wealth trickled down to the broad mass of the population), the disparity of living standards to the north and south of the Mediterranean has widened still further. Nevertheless numerous bridgeheads across this divide are now in place as a result of mass migration during the sixties and seventies, and although fortress Europe is now committed to bringing that inflow to a halt, it still continues almost inexorably. Economic inequality across the Mediterranean has steadily increased the pressure to migrate, and even though new arrivals from the Islamic world are only too aware of the intense hostility they can expect to encounter, moving north offers at least a *chance* of prosperity, however remote. Staying put seems to offer nothing but a dead end.

Last but not least, the collapse of the Soviet Union has produced a seismic shift whose aftershocks are still with us. Firstly Europe's eastern boundaries are beginning to crystallise more clearly than ever before. Ever more salient conflicts are now erupting between the Russians and their allies such as the Ukrainians, the Georgians and the Serbs on the one hand, and assorted Muslim groups such as the Turks, Chechens, Azeris, Uzbegs, Tajiks, and Khazakhs on the other; a fault-line is once again emerging at the boundaries of Christendom. A second consequence of the demise of the Soviet Union is that the internal division between Eastern and Western Europe which once generated such obsessive concern has now largely disappeared, and with it the utility of 'militant Communism' — or indeed its predecessor, 'The Zionist conspiracy' as a focus for paranoid concern. Instead Islam has been brought back from abeyance to fill once again its former symbolic role as the antithesis of European civilization and all it stands for.

Yet despite the many structural parallels between the contemporary situation and that which emerged a millennium ago, there is one crucial difference between the two. In the original scenario it was Christendom which stood in a position of political and economic disadvantage, but in the contemporary context those roles have been comprehensively reversed. But if Europe's contemporary inhabitants consequently stand in sharp contrast to their tenth century predecessors, since they have no immediate need to fear either the military power or the economic wealth of their Islamic neighbours, the contradictions across this disjunction have by no means been eliminated. If Europeans now feel threatened by their Muslim neighbours — as indeed they do — it is for precisely the opposite reasons. The more Muslims seek to reduce current inequalities, the more they are bound to challenge the position of economic and political *privilege* which Europeans currently enjoy.

Not only are such challenges already being mounted both internally and externally, but they are also beginning to be articulated in ideological as well as material terms; not surprisingly, defensive responses to these challenges have now begun to be devised. While the reinforcement of Fortress Europe through the introduction of ever more draconian immigration controls is one such response, another is the ever-increasing tendency to demonise the ten million or more Muslims who are now resident within, most particularly when they make an effort to articulate their own material, religious and cultural and cultural concerns. For although Europe's Muslims are anything but a homogeneous group, they all have certain common interests. All are worried about the level of exclusion and discrimination they encounter, and wish to challenge it; and although their understandings of what Islam consists of are extremely varied, all incorporate some kind of commitment to an Islamic agenda in their personal lives, and hence, for example, would wish to see that agenda treated with greater sympathy by the local educational system.

What is striking, however, is the intensity of the hostility which very presence of a Muslim population, let alone the articulation of the mildest of such Islamic demands is currently precipitating in virtually every corner of Europe where they have settled, so much so that there is good reason to suggest that the visions of difference originally erected a thousand years ago are now being both revived and revised.

While an explicit attempt to pillory Muslims as followers of the anti-Christ could not be expected to make much impact in a contemporary context, a careful examination of the pattern of structural oppositions set out on page 10 in the light of current obsessions reveals some disturbing parallels. On the face of it 'licentiousness' might now seem to be a quite meaningless charge — until one remembers that the super-sensuous harem remains an image of considerable force, while a favourite criticism of Islamic lifestyles is that its gender conventions are innately oppressive, and allegedly sanction a comprehensive degradation of women. However the view that Islam necessarily renders Muslims violent, vicious, duplicitous and mad chimes more directly with contemporary views, and is supplemented with an even more popular image of Muslims as over-committed fanatics, or in other words as 'fundamentalists'. Not only have the terms 'Muslim' and 'fundamentalist' become virtually synonymous, particularly in the popular press, but the very idea that a program of social and political mobilization might be articulated in religious terms is perceived as the antithesis of rational, scientific and indeed modern behaviour. Muslims are therefore routinely presumed to have an authoritarian and anti-democratic in outlook, to be hostile to any kind of joy or gaiety, and to be such blind followers of convention as to be outside the bounds of rational thought and reflection. While the accuzation of impurity has now largely lapsed — even if they are still routinely perceived as dirty and/or smelly — the vision of Muslims as black appears both to have been redefined and given a new vitality. Moors may no longer be assumed to be as coal-black as Shakespeare's Othello, but skin colour remains a crucial differentiator: the feature which is held ultimately to differentiate Europe's non-indigenous population (and of which Europe's Muslim neighbours are the most immediate exemplars) is their nominal possession of a significantly darker natural skin colour.

Bearing all this in mind we can now construct a revised set of oppositions which builds upon those originally erected by the crusaders:

European	: Muslim
Gender-equal	: Gender-oppressive
Democratic	: Authoritarian
Progressive	: Backward-looking
Modern	: Traditional
Liberal	: Fundamentalist
Governed by reason	: Fanatical
Joyful	: Kill-joys
Civilized	: Uncivilized
White	: Not-white

If this analysis holds, it follows that the Islamic world has now been restored to its former position as Europe's primary *alter*, and that in this process Islam has once again been represented as the antithesis of just those characteristics which Europe and Europeans would like to believe that they themselves epitomise.

Contingency and specificity in the construction of Europe

Much of the argument which has been presented so far is little more than a synthesis of the perspectives developed in a wide range of more specialist analyses, although it will also be obvious that I owe a particularly heavy debt to the work of Edward Said. Yet to break off at this stage, as almost all other analysts do, avoids what I would suggest is the most important challenge of all. While the approach we have taken so far serves very effectively to illuminates why it is that the boundaries of Europe (both internal and external) are located where they are and at least gives an inkling of why they are defended with such passion, it also opens up a yet more fundamental question still. Is Europe's contemporary vision of itself, and most especially the means by which it constructs it boundaries, simply the product of a long series of historical contingencies, or is it an intrinsic — and hence distinctive — feature of European culture itself?

That the developments highlighted here are the outcome of a multitude of historical contingencies is self-evident, as is the prospect that Europe's definition of itself will continue to develop in response to further (and necessarily unpredictable) contingencies. To suggest otherwise would be to adopt a position of manifestly indefensible essentialism. Likewise antithetical boundary construction is anything but a uniquely to European phenomenon, as current eruptions of near-genocidal ethnic polarization in contexts as widely separated as Biafra, Rwanda, the Lebanon, Punjab, Sri Lanka and East Timor make only too clear. Moreover numerous ethnographic reports demonstrates that the tendency to envisage distant neighbours as occupying an inverted world in which anti-humans walk on their heads and insert food directly into their stomachs, where rivers flow uphill and the seasons are chaotic is an equally global phenomenon.[14]

Yet despite all these reservations and contra-indications, I would nevertheless suggest that although exposure to social, cultural and religious pluralism has long been a *normal* part of human experience — if only because few societies are or ever have been so small, so homogenous and so isolated as to lack any such internal diversity — for at least the past millennium the inhabitants of Western Europe have felt this experience to be far more challenging than most. Yet although antithetical polarization is now quite manifestly a global phenomenon, it was not always so: in every single extra-European context listed in the previous paragraph (and it would be easy to construct a much longer list) the current condition of apparently unbridgeable polarization turns out, on careful examination, to be a *recent* phenomenon — in sharp contrast to the popular (Western) assumption that such conflicts are nothing more than eruption of ancient and irrational tribal hatreds.[15]

Although it would be idle to suggest that we can extract ourselves from past mistakes through a simple inversion of conventional polarities, or in other words through a romantic attribution of moral perfection to all things non-European, there is nevertheless a great deal of historical evidence to suggest that in much of the rest of the world inter-ethnic and inter-religious relations have — at least until very recently — long been broadly cordial, and that it is Western Europeans' involvement in religiously inspired genocidal war which is relatively exceptional, both with respect to its historical depth and to the bloodiness of its outcomes. This suggests a further set of questions. Why did Europeans and proto-Europeans exhibit both such an early and such a vigorous commitment to constructing non-negotiable boundaries? And while the success of the Imperial project may now have led to the globalization of this mode of thought and practice, might it not be that its origins are in some sense specifically *European*? And if so, where and in what contexts might its roots best be identified?

The Augustinian roots of hostility to pluralism in Catholic Christianity

Although the arguments advanced here have ranged widely through time and space, one common theme nevertheless emerges from them: all are located close to, and are very often at the core of, Europe's *religious* development. This suggests that a careful exploration of Christian theology, and especially its western and Latin forms, might well prove helpful. At first sight this focus might seem surprising, on the grounds that the teachings of Jesus of Nazareth are an unlikely source of such violent and inhuman attitudes: indeed given Jesus' powerfully articulated commitment to openness, tolerance and justice, quite the opposite outcomes might have been expected. However I would suggest that it is not so much on the teachings of the founder himself which are at issue here, but rather on those of a key figure in the development of Western Christianity: Saint Augustine, the fourth century bishop of Hippo.

In focusing on Augustine I certainly would not wish to suggest that all the theological arguments with which he is associated were entirely his own creation, for they manifestly grew out of his close association with figures such as Ambrose and Jerome. However from our perspective the significance of his teachings arises firstly from the fact that he formalised his position just as the split between the Catholic and Byzantine traditions was taking place, and secondly because theologians in the Western churches — both Catholic and Protestant — have been referring back to his teachings ever since.

In cosmological terms — for it is Europe's vision of its place within the social universe that is our central concern here — one of the most striking aspects of Augustine's theological perspective is the extent to which his youthful commitment to Manicheism continued to influence his thinking. Of course Augustine subsequently went out of his way to distance himself from that tradition, but many aspects of his theological vision, which saw light as pitted against darkness, reason against passion, spirit against matter, and truth against wholly misguided heresy, was profoundly dualistic in character. To be sure Augustine differed from the Manicheans on certain crucial issues, not least in his rejection of their radical asceticism, and his contrary insistence that God's grace, mediated through Christ and the Church, could nevertheless provide Adam's intrinsically sinful offspring with a route to redemption and thus salvation. As a result his most influential doctrinal development of all — the notion of original sin — became the very core of Catholic theology, so as it were Christianising the Manichean's comprehensively negative evaluation of the existent world.

Although a full exploration of Augustine's theology far beyond the scope of this brief essay, the very dualism of his thinking makes it relatively easy to use the analytical approach deployed earlier in order to delineate the broad outline of his conceptual vision:

Light	: Darkness
God	: Satan
Good	: Evil
Catholic	: Heretic
Christian	: Pagan
Salvation	: Damnation
Spirit	: Matter
Mind	: Body
Reason	: Passion
Celibacy	: Sexuality
Civilization	: Barbarism
Culture	: Nature

Augustine's powerful influence over many generations of thinkers in the Latin tradition, both Catholic and Protestant, is universally acknowledged, as is the impact of his theological vision on the development of European religious and cultural ideology. But what is also quite astonishing in this context is the closeness of the congruence between Augustine's cosmological vision and those which we have extracted from subsequent contexts. To be sure the others in opposition to which these subsequent structures were erected were quite different from the Manicheans, Donatists and Pelagians against whom the bishop of Hippo directed his scathing rhetoric. With the exception of the Jews, those later targets were either of little concern to Augustine, as with the inhabitants of tropical Africa, or had not yet come into existence, as with Islam. But what is most striking is that every single component in the patterns of structural opposition identified earlier has a parallel in one aspect or another of the pattern set out above.[16]

Nor is this tendency to construct outsiders as evil, alien and comprehensively despicable restricted to formal theology, or even to what has now become a relatively narrow sphere of Christian commitment. On the contrary this mode of thinking is equally deeply entrenched at the very heart of European culture, and at all possible levels. Apart from the Tarzan myth mentioned earlier, just three illustrative examples of the extent of its influence will have to suffice here. First in Shakespeare, three of whose most significant plays, *Othello*, *The Tempest* and *The Merchant of Venice* focus primarily — albeit from a critical perspective — on myths of otherness about Muslims, Black Africans and Jews; secondly the Rushdie affair, which gave rise to the most astonishing amount of vituperation against the Islamic tradition as a whole, and which was most vigorously articulated not by the Churches but by secular radicals.[17] And finally contemporary France, where the concept of *laicité* is currently being used to challenge the legitimacy of any kind of public commitment to Islam amongst its Muslim minorities, so much so that attempts by schoolgirls adopt the *hijab* are construed as constituting a wholly unacceptable challenge to the integrity of the Republic.

Moreover of the various latent *alter*s available to Europe, there can be little doubt that it is Muslims and Islam which currently generate by far the highest level of paranoia. Hence whilst that part of Europe's population which is of non-European descent also includes many non-Muslims, and even in Britain where the non-Muslims form a clear majority within the visible minorities, popular hostility is at present overwhelmingly directed at the Muslim presence.

Europe in Comparative perspective

In order to throw the apparent normality of all this into some kind of perspective, it is highly instructive to consider how those traditions which did not root themselves in Augustine's tortured and often near-paranoid dualism responded to encounters with religious and ethnic difference; nor do we even need to look beyond Christianity itself to engage in such an exercise, since the Orthodox traditions of the Eastern Church offers an ideal test-bed for comparison. Firstly at an empirical level, its followers normally appear to have been far less perplexed by religious difference than their Western counterparts: hence though physically far closer to Jerusalem, they never perceived it as having been 'lost' in the sense which seemed self-evident to the Crusaders. This difference in perception, which was also repeated in numerous other contexts, has very clear theological roots. Thus while the Orthodox tradition certainly accepted the notion of the Fall, this was not — *pace* Augustine — construed as giving rise to an inescapable condition of original sin, nor was material and physical existence perceived as inherently evil. Quite the contrary: Orthodox cosmology views the created universe as a manifestation of the divine essence, and hence it is a vehicle through which a realization of God's majesty can be achieved, rather than an obstacle to salvation. And because such a realization can take place directly, rather than requiring the necessary mediation of Christ and the Church to remove original sin, Orthodox cosmology is prepared to accept that even the unbaptised may still gain salvation; hence it provided conceptual space within which alternative spiritual traditions — including those which owed nothing to Christianity — might still be recognised as at least partially legitimate. Hence I would argue that it is precisely because they were not constrained by the dualistic absolutism of an Augustinian heritage that Orthodox responses to religious and cultural diversity have (at least until very recently) displayed so few parallels with Western developments, such that those inspired by Eastern Christianity have normally found it far easier to cope with conditions of pluralism than have their Protestant or Catholic counterparts.

   In this respect one of the most distinctive features of the western European cultural tradition is the depth of its tendency towards dualistic thinking, accompanied by an equally strong tendency to evaluate the physical (as opposed to the moral and spiritual) world in negative terms. But although these ideas can be traced back to Augustine's manichean heritage, it worth emphasising that dualism by no means necessarily leads to these conclusions: in its classic Zoroastrian form, physical existence is regarded as intrinsically good, even if under constant attack from hostile forces of darkness and decay. And if we look still further afield, we find that Hindu tradition (together with virtually all of its Buddhist variants) also takes a similarly positive view, albeit by a different route and in the context of a radically different cosmological vision. Thus while most parts of the Indic tradition posit a cyclical (as opposed to a linear or dualistic) cosmology, such that the existent world of *samsara* is routinely perceived as impermanent and therefore illusory, it is also by definition a manifestation of the otherwise unqualified Ultimate. Nor does either tradition appear to have had any great difficulty in coping with pluralism, for variety was viewed as necessarily intrinsic to positively evaluated existence.

What, though, about that *bête noir* of the Western world, Islam? While popular opinion may hold that Islam is intrinsically hostile to all non-Muslims, the Qur'an itself includes a clear injunction that the 'peoples of the book' should be treated with respect, even if orientalist scholarship has put a great deal of effort into seeking to demonstrate otherwise. Yet although certain aspects of the Shari'a (as well as recent political developments) may seem to support such a conclusion, it would be quite wrong to suggest that such an outlook is a necessary characteristic of Islamic practice. To take one immensely influential example, the sufi philosopher Ibn Al-Arabi (1165-1240 C.E.) developed the doctrine of *wahadat al-wujud* (the unity of being) to argue that because everything that exists is God, or to be more precise a manifestation of the otherwise transcendent divine essence, and since there can be no exceptions to this truth, it follows that even those religions which stand right outside the inheritance of Abraham and Moses are nevertheless components of the divine theophany. Hence no matter how far the practices of those who follow such alternative traditions may diverge from conventional Islamic expectations, all both manifest and reflect an awareness of the One, and must therefore be respected.[18]

Once set in this kind of comparative context, the far reaching consequences of Augustinian theology on Western Europe's vision of itself, and most especially on the way in which transactions with others might be handled can be brought more clearly into focus. Whilst most other civilizations found it quite unnecessary to demonise otherness, the negative dualism which lies at the heart of Western Europe's religious and cultural heritage led to a different, and indeed a very distinctive, conclusion. In Augustine's theology there is only one path to salvation, which can in turn only be followed by an elite which seeks self-consciously to distance itself from the fallen world — or to put it another way, if there is but one route to Civilization in the face of an otherwise violent, squalid and impassioned state of nature; and while the elect may well be sorely tempted to indulge in that which they so determinedly deny themselves — as indeed was Augustine himself — the line must be held: those who deviate (whether by accident, design or sheer ignorance is immaterial) necessarily threaten everything that is good and true.

While it would be quite absurd to blame Augustine for the way in which his theological outlook was subsequently developed, there is nevertheless good reason to suggest that it is within this mould — albeit mediated by a host of historical contingencies — that his intellectual heirs have continued to construe human otherness. But to complete the argument, one last caveat must still be dealt with: the plain fact that in the contemporary world such modes of thought, which so easily lead both to religious polarization and to genocidal ethnic cleansing are by no means an exclusively Western European phenomenon. Does this destroy my argument? I think not.

Firstly wherever such polarization has erupted in non-European contexts, this has invariably been *against* the trend of long-standing local moral and cultural expectations, rather than in congruence with them; secondly virtually all such eruptions — whether we focus on the rabid anti-Islamism of a Slobodan Milošević in Serbia or the Vishva Hindu Parishad in India, or indeed the equally rabid anti-Western and anti-Christian rhetoric of groups such as the Jamaat-i-Islam or the F.I.S. — are best understood as responses to the same historical contingency: a bruising encounter with the political, economic and ideological impact of Imperialism. It is precisely because of the success of that process that the impact of Augustine's intellectual heritage has now gone global.[19] Yet if 'fundamentalist Islam' has consequently emerged as Europe's collective nightmare, there is a powerful sense in which Europeans are now beginning to reap a harvest whose seeds they themselves have sowed. If Islamic activists now find it strategically advantageous pay those who have for so long disparaged, excluded, exploited and oppressed them back in their own money, no-one should be surprised. Europe is receiving no more than its just desserts.[20]

Conclusion

Nevertheless we still face a pressing question: how might the intensifying process of polarization in which we are currently enmeshed best be unwound? If my analysis is sound, a number of much recommended solutions can only be dismissed out of hand. Firstly any attempt to resolve the problem by further excluding Muslims — whether by reinforcing the walls of Fortress Europe, by introducing repatriation programs, or by denying European Muslims the right to build their own lives on their own terms — is doomed to failure, since such policies actually constitute an open invitation to minority communities to close ranks to reinforce their distinctiveness, the better to defend their interests. No matter how alien such developments may see, Muslims and Muslim communities are an integral part of Europe's social order.

Yet as just what sort of Muslims? This gives rise to a second line of argument: that if only European Muslims would adopt less alien, less aggressive (and indeed less 'fundamentalist') modes of behaviour, they would encounter much less hostility and much greater acceptance — or so it is often suggested. Yet although the Islamic tradition as a whole is much less aggressive, much more easy going and above all far more intellectually sophisticated than most Europeans have ever been able to acknowledge, the suggestion that Muslims can earn greater respect by acting in a less challenging way is not only grossly historically mis-informed, but wholly misses the point. Current Muslim aggressiveness (of which only the first stirrings have yet begun) is by no means an innate feature of the Islamic tradition: rather it is best understood as a strategic vehicle which is currently being deployed as a means of challenging exclusion and devaluation. Since this strategy has caused so much alarm and confusion amongst their excluders, the prospect of it being abandoned is remote.

As meaningful options have shrunk, so a third — and apparently much more reasonable — strategy has come to the fore: the suggestion that Europeans should make a much greater effort to inform themselves about Islam. Yet although such a commitment can only be regarded as welcome, even if it were implemented there is still good reason to suggest that the availability of more accurate information about Islam would have any significant impact in its own right on current attitudes. After all Europe has had the Islamic world as its neighbour for more than a millennium, but as Daniel (1975) shows, it has never felt able either to acknowledge its *alter* as an equal, or to take its cultural or religious traditions seriously. Having spent more than a millennium reading Islam through the distorting prism of their own deeply entrenched assumptions, more information, however accurate, is unlikely to make much difference to conventional European judgements.

Is there any solution? I believe there is, although by a route that is so deeply uncomfortable that the very need to embark on it is likely to be tenaciously resisted. The logic of the analysis presented here is that the most urgent priority is not for Europe to understand its *alter*s better, but rather itself and its own history — for it is within Europe's own long-standing structures of self-definition that pluralism in general, and the Islamic presence in particular, have been rendered into nightmares. If so, it is Europe itself which stands in urgent need of therapy. But as yet the patient is still in denial, and as any psychotherapist would confirm, those who refuse to acknowledge the seriousness of their self-generated plight find it far easier to engage in a process of transference. Rather than confronting the illusory character of their own mental constructions, they prefer to ascribe the very behaviour which they refuse to acknowledge in themselves to those whom they believe are harassing them.

Can Europe afford to stay in denial? Half a century has passed since six million souls were consumed in an earlier effort to extirpate such fantasies, but despite all the consequent guilt and shame Europe has managed to find itself another collective *alter*, about whose very presence some all too familiar arguments are now developing. Yet despite these disturbing parallels, any future confrontation may well have a far greater impact on Europe's comfortable majority than did the last. Europe's Muslims have already begun to resist denigration and exclusion far more actively than did their predecessors; and Europe's Muslim population currently roughly similar in scale to that of pre-holocaust Jewry, their global presence is very much larger. If conflict should erupt across that disjunction — which God forbid! — casualties would not be restricted only to one side. Unwelcome and uncomfortable though the prospect of therapy may be — for it will necessarily entail a root and branch scrutiny of Europe's entire conceptual and cultural heritage — only one diagnostic conclusion is available: if Europeans choose to maintain their long-standing condition of denial, it is at their own peril.

Notes

[1]   In Britain 'Oriental Languages' are routinely taught only in Oxford, Cambridge, and at the specialist School of Oriental and African Studies in London.

[2]   Egypt's Coptic population includes approximately 7 million people.

[3]   In a much commented upon article in *Foreign Affairs*, Huntington (1993) not only predicts that "The next world war, if there is one, will be a war between civilizations-", but also indicates that the most likely location of such a war will be across the fault line between Western and Islamic civilizations.

[4]   In his analysis of the way in which the second century B.C.E. Book of Jubilees expands on Genesis X, Alexander (1982) shows how its author has effectively superimposed a Biblical view on earlier Greek understandings of circum-Mediterranean geography to produce the now-familiar association between Europe, Asia and Libya (=Africa) and Noah's three sons Japhet, Shem and Ham. However Alexander also shows that the author of Jubilees follows Greek precedents in identifying the boundaries of these regions as the river Don, the river Nile and the straits of Gibraltar, and that although these divisions subsequently proved to be a very fertile source of myth making, their social and political implications at that time were quite different from more recent conceptualizations of their significance.

[5]   In his much criticized and even more profoundly misunderstood *Satanic Verses* Salman Rushdie made an extremely very well-informed attempt to reinvert these inversions, even if the ultimate outcome of his efforts was a complete disaster.

[6]   These views and their consequences are reviewed in considerable detail in both Daniel 1975 and Maalouf 1983.

[7]   Stories of battles between Richard the Lion-heart and the violent and heartless Saladin remain a staple of English children's fiction. Needless to say a more historically-informed assessment of the character of the two leaders reverses most of the judgements which are central to those stories.

[8]   Introducing his analysis of the relationship between medieval Latin Christianity and Islam, Daniel (1975: 23ff) tells the extraordinary story of the ninth century martyrs of Cordoba, who went out of their way to insult the prophet Muhammad in front of the Islamic authorities; censure was inevitable, but the *provocateurs* were very determined. By deliberately repeating the offence, they left eventually left the Cadi with no alternative but to order the ultimate sanction of death. Both the martyrs and their

admirers were well satisfied with this outcome, which 'proved' their theory that Islam was merciless and addicted to violence.

9   This is precisely the conclusion to which Daniel (1975) is driven in the course of his masterful review of the history of ideas in Medieval Europe.

10   It is striking that in the Indian Ocean and the Far East European adventurers are best understood not so much as having established trade routes, but as having eclipsed their (largely Muslim) predecessors. And they did so not so much by virtue of greater commercial skills, but by enforcing better terms of trade quite literally down the barrels of their cannons.

11   At least a part of this decline can be traced to the fact that having circumvented the Islamic obstacle in a way which had never been open to Venetian merchants, Spanish, Dutch and English merchants took over the oriental trade routes which had been a source of much of the prosperity of the Islamic heartlands.

12   Martin Luther and his associates were responsible for articulating, and thus legitimating some particularly vicious forms of anti-Jewish rhetoric (Webster 1990)

13   It seems most unlikely that the inhabitants of territories not subjected to German occupation would have behaved very differently from those that were. While most of Britain was not put to the test, the Jewish population *was* removed from the only part of its territory which was so occupied — the Channel Islands.

14   Middleton's account of Lugbara Religion (1960) offers a classic account of such a vision.

15   Such expectations can also be related to the long standing European view that all the populations of all its colonial possessions were so riddled with barely suppressed tribal and religious rivalries that in the absence of firm Imperial guidance even the slightest disturbance was bound to precipitate a bloody civil war. Such myths served to legitimate the Imperial presence whilst also sanctioning policies of divide and rule.

16   Further parallels can also be found elsewhere. Although concerned primarily with issues of gender, Plumwood (1993: 43) presents a very similar pattern of oppositions which she also suggests are 'key elements in the dualistic structure of western thought'.

17   One of the clearest and most vituperative examples of such hostility of which I am aware is Fay Weldon's pamphlet, *Sacred Cows* (1989). The issues are more fully discussed in Akhtar (1989) and Kabbani (1989).

18   A fuller account of Ibn al-Arabi's teachings, as well as a masterly overview of the realities of Islamic history can be found in Lapidus (1988).

19   One of the most ironical consequences of this development is that if a contemporary Augustine who followed his footsteps from North Africa to Milan, and even more so to France, he would be automatically classified as an Arab, and hence be subject to suspicion as a potential member of the F.I.S.

20   While this strategy certainly proved a very effective means of causing external alarm and confusion, it is still a much more open question as to whether the adoption of some of the West's worst traits — albeit dressed up in Islamic clothes — is having anything like as positive an impact on the internal structure Muslim societies.

2

Muslims in France

Catherine Wihtol de Wenden

For the last ten years, Islam has been a very important issue in the French political debate: Conflicts in the car industry using the allegiance to the Muslim community as a mobilization factor (1983-1984), a first debate on the reform project of the nationality code questioning the allegiance of Franco-Maghrebians (Can one be French and Muslim?) (1987), the Rushdie affair (1988), the Scarf ("foulard") affair in France (1989), the Gulf War (1991), the debate on an Islam of France (1989-1990) as well as many local conflicts around the visibility of prayer rooms and mosques (Lyon, Marseille, Charvieux-Chavagnieux ...), or even the market of halal meat are the "elements" of the debate.

Undoubtedly, Islam as a religion as well as a collective identity, is now part and parcel of the French political space. It brings many challenges in the public opinion concerning French identity, secularism, citizenship, allegiances, intrusion between external and internal political order (Algeria), and assertion of alternative allegiances facing with a society which excludes populations of Muslim culture ("It is better defining oneself as Muslim than as an unemployed").

But what characterises most Islam in France is its diversity (Maghrebians are the majority, but there are also Black Africans, Turks and some Asians from Pakistan) (I), compared with other European countries, and its emergence in the French landscape (II).

Diversity of Islam in France
Factors of visibility

It seems difficult to give precise figures of Muslims in France because, since the census of 1968, membership to a religious faith is no more asked for. We can, however, assert that they represent between 3 and 4 millions if we include not only the foreigners of Muslim culture but also those who have acquired French nationality by birth, as well as the "harkis" (500,000) who fought with the French army during the Algerian war and who were repatriated in France after 1962. (They had to choose for French nationality until 1967.)

So, in spite of the frequent references to the Islamic community in France, Islam is far from homogeneous. It is less and less so because of a plurality of cleavages of nationalities, age, sex and trends linked to various periods of immigration and identification points, even though all these features are not a decisive factor for the degree of homogeneity of a community.

Islam was first brought by foreign workers: the first ones during the First World War (colonial soldiers and workers recruited by the French army from Kabylia), some of whom stayed in France after 1918. A second wave arrived during the thirty years of growth (1945-1974), especially at the end (1960-1970). It consisted mainly of Tunisians and Moroccans. Most of them were young and tended to relegate Islam to their old age, when they would return home. Religious practice, when it existed in firms and collective housing for immigrant workers was hidden, private, nearly shameful.[1]

In 1962, a third wave was brought by the "French Muslims", a name applied to the *harkis* of the Algerian war. Coming mostly from Aurès and Kabylia and young, their religious practice was all the lower as they had adopted a French allegiance. But some were also linked to traditional religious leaders (the most famous one was the Bachaga Boualem who settled at the Mas Thibert, near Marseille), and had chosen a French allegiance.

In the seventies, a fourth wave arrived with the Turks in some regions such as Paris, but also Alsace and Franche-Comté, while a fifth wave came with the Black Africans from the valley of Senegal river (Mali, Mauritania and Senegal). Among them, only half were Muslims, the other half being Christians.

But another event, perhaps more important for the settlement of Islam in France, was the stopping of immigration flows of workers decided in 1974: its unexpected effect was the acceleration of family reunifications.

By this the landscape of the immigrant community has changed. Yesterday it was work, unionism, coffee-shops, hotels. Now it was going to be suburbs, school, family housing. Some claims which were expressed in the work place or around it were now being asked for in the city.

Some evidence of this change was given by the Sonacotra strike (1976-1980) when French public opinion began slowly to discover that migrant workers had a religion: Islam, while they were seen before as proletarians. The visibility of Islam began to appear in day-to-day life: prayer rooms in the suburbs, specific places for Muslims in cemeteries, a market of halal meat and Islamic libraries.[2]

Another factor of the settlement of Islam, along with the family reunifications and the agreeing of the populations, was the freedom of associations which was granted to foreign associations in October 1981: Muslim associations were developing (up to 650 in 1985), some Franco-Maghrebians were stressing their collective belonging to Islam in French society (inside the claim for a "right to be different") while severe strikes in the car industry (Citroën, Renault 1983-1984) were using the strength of the "umma" as a mobilization factor.[3] This growing visibility of Islam brought much confusion in the French political debate,[4] especially within the political issue of the Iranian Revolution. But the visibility of Islam is not necessarily followed by a rise of its practice.

The French specificity

All these conditions of the birth of Islam in France have progressively drawn the characteristics of its specificity: the overwhelming majority of Maghrebians is a population weakly educated in religion and belonging to the lower classes in France (an "Islam d'OS"): a popular Islam, essentially quiet, of settled people becoming older (un "truc de vieux")[5] giving to the French public opinion the miserabilist image of a religion of poor and formerly colonised people.[6]

Sunnite in its majority, Islam in France is dominated by Maghrebians who "give the tune". Although Islam has no institutional framework, it was first represented in France by the Paris Great Mosque, built between 1924 and 1926 to thank the Muslim warriors during the First World War of 1914-1918, inaugurated by Lyautey, with a rector appointed first by

France.[7] When Algeria became independent the rector who was on office, Si Hamza Boubakeur, succeeded to be in office by virtue of being appointed by Algeria (1957-1982). The following Algerian rectors, Cheikh Abbas and Tidjani Haddam were so, too. It is only with the appointment of the present rector, a Frenchman, Dalil Boubakeur (1992), son of the first rector, that France has recovered its authority.

a) *Maghrebians*

Even if "Maghrebian Islam" has become more and more a French Islam, because of the French nationality of those who possess a Muslim cultural background, it comprises the most numerous groups: young Franco-Maghrebians (one million), Maghrebians of Algeria, Tunisia and Morocco (1,412,000 at the census of March 1990), Black Africans (178,000, half of whom have a Muslim cultural background), Turks (201,000), French Muslims (harkis: 500,000), Pakistanese and others (50,000), and converted French (50,000).

In its majority, this population, for its oldest component has a very low rate of school attendance, Islamic education included and its religious practice is both derived from traditional rural customs and recent Islamic trends which became active in the eighties (Muslim Brothers, Afghans and Iranians).

Moreover, the evolution of countries of origin brings specific tendencies to each national group: the entrance of the Algerian FIS (from Algeria) into French suburbs, negotiating its presence against a promise of social peace and getting rid of drugs and alcohol,[8] the political and religious place of the King of Morocco as Commander of the Believers to fight against integrism even in the French space (involving, among others, a speech to the three Moroccan girls wearing a scarf in 1989 at the French TV), and, at the margins, the influence of some extremist groups coming from Tunisia such as the "Mouvement de la Tendance Islamique" which created in France the GIF[9] and introduced literature of the Muslim Brothers and the "Tabligh" (*Foi et Pratique*), a fundamentalist move-ment[10], and proposed to read the Qoran and to pray.

All these trends may touch the Franco-Maghrebians in France: the oldest because they have abandoned the myth of return and know that they will live and die in France. So they cannot postpone their coming back to Islam, all the more since the other structures of socialization have been strongly weakened by unemployment, bringing them towards a private life and to developing a cultural or religious identity. As for the youngest, Islam grows all the more as exclusion increases: in some suburbs, the beard-wearing men ("barbus") are the only present to propose them structures of belief, of life, even a family or a job and sometimes a valuable identity: "It is better to say we are Muslims than unemployed". But the leaders come also from elsewhere (Maghrebian students from middle classes), considering France as a "terre de mission".[11] In the meanwhile, the relative failure of the associative movement for civic rights (the young Franco-Maghrebian movement of the eighties stressing the fight against racism, new citizenship, allegiance to French society) pushes the most desperate ones to the alternative model of Islamic identity as a way of life and a way to disturb the French political game. Some first examples of such a behaviour appeared during the Gulf War among the excluded who liked to refer to: "Vive Saddam" facing the journalists, while the associative beur movement tried to calm their troops.[12]

b) *Africans*

Very strongly hierarchised, Islam of Black Africans is comparatively a practice of foreign workers of the first generation. Half of Black Africans in France have a Muslim cultural background, a more "soufi" one, with "marabouts" and brotherhoods. Four of them are namely present in France:[13] the Qadiriyya, the Tidjanis, the Murids and the Tablighis. The "marabout" plays the role of a leader, travelling in France to help the young workers to come back to Islam, often taken in charge by the immigrant community itself. But one must not be misled by false marabouts "à carte de visite" who propose magic interventions in love-affairs or work to poor and credulous people.

c) *Turks*

Very isolated in France, ignorant of the Arabic language, Turkish believers rarely join other Muslims in France from whom they hold a distance because of their experience of secularism (1924). Among them, there is a double scission between Kurds (40% in emigration against 20% in Turkey) and others, and between Sunnis (the majority) and Shiites (the Alevi minority). Shiites are called "red heads" and do not practise proselytism (they were born in this religion and remain so) but consider themselves as belonging to a religion of the excluded. Many networks are structuring

Turkish allegiances, organised across the associative movement, ranging from the followers of the Turkish political leader Erbakan, to fundamentalists who want to control the population in exile (Milli Görüs), and to the nationalist "Grey Wolfs", who are powerful in Germany.[14]

We must also take into account some brotherhoods which structure themselves clandestinely: some of them are Shiites and other Sunnites. They appear as religious associations in France (Union des Centres culturels islamiques) as well as in Germany. Today the main aim of such groups is more to take control of the teaching of religion than to socialise the immigrants.

Along with these three main cultures, we must mention some thousands of converted French whose leaders (Jacoub Roty, Daniel-Youssef Leclerc, Didier-Ali Bourg) have taken responsibilities in the organization of Islam in France and creating universities to teach it.

The stakes of Islam

Actually the stakes of Islam in France go further than its religious practice which is rather low (10% and 1% fundamentalists) if we take into account the five pillars of Islam (faith, prayer, Ramadan, taxes and Mecca pilgrimage), but the identitary consciousness grows among the 16-24 years old.[15] The same holds true for visible communitarist practices such as Ramadan (declared to be observed by 75% of them).

The political challenge on Islam in France is mainly observed in three domains:

1) *The representation of Islam in France*

France is a secularised country, which considers that secularism is an element of the republican values. The law of 1905 on the separation between the churches and the state precises that the State does not recognise nor give subsidies to any religion in France. Associations ruled by the law of 1905 organise the life of religions in France (but most of the roughly 1000 Islamic associations registered are ruled by the law of 1901 because of their cultural activities at local levels). This status is not implemented in the three departments of Alsace-Lorraine (Haut-Rhin, Bas-Rhin and Moselle) because they were part of Germany in 1905 and they thus live under the Concordat of 1801.

Many of the thousand associations have been structured at the national level since the eighties, with the aim of gaining a representativity vis-à-vis the public powers in France: the FNMF (*Fédération Nationale des Musulmans de France*), created in 1985, represents a "Gallican" Islam, an Islam of France federating 150 Islamic local associations; the UOIF (*Union des Organisations Islamiques de France*), created in 1983, whose ideas are not far from the Muslim Brothers, is inspired by Tunisians and challenges the power of the FNMF, ruled by Moroccans; the GIF (*Groupe Islamique de France*), created in 1981, of Tunisian origin; the AIF (*Association Islamique de France*), born in 1984; the UJM (*Union des Jeunes Musulmans*) born in 1987, among the "beurs" of Lyons.[16] The Mosque of Paris, built in 1924 and which wants to develop a moderate form of Islam also fights for representativity.

Another political challenge was formulated by the French public powers at the end of the eighties, viz. about how to dialogue with Islam in France. Some local affairs had remained unresolved by the mayors and the demand of Islam was requiring a French answer: market of hallal meat, building of mosques, scarf affairs, muslim places in the cemeteries, etcetera. In 1989, the CORIF (*Conseil de Réflexion sur l'Islam en France*) was created by the Home Minister Pierre Joxe to be an interlocutor with public powers, and the ensuring debates on an Islam of France, a "gallican Islam", were very rich.[17] This consultation structure of nine wise men, which was not really representative of all the trends of Islam, has not been consulted by Charles Pasqua since 1993 and the Head of the Great Mosque of Paris, Dalil Boubakeur, has given birth to a new structure in November 1993, the "*Conseil Représentatif des Musulmans de France*". It consists of 25 members, but lacks the participation of the FNMF and the UOIF. It aims at occupying itself with the training of imams. In January 1995, the Rector gave to the Home Ministry a "Chart of The Islamic Religion in France", reasserting the respect of the republican rules.

This last stake has acquired a central role in the French debates since the very last years, with a kind of war between the Institutes. In 1991, a University was created in the department of Ain at the initiative of the UOIF and financed by Saudi Arabia, followed by an institute of training (the CERISI of the French convert Didier-Ali Bourg whose association is member of the FNMF) financed by some countries of the Gulf, and by the Institute for the training of imams of the Paris Great Mosque (November 1993). The challenge is actually very strong, in a situation where established elites among Muslims in France are lacking, faced with the necessity to adapt Islam to secularised western societies, the disintegration and exclusion of the youth, and the subsidies offered by Saudi Arabia.

Another debate lies in the visibility of Islam in the French landscape. Have we to go on with a thousand mosques, but many of them living in a kind of clandestinity in cellars and undergrounds, or to encourage "mosquées cathédrales", giving more legitimacy to Islam but with the risk of exacerbating a part of the French population? Although there are only five "mosquées cathedrales" in France (Paris, Roubaix, Mantes-la-Jolie, Every and the last one of Lyon since September 30th, 1994) it seems that beautiful great mosques tend to banalise Islam, to oblige such mosques to gather several trends and nationalities around a quiet Islam, to avoid the creation of suburb heros, and to give a more positive image of Islam than the negative one of poor men praying in the street.[18] In most cases, it is the poverty and the discretion of the prayer rooms which strike, in spite of the negative image of mosques in the neighbourhood in French public opinion, rather than the challenge to French identity brought by "minarets" in the French landscape.

2) *The game of allegiances*

At several occasions, the allegiances of populations of Muslim culture have been questioned in the French political debate: at the occasion of the reform of the Nationality Code (can one be French and Muslim?), during the Gulf War (weren't we facing with a fifth column whose allegiances were doubtful?), and with regard to the Franco-Algerian agreement on military service (signed in 1983) which allows the applicants to take the French nationality even if they have served in the army in Algeria (in fact only a very few of them, hardly 5%, do so in Algeria).

The Gulf War was the best opportunity to appreciate the nature of such questioning about allegiances. As soon as the Gulf War began, religious authorities in France (Catholic, Protestant, Jewish, Muslim), as well as communitary associations and some mediatic leaders of the "show bizz" wanted to preserve the dialogue between communities and refused to bring in France the Middle-East dramas. The overwhelming feeling was less the political or ideological passion or the desire to influence the events, than the anxiousness to preserve daily life (suppression of external and collective activities or leisure).

However, the Gulf has provoked a steady gap between the main trend of French public opinion and the four million people of Arab-Muslim culture: a SOFRES poll of January 25th 26th, 1991, showed that 68% of the Muslims were hostile to the American military intervention in the Gulf (against 75% of French population in favour of it). But there has been no manifestation for or against the French Government and no conflict between those populations and the police about the Gulf War.

As Dominique Schnapper[19] showed, the sympathy of Franco-Maghrebians has remained prudent: 74% declared at the SOFRES poll that they would not fight in the Gulf, neither on the side of Saddam Hussein, nor on that of the French army. But the proximity to Saddam Hussein is stronger among the youngest (15-24 years old) (27%). At the same time the rise of political consciousness among the most scholarised in the suburbs appears with the support to the Palestinian cause and the hostility towards Israël, according to a symbolic arabity and a support to the PLO.[20]

However, they felt insecure. They were critical rather than proud when Saddam Hussein launched its missiles on Israël, according to the SOFRES poll. Most of Franco-Maghrebians were systematically nearer to non Muslim French people than to the rest of the Muslim community because they were strongly concerned with their life and future in France. Their reaction to the Gulf War has showed once more that community-feeling was less strong than their belonging to the French political identity.

This majority must not hide a minority of activists of a high level of scholarship, leaders of Muslim associations, holding an anti-Western and anti-Sionist discourse as a response to rivalries with the successful Jewish organization. They were in search for dignity and consideration in French society: for them, the war has been an opportunity to show their Muslim identity.

As for the most integrated, they have had the feeling to go through a trial, to be unfairly suspected of double allegiances: their identity was hurt in spite of their adhesion to universalism and French values. They have had the impression to have been victims of the hypocrisy of the Western world.

Today, the Palestinian movement is not very strong in France, unlike the situation in Germany and Great Britain. Except for some trends such as Muslims Brothers' networks, the concern of Franco-Maghrebians seems now much more focused towards Algeria than towards the Middle East. But here also, the reactions and allegiances are not very strong.[21]

In fact, all field surveys[22] on Islam and citizenship illustrate the various forms of combination of values: a secularized Islam, not necessarily practised, among the most scholarised, of a high cultural level; a rather diffuse Islam, quite popular and identitary, lived day-to-day, negotiated through the mediation of local leaders (mosques of the districts and suburbs); an Islam of the margins, linking Islamic propagandists to the excluded in search for an alternative model to citizenship and Western values and a rebuilt identity proposing Islam as a way of life; and an Islam of "elsewhere" maintained through transnational networks which try to preserve religious values (flows of marriages between France and the Maghreb) or to bring new ones (flows of Islamic leaders).

In these last examples, the communitarist dimension of Islam appears as the alternative to desocialization (failure of universalism, individualism, secularism, citizenship brought by civic associationism of Franco-Maghrebian during the 80's), but there are many "bricolages" of identities. Allegiance to French values predominates. The urban policy, set up since 1989 seems however in some places to have failed compared with the local success of some beard-wearing men ("barbus"). Is this new trend an emerging set of references, shifting between cultural mediation and urban violence, able to define new social movements, ethnic lobbies or new citizens? Most of them are merely asking for respect and dignity, while revealing a complexification of the allegiances in contradiction with the logic of the Nation-State, both at internal and at external levels.

Some of these allegiances are visible in the various games played by local associationism: in the suburbs of great towns we can observe several types of these associations: on the one hand, municipal associations with religious aims whose role consists in fighting against the lack of social structures in the district and against religious quietness contrasting with the disturbances all around and which try to develop proselytism; on the other hand, civic local associations but infiltrated by Islamic leaders who aim at becoming strongly settled mediators for the public powers, with a political project in France built on the so-called Anglo-American model of ethnocommunitarist lobbying and expressing values opposed to Western democracies. As for the other structured networks warning to introduce the Algerian civil war in France, the factors of adhesion to such groups are different in France and Algeria and the aims and context strongly differ. Moreover, some networks in France are, owing to immigration, bringing funds to armed groups in Algeria. Developing terrorism in France and provoking the suspicion of the police on a large scale would mean destroying the main financial support. Otherwise, reislamization in France mainly emerges outside the control of the ex-Algerian islamism and terrorism, viz. in the form of pietism, as a search for a strong communitarist identity which must be distinguished from political integrism.

3) *The questions about "ingérence": Is the Algerian war crossing the Mediterranean?*

The Folembray affair of August 1994, when twenty so-called "islamists" were expelled from France[23] has awakened in France new fears about possible integrism imported from Algeria. It also revealed the possible existence of illegal networks helping the Algerian "underground" from France and bringing the "djihad" to France. Other affairs stressed the same challenge: in some suburbs, the new scarf affairs caused by the circular of François Bayrou, Minister of Education, in September 1994 stressed the islamist support of several girls (around 2000 wore the scarf in September and around 400 since the circular; according to official data 79 girls were excluded from school). In December 1994 some of their supporters held placards with "Vive la France musulmane", trying to pursue proselytism. Then, the Algiers-Paris Airbus affair, on the eve of Christmas '94, went on to bring new fears about transposition to France of the Algerian civil war. Most recently, the terrorist attacks in Paris and Lyon in the summer and autumn of 1995 have reinforced the suspicion of political intrusion.

If proselytism emerges, with an exportation of the Algerian crisis to France, the causes of the expansion of Islam are not the same here and there. In France, the radical forms of religious behaviour among the youth are inspired by the new prophets of the American ghettos where Black Muslims are emerging on foot-ball grounds, squats and playgrounds. But in the French context this is somewhat different. New wave imams are using the loss of identitary values and the feeling of exclusion to develop a "catch all" strategy all around. Across their networks of so-called cultural associations, some of them are socializing the excluded to integrism, intolerance and radical Islam as a denial of citizenship. But all the Islamic associations are not alike: for some, the teaching of the Qoran may also give a new sense of life to both teachers and children. Others have left their families to flee from a too heavily tightened social control and they practise Islam to acquire independence from their parents (it is one of the several meanings of the scarf-wearing among girls in the university and high schools) without any definitive conflict, in an acceptable freedom, while asserting for themselves what is "haram" and "halal". So, it is difficult to answer whether Islam is or is not a danger for secularised societies such as France. Has French society to tolerate its expansion or to fight against it? Assimilating it to the worst does not seem to be the right way for public powers and opinion, even if some forms of proselytism appear as a denial of citizenship and secularism.

Another question is about the links with the Algerian armed terrorist struggle. During 1994, 300 persons were arrested and among them 83 in the surroundings of Paris, following six months of police enquiries on an external branch of the GIA. Some associations, presenting themselves as a help to excluded young Muslims, are a logistic support to the Algerian "underground", financed by drugs, by wealthy shopkeepers who belong with all their families to illegal networks. Other financial help is provided by the "Islamic tax", a kind of racket on Muslim shopkeepers. Some places in the far countryside serve as military training areas for suburban youth who don't fear to be killed in Algeria. Some of the youngsters have a radical feeling of revolt, less because of the Algerian situation which they don't know very well but because of their conditions of life in France.[24]

So, the Islamic threat in France is two-sided: against citizenship and democracy in France or turned towards the Algerian conflict, with links between the two, but these are neither automatical nor frequent. Other European neighbours, such as Germany, are showing their fear towards the heterogeneous mix of leaders of Maghrebian and Middle-Eastern islamism, young suburban activisms and weapons or drugs networks. The two leaders of the former FIS in Europe - Cheikh Abdelbaki Sahraoui in France and Rabah Kébir in Germany - were severely controlled. But other countries such as Italy, Spain, Belgium or Eastern Europe, strongly concerned by those Islamic nations, are diversely worried by the threats of political extension of such trends on their own muslim communities. And where nation-states have a strong and long tradition of democracy, such as in Great Britain and Switzerland, the Islamic cause does not seem to be promised a long future.

Conclusion

Islam in France is raising two main questions: the first one is about its image in the French public opinion. Several representations are observed: cultivated Islam, sociological Islam, Islam as an implementation of the Qoran stricto sensu, Islam as an alternative to political expression and citizenship, Islam as an emergence of external political disturbance in the internal political order, etcetera. But the specificity of Islam in France lies in the fact that it is mainly viewed as a religion of colonised, of poor people, of obscurantism, unable to adopt itself to French values (the term of integration is very often used about people of Muslim culture) and in contradiction with French political rules. The image has now changed with collective identitary expressions of the excluded youth, using Islam as an instrument of communitarist expression or as an alternative way of life. However, the public representations tend to amalgamate all these new Muslims to integrism and political terrorism. Thereby, several examples are adduced, such as the murders of Paris, in September 1986, the fear of violence which led to preventive police operations during the Gulf War in 1991, the expulsion by Charles Pasqua of the Muslim leaders in Folembray in August 1994, and the most recent terrorist action in France in 1995. It is only if we will reach a "banalization" of Islam as a religion among the others, that this great gap will be crossed.[25]

The other question is about the new expressions of Islam as a political alternative to democratic and Western values, a negation of citizenship. If it can be considered merely as an identitary behaviour of the youth (16-24 years old), perhaps is it only a question of contingency. But, with the permanence of exclusion and unemployment, the failure of traditional pools of socialization, it may appear as a middle-term answer to urban disturbances, with its positive heroes, its missionary program ("France terre de mission"), its external links to Arab countries ("ingérence"). In that case, it would mean that communitarism would have gained against the French model of citizenship in some margins of society where universal values would have lost their meaning.

Notes

1 See Linhart: 1973.
2 Kepel: 1987.
3 Wihtol de Wenden: 1988.
4 Mauroy, P: in 1983 (cf. Catherine Wihtol de Wenden: *Les immigrés et la politique*. Paris, Presses de la FNSP, chap. 5, 1988).
5 Gilles Kepel: *Le Monde*, 13 October 1994.
6 Wihtol de Wenden: 1991.
7 Boyer: 1993.
8 Wihtol de Wenden: 1993.
9 GIF: *Groupe Islamique de France* created in 1980.
10 *Société pour la propagation de la Foi et pour l'appel de Dieu* created in 1972.
11 Kepel: 1994.
12 Wihtol de Wenden: 1991.
13 Diop: 1989.
14 Gokalp: 1986.
15 Kepel: *Le Monde*, IFOP Survey, 13 October 1994.
16 Cesari: 1994.
17 Etienne: 1989.
18 The photograph of the Mosque of the Rue du Bon Pasteur, in Marseilles, with faithful men on their knees in the street was reproduced several times in newspapers and magazines and tends to give an image of a fanatic religion.
19 See Schnapper: 1993.
20 See Geisser: 1995.
21 See Belaid: 1995.
22 Such as the one conducted by the CERI from 1987 to 1989: *Modes d'insertion des populations de culture musulmane dans le système politique français.* (dir.: Rémy Leveau and Catherine Wihtol de Wenden), déc. 1990.
23 Most of them were expelled illegally and have gained their procedures against the French Government. See Joseph Krulic; L'affaire des ressortissants algériens retenus à Folembray. *Revue française de droit administratif*, mars-avril 1995.
24 See Moi, Khaled Kelkal, interview by Dietmar LOCH, *Le Monde*, 7 october 1995.
25 Wihtol de Wenden: 1992. See also the same author: 1990.

3

Religious Traditions in the Public Sphere:

Habermans, MacIntyre and the Representation of Religious Minorities

David Herbert

In early 1989 Rushdie's *The Satanic Verses* hit the headlines of British newspapers after its burning in protests by Bradford Muslims was followed in uncomfortable succession by Khomeini's *fatwa*. At the time I was an undergraduate studying religion, psychology, social policy and literature, a combination of subjects which seems fortuitous for analyzing the controversy. Yet the lack of communication I perceived between specialists operating within these fields led me to the conclusion that while illuminating accounts of the controversy multiplied, there remained no academic discourse capable of representing together the integrity of the diverse groups of people reacting to the controversy. This academic division was mirrored at a popular level, judging by media representations of the controversy, and continuing debates in the areas of race, ethnicity and religion.

In subsequent research I have been concerned with the representation of religion in public contexts, including the media, law, education and politics. This paper considers two debates in the borderlands between moral philosophy and social theory, with the intention of shedding light on issues involved in the political participation of religious minorities in secular societies. Most of the examples used concern Muslims in Britain. The two debates have been stimulated by Habermas' account of the structural transformation of the public sphere (1962; English translation 1989), and by Alasdair MacIntyre's account of encounter between traditions.

Habermas' early work offers a historical perspective on the development of the ideas and practices of 'publicness' in Western societies, albeit one which needs supplementation and correction by other narratives. In particular he provides a perspective on the development of public debate and political participation in these societies. While critical of these developments Habermas expresses hope that the quality of public debate glimpsed amongst the bourgeoisie of the Enlightenment can be recreated on a wider stage today. By contrast MacIntyre is deeply critical of Enlightenment culture, drawing instead on Aristotelian and Thomistic thought to re-imagine society on the basis of traditioned communities. Yet in his modelling of encounter between traditions MacIntyre commits himself to the possibility of rational negotiation between traditions, and it is at this point that the two contrasting theories converge, and why they warrant attention in societies where existing practices often seem inadequate to represent new diversities.

After introducing these debates I shall consider an example of how they might inform empirical work. In 1993 the Policy Studies Institute (PSI) published a report entitled Britain's Ethnic Minorities (Donaldson (ed.) 1993), whose findings were used in the making of a controversial BBC *Panorama* documentary *A New Underclass*? This broadcast drew strong protests from British Muslims for its portrayal of Muslim women and youth. In citing this study I intend to argue for a more explicit thematizing of religious and cultural difference in studies of ethnic minorities in secular societies, using models suggested by the debates surrounding Habermas and MacIntyre. Finally, I shall consider the implications of the argument advanced for what Charles Taylor calls "the politics of recognition" (1991); the demands of minority groups for differential treatment to preserve their traditions, and thus sustain a complex equality based not on individual sameness but on a combination of individual rights and collective identity.

To speak at all of religious 'communities' in post Enlightenment societies is immediately contentious, for in such contexts religion tends to be seen as a private matter, so that suspicions arise about the purposes the imagination of such 'communities' serves. Indeed, the mobilization of collective identity through religion may be used to suppress diversity within an imagined community, and to consolidate the power of those recognised as leaders of the designated group. But questions may also be asked as to whose interests the suppression of such identities serves. It is not surprising that designations of publicness and privacy reflect the balance of power within a society; however, this paper seeks to ask how reason and justice can interrupt the play of power, where understandings of reason and justice are themselves contested.

A sketch of two debates

As summarised by Nancy Fraser, Habermas' concept of "the public sphere... designates a theatre (sic) in modern societies in which political participation is enacted through the medium of talk. It is the space in which citizens deliberate about their common affairs, and hence an institutionalised arena of discursive interaction" (Fraser 1992: 110).

The public sphere is distinct both from the state, and from the economy, distinctions essential to democratic theory. In the English coffee houses, French salons and German table-societies of seventeenth and eighteenth century Europe, a culture developed in which it came to be believed that the debate which drives political decision should be open to all private citizens, and that the outcome of such debate should rest upon the quality of argument and not the status of participants. It is in these institutions that Habermas discerns the genesis of the modern public sphere, and the birth of the ideal of modern participatory democracy.

In *The Structural Transformation of the Public Sphere* (1962, English translation 1989) Habermas seeks both to reclaim this concept as an ideal with emancipatory potential, and to explain what he diagnoses as the decline of this sphere in the nineteenth and twentieth centuries. Thus the model provides both a historical narrative to locate contemporary contexts of political participation in Western societies, and an ideal model of public discussion. This could be a useful perspective from which to view the political participation of religious and cultural minorities, for it counters a liberal tendency to assume that rational discussion has a neutral, ahistorical character, and provides a structure to narrate the reasoning and history underlying present practices.

Habermas' account is not without its problems. It is striking that he considers the quality of political participation to have declined since the eighteenth century, for during this period the inclusiveness of participation,

at least at a formal level, has vastly expanded, as witnessed by the enfran-
chisement of women, the landless, and members of religious and cultural
minorities. Habermas' evaluation privileges a particular form of participation by focusing on the bourgeois public sphere. Hence the themes of
quantity and diversity of participation need to be theorised alongside the
quality of participation emphasised by Habermas.

In the historic bourgeois public sphere it was held that equal participation is enabled simply by ignoring or 'bracketing' status differences.
However, it has been shown that such bracketing may only mask the way
in which status effects formally equal discursive contexts; thus studies
have repeatedly shown that men say most and interrupt women more often
in the formally equal settings such as business meetings and academic
seminars (Fraser 1992: 119).

Furthermore, the notion of a single public sphere depends upon the
effectiveness of bracketing procedures, because if in practice all voices are
not heard equally, then the principle of decision by quality of argument
alone is undermined. Thus it is likely that plural public spheres will better
allow marginalised voices to emerge in stratified societies (Eley 1992). So
a model which also theorises the relationship between different and often
competing public spheres is required.

Distinctions between public and private assumed by both the bourgeois
ideal and contemporary liberal theory also need to be challenged; as
Benhabib argues (1992: 84), such boundaries are politically defined and
can be transformed through political contestation, as the publication of the
domestic arena by women's movements or the publication of sexuality by
gay and lesbian movements both illustrate. Religious and cultural minorities may also dissent from the dominant liberal formulations of private
and public.

In short, Habermas' theory needs to thematize difference, a process
which problematises the simple egalitarianism of the bourgeois model
central to his thesis. MacIntyre can help towards such thematization. But
as I commend attention to the debate initiated by Habermas rather than an
uncritical adoption of his early ideas, so I commend MacIntyre's account
of tradition with qualifications. However, I shall argue that MacIntyre's
theory of tradition promises to provide both a way of respecting the
integrity of the traditions of diverse communities, and a mode of rational

conversation between traditions.

MacIntyre uses the term 'tradition' in two senses, both as intellectual "traditions of enquiry", and as "those larger social and cultural traditions within which traditions of enquiry are embedded" (1994: 292). He argues for a reconnection of culture, value and reason disconnected by the Enlightenment, appealing to schemes developed from Aristotle and Aquinas. I suggest that his emphasis on the importance of embedding in culture and history for both for individual identity and purpose, and for rationality, is crucial to understand minorities' demands for what might be termed 'cultural survival', demands which range from British Muslims' appeals for separate state funded schools to Canadian Inuit demands for special land rights to preserve their traditional lifestyle.

This way of thinking challenges the limited conceptions of 'culture' and religion' often implicit in multicultural and multifaith policy and practice, for example in confining culture to aesthetic and domestic spheres, while assuming the superiority of Western traditions in such public domains as intellectual enquiry, economics, and politics (Hulmes 1989). It also makes sense of connections between social and ethical practices obscured by a Western ethics premised on the autonomous individual of Kantian moral theory, for example the connections between South Asian hospitality codes, honour, loyalty and obligation.

In highlighting the capacity of traditions of enquiry to generate solutions to problems from their own resources attention shifts to the traditional resources of religious and cultural minorities and away from wholesale adoption of Western practices. Regarding Islamic law (*sharia*), such internal resources for change are illustrated in the historic controversy amongst Sunni jurists over the validity and scope of new interpretation (*ijtihad*; literally 'effort'), and especially *istihsan* ('preference'), which can involve an appeal to higher principles within *sharia* (Kamali 1991), in contrast to the natural law basis of Christian shaped Western legal systems, which appeal beyond positive law to a 'natural' order. Such resources may provide responses to some of the challenges of modernity, and at least challenge the view that *sharia* is frozen in medieval form.

MacIntyre suggests that where traditions meet, as in modern plural societies, members of one tradition may learn to understand another tradition as "a second first language", and in doing so may recognise that within another tradition resources which solve problems identified but unresolveable within their own tradition (1977; 1988: 349-369). Here is the promise that culturally rooted rational exchange rather than superior force can shape encounter between traditions. For example, it is possible to argue that some contemporary Muslims recognise in democracy a solution to problems of legitimacy which arise under modern conditions and for which Islamic political theory had no prior solution. At the same time, their tradition enables them to critique western forms of democracy, and to draw on practices of consultation (*shura*) already present within the tradition (e.g. Mernissi 1993, Ayubi 1991).

However, their contrasting evaluations of the Enlightenment question whether Habermas and MacIntyre's work can be viewed as complementary, Habermas seeking to fulfil the Enlightenment project, MacIntyre to replace it. Yet both share a commitment to the possibility of rational negotiation between diverse parties in plural societies, rejecting alternatives as at best constrained coercion. Both have enacted this commitment in ongoing dialogues with academics across conventional disciplinary boundaries and spanning several decades. Furthermore, both emphasise the relationship between ethics and culture without reducing this relationship to relativism, and insist on the importance of reclaiming history for understanding the present and transforming the future.[1] Thus both provide an alternative to liberal theories, which presuppose the internal liberalization of minority communities, and to postmodern theories, which deny the possibility of reasoned public dialogue, and thus abandon the public arena to the play of force. I now turn to apply these suggestions to the PSI study.

'Race' and religion: The PSI's 'Britain's ethnic minorities

The first problem to be considered is the dominance of the constructs of 'race' and 'ethnicity' which privilege colour in collecting data about minority groups, and in particular the assumption that colour is the principal determinant of discrimination, to the extent that other factors can be disregarded. One result is that religious factors are excluded *a priori* because they simply do not feature in the raw data. A second is that most emphasis is placed on the agency of the majority in oppressing the minority, so that the creative response of minority groups to oppressive conditions is neglected (Ballard 1992). Thirdly, the absence of a positive account of minority tradition can mean that where explanation of discrimination on the basis of colour fails, an impoverished and negative portrayal of minority cultures may feature as a post hoc explanation.

Each of these features is illustrated in the Policy Studies Institute's (PSI) Britain's Ethnic Minorities (Donaldson, ed. 1993).[2] One section of the report seeks to explain differences in relative economic deprivation between ethnic minority groups in the UK. It found Pakistani and Bangladeshi groups were the most deprived, while East African groups, mostly twice-migrants from the subcontinent, were the best off (Donaldson ed. 1993: 151-4). Trying to explain these findings, the report dismissed the possibility that differential discrimination against these groups could be a significant factor, since, "Previous research found that racial discrimination was experienced equally by all ethnic minority groups" (Donaldson ed. 1993: 155). The report continues by arguing that this situation is highly unlikely to have changed, since "both the most and least successful of the groups in the ethnic minority population *have a similar skin colour*" (1993: 166, emphasis added).

But is it plausible to maintain that skin colour is the only criterion of discrimination? Are the secularised clean shaven Asian professional in a smart Western-style suit and the *mullah* in traditional dress with full beard discriminated against solely in the same way, i.e. on the grounds of colour? Do history, and immediate context, not influence perception? Are Western media reactions to revolutionary Iran, to *The Satanic Verses*, to the Gulf War, irrelevant to discrimination in the UK.?

In fact, there is some evidence of differential discrimination, both against Muslims as a group, and between other minorities on the grounds of cultural difference, in spite of an overall scarcity of research in this area.[3] Thus in the Britain a 1991 MORI poll found that 24% expressed an unfavourable attitude to Islam compared with only 12% favourable, while between 35% and 50% saw potential conflicts with the 'British Way of Life' in the Muslim practices of *halal* slaughter, separation of the sexes for health care and five times daily prayer (IQRA Trust 1991).

Such evidence suggests that a model which considers cultural and religious difference, both in terms of discrimination against minorities and the adaptive responses of minority communities, would be better placed to analyze the complexity of community relations than one based solely on prejudice arising from colour discrimination.

In the PSI study, the choice of variables meant that a number of significant facts did not emerge at the empirical level. These include the facts that Bangladeshis and Pakistanis are predominantly Muslim, while East Africans are of mixed Sikh, Hindu and Muslim backgrounds, and that the latter are likely to be more secularised than the former, coming from urban rather than rural sending communities. Such factors only emerged *post hoc* when a colour based explanation failed, and then only in terms of alleged disadvantages of a Muslim background, namely educational deprivation and low economic activity amongst women (Donaldson ed. 1993: 158). In the PSI report these comments are expressed cautiously and the lack of empirical support acknowledged, but in the *Panorama* documentary this caution was absent.

None of this is to deny that the practices of Muslim communities may restrict the economic and educational activities of women (although this remains needs to be demonstrated rather than asserted), but rather to show that the PSI's model of investigation left no other avenue of explanation open. By contrast a model like MacIntyre's, which takes seriously the religious and cultural complexity of both minority and majority communities, could look at both the possible impact of differential discrimination by the majority community, as well the complex of values which may produce restrictions on the activities of women and the reasons which may be given for such restrictions. Thus Muslims may argue that sustaining of greater family coherence may be a benefit of practices for which these restrictions may be the cost. Such reasons may prove unacceptable in a liberal society, but to conceal them, and to refuse to consider the value system within which they make sense, serves only to reinforce mutual ignorance.

This last point raises a controversial aspect of representing religious and cultural difference, that is prejudice not just against but within ethnic minorities, or rather the variety of ethical systems sometimes at variance with secular ethics which minority communities may sustain. The status of women within *sharia* or Hindu *dharma* demonstrate such ethical diversity, indicating ethical systems based on forms of reciprocity embedded in communal and hierarchical rather then individualistic and egalitarian relationships. How is such ethical diversity be represented in the public spheres of secularised democracies?

It must be recognised that minority communities are diverse, containing groups and individuals ranging from secularist to fundamentalist. Also, the behaviour of individuals varies with different relational and social contexts, defying classification into monolithic religious or secular categories.[4]

Thus there is a danger that presenting minority difference can create a new artificial homogeneity, not of colour but of religion, culture or value. Such difficulties are exemplified in an exchange in the pages of *New Community* between Richard Ballard (1992) and John Goering (1993). Ballard attacks the American derived model of 'race relations' based on 'deprivationism' and argues passionately for a recognising religious and cultural difference, citing the mobilization of South Asian kinship networks in economic production as a response to discrimination generated from traditional resources, "mental, spiritual and cultural" (1992: 485).

In response, Goering counters that Ballard's arguments pays insufficient attention to macroeconomics and reinforces stereotypes of the religious, hardworking Asian, denying the legitimate aspirations of members of minorities to the same things as the white population (1993: 140).

Furthermore, as the *Women Against Fundamentalism* group argue (Saghal and Yuval-Davies 1992), the public recognition of religious or cultural 'communities' can serve to shore up patriarchal authority structures. Indeed, as Yasmin Ali contends, patriarchal structures in local government may reinforce patriarchal structures amongst ethnic minorities, thus combining to replicate colonial systems of representation (Ali 1992). Such recognition may also lead the second and third generations to believe that the only path to political influence is by identifying with such communities and participating in such structures.

Thus the representation of collective difference is fraught with democratic danger. Yet the argument that the self-esteem, achievement and integration of minority groups depends significantly upon positive public recognition of their distinctive identities appears compelling. Therefore, to represent the interests of minority groups it appears necessary to represent their diversity in terms of both fundamental individual equality with and some measure of shared difference from the majority population, which itself also needs to be seen as diverse.

Liberalism and the 'politics of recognition'

However, individualistically oriented liberal theories of justice have difficulties in recognising demands springing from collective differences. MacIntyre's approach suggests we examine the history of these difficulties. Modern forms of liberalism have tended to reject claims of cultural rights based on collective difference, particularly since just such rights have been tainted by association with Nazi ideology (Kymlicka 1988). Yet rights based on collective difference have since been invoked both by migrant groups, like British Muslims, and indigenous minorities, like the Canadian Inuit (ibid.). These collective claims may conflict with the rights of individuals both within and outside such communities. For example, Muslim struggles for recognition as a collectivity, expressed in the UK in demands for separate schooling or provision in religious education (UKACIA 1993), may conflict with demands by others in those communities to be recognised as autonomous individuals, as expressed by the *Women Against Fundamentalism* group (Saghal and Yuval-Davis 1990, 1992).

While the American civil rights struggle in 1960's formed thinking about community relations both in the West in terms of colour and individual equality, patterns of immigration and political developments have generated challenges to this paradigm. Thus Habermas asks, "Can a theory of rights which is so individualistically constructed deal adequately with struggles for recognition in which it is the articulation and assertion of collective identities which is at stake?" (1994: 107).

Rawls (1973, 1993) provides an example of a liberal response to this challenge,[5] shifting the scope of his theory from the universal to the particular form of the Western democracy. Yet the retention of devices such as "the Original Position" and "the Veil of Ignorance" show that he continues to assume the universality of the individualist, autonomous subject, a cultural product of the Western capitalism, and hence does not allow for the possibility that cultural difference amongst the West's new inhabitants may be more than skin deep.

Bhikhu Parekh finds the liberalism of Rawls and his contemporaries Dworkins and Raz fundamentally unchanged since the writings of JS Mill, an East India Company employee who rejected even British parliamentary control of India, and thus sees the work of contemporary liberals as embedded in an "arrogant colonial mode of thought" (1994: 13).

In his analysis of liberal difficulties, Taylor argues that a new conflict has developed between what he terms a "'difference-blind" liberalism" (1994: 62) and what might be termed a 'difference-aware politics of equality', the latter demanding that recognition of identity based on collective difference is respected as a human right. Taylor argues that individualistic theories of rights cannot adequately represent the needs of groups who feel that their 'cultural survival' is at stake. By contrast, MacIntyre can help make sense of these needs. Cultural survival depends upon a complex network of community and practices in which the individual is embedded, and thus cannot be adequately represented as a commodity to be chosen or rejected by the autonomous individual. Therefore such needs cannot be represented in an individualist theory of justice, either as a good to be chosen or as a right to enable such choice. However, MacIntyre's concept of tradition provides a way of representing this difference, while Habermas' concept of the public sphere can help to analyze the discursive and institutional contexts in which such claims are made.

Exemplars of the new politics of difference discussed by Taylor include not only ethnic and religious minorities, like British Muslims, but also 'lifestyle minorities' like lesbians and gays or New Age travellers. Such examples suggest that this politics differs from a simply nostalgic appeal to premodernity. In contrast to the unreflexive communal solidarity ascribed to premodern collectivities, these demands for recognition depend on a mode of subjectivity characterised by reflexivity, whose history is traced by Taylor to Rousseau, an Enlightenment advocate of both collective purpose and individual subjectivity (1994: 44-51). So this politics should not be seen as the last cries of dying cultures contingent on organic social systems and hence doomed to extinction under modern conditions, but as a new identity politics, at home in the modern world.

Thus we might reflect that in the case of British Muslims, advocates of an assertive Muslim identity are not usually first generation migrants, but second generation or at least Western educated.[6] Furthermore, though it may not represent itself as such, the political Islamism espoused by radicals is distinctively modern, for the various theories of an Islamic state post-date the demise of the caliphate in 1922, and the same modern origin can be argued for moderate Islamic exponents of democracy (Ayubi 1991: 1-34, 201-13). So cultural survival is defended using modern methods, by citizens or would-be citizens anxious to assert their rights.

Conclusion

The politics of identity has become the means through which diverse groups express their incommensurable demands. Two recent dramas of protest and counter-protest graphically illustrate this. In 1989 *Women Against Fundamentalism* counter-protested at the Hyde Park demonstration against *The Satanic Verses*, while on 13 August 1995 the lesbian and gay group *Outrage* marched in protest at the *Hizb-ut-Tahrir* demonstration in Trafalgar Square. How might the concepts of public sphere and tradition help us to make sense of such encounters, to do some kind of justice to radical oppositions expressed by avoiding the reduction of either party to stereotype or caricature?

Habermas reminds us that without public forums and vocabularies capable of sustaining rational discussion such participation is reduced to public posturing. But the demonstrations and confrontations, which avoided violence if not ill-will, themselves point to the limitations of Habermas' focus on rational discussion, and indicate alternative legitimate means of political participation. The examples also suggest that Habermas may overemphasise the importance of consensus as the outcome of rational discussion. Where there are fundamental disagreements concerning the common good rational discussion will not result in consensus. But other outcomes may can reflect the contribution of rational discussion, providing hope that outcomes may be more than the aggregate of power relations. The contribution which public demonstration and other means of lobbying may also make to such outcomes reinforces this hope. As Thomas McCarthy argues, "*rationally motivated* agreement as a moral--political alternative to coercion may well involve elements of conciliation, compromise, consent, accommodation, and the like. Argument ... can play a role in shaping any and all of them. And (this) ... as well as consensus in Habermas' strict sense, can give sense to participants' argumentative practices. The only supposition that seems necessary for the genuine give and take of rational discourse is that the force of the better argument contribute to the final shape of *whatever* agreement is reached." (1992: 67)

This position is compatible with MacIntyre's understanding of competing rationalities, since rational argument in terms of the diverse participants can be seen to contribute to the outcome. This is not pure relativism, for as I have already argued, MacIntyre provides a model of rational exchange between traditions of enquiry. However, it should also be noted that MacIntyre (1981: 62-78) sees protest as the characteristic form of ethical expression in morally fragmented post Enlightenment culture. A culture which denies its traditionality and sees its ethical judgements as free floating deprives itself of rational means of engagement with different judgements, since on MacIntyre's understanding such engagement comes only through mutual recognition of different historically embedded rationalities, and without this we are reduced to the shrill and shriller sounds of protest and counter-protest.

Yet a modified form of Habermas' theory can give meaning to the practice of rational argument even in the face of basic disagreements, while MacIntyre's call to provide a narrative of tradition which links history, culture and thought supplies a basis upon which mutual recognition, as a precursor to rational discussion, can occur. So while the debates stimulated by MacIntyre and Habermas cannot resolve fundamental disagreements, they can provide a framework which gives meaning and purpose to the arguments of participants from diverse traditions, and suggest new directions for research across conventional disciplinary boundaries. Thus they promise alternatives to liberal cultural imperialism and postmodern despair.

Notes

[1] This commitment to history makes them both vulnerable to criticism of the quality of the histories which they write, but such criticisms are fundamentally in accordance with the methods they propose.

[2] It should be noted that the criticism of failing to thematise religion does not apply to other PSI work; see for example *Shifting Ethnic Identities* (Modood et al. 1994).

3   Regarding differential discrimination more generally, Bagley and Verma (1978) found what they termed 'specific racism' against particular minority characteristics in areas of high contact between ethnic groups. Kawwa (1968) found greater prejudice against Cypriots than West Indians in London, the reverse of skin colour difference from the white majority, but in arguably in line with cultural, and certainly linguistic difference. As long ago as 1960 Rokeach argued for the importance of differences in beliefs and attitudes, as well as perceived physical characteristics, in determining racial discrimination.

4   Rather, people exhibit what Vertovec has termed 'multiple cultural competence' in different social settings and relationships (in Jackson and Nesbitt 1993: 174).

5   For alternative liberal responses see Kymlicka (1989) and Galston (1991).

6   E.g. Shabbir Akhtar, Cambridge graduate; Kalim Siddiqui, former *Guardian* journalist; Yusuf Islam, convert and former pop singer.

4

The Muslim Presence in Spain:
Policy and Society

Montserrat Abumalham

The presence of Muslims in Spain is nothing new. Nevertheless, this phenomenon has indeed changed with the passing of time. In this paper I will try not just to analyze, or rather to pose questions about the matter concerning us, but to offer a general view of the effects of the Muslim presence on the Spanish society and of the resulting response given by the society and the political authorities.

Mythical Islam

Before trying to describe the present reality, a few words must be said about the relationship between Spain and Islam, from a perspective I would like to call "mythical."[1] Remarkably, every time subjects such as the Arab World, the Arabs, North Africa or Islam are approached, they are discussed as if these were an indivisible, synonymous or interchangeable whole. Hence, sometimes Iran and the Iranians are discussed as if they were an Arab country - this can be often heard in both private conversations and in the media - and, for example, the Moroccan fishermen are talked of as Muslim fishermen.

It is also frequent to make sort of a temporal distinction (a-temporal or a-historical, I would say) whereby the *Arabs-Muslims-Middle Easterners-North Africans* of the past are regarded as valuable characters who contributed to the progress of the sciences and technology, composed beautiful and exotic poems or built remarkable edifices full of precious decorations. In this context utterances can be heard like the following: "Just seeing the Alhambra one can realize the creative capacity of those people." The preceding sentence usually is followed by an assertion such as: "But today, just look the way they live and how they produce nothing good!"

If we turn to the so trite issue of the religious wars darkening the current political scene, ex-Yugoslavia, the attacks of confession against confession in India and Pakistan, or even the Palestinian-Israeli problem, we are likely to hear about how in Medieval Spain we had a perfect model of peaceful coexistence of the three monotheistic religions cooperating and communicating fluently and with great tolerance. We will even hear that everything went askew due to the advancement of Christianity, a less tolerant religion than Islam.

On the other hand, when a terrorist attack takes place anywhere, the authorities or the security forces are quick to blame it on the radical Islamists who have been seen wandering around the area. The most noticeable example is the Oklahoma massacre, that initially was blamed on someone who did not have a dark skin, supposedly of Muslim religion. In Spain the situation is not as extreme, since it goes not further than requesting the identification papers from those appearing to be from somewhere south of southern Spain. However, this image given by the media has a decisive influence on the opinion of the average Spaniard.

In short, there seems to be two Arab-Islamic worlds: that of an imagined, 'a-historical' past, a perfect place endowed with all goodness, which every Spaniard is willing to join claiming either a Muslim or a Jewish ancestor. And another world, equally 'a-historical' or unreal, to which are attributed all wrongs and perils. These magical and mythical visions must be paid adequate attention since they are the intangible prism through which realities are often observed. Even worse, they force the eyes of goodwilled people to see what is not.

The truth is that there exists an old historical relationship between Spain and Islam that we are not going to discuss here, but obviously it is not only marked by mutual tolerance and enrichment. Neither tolerance nor inter-culturality are functional concepts in past centuries. Even today these are terms whose exact meanings are yet to be defined, and the implementation of which needs yet to find its safest channels.

The real Muslim presence

In very recent times, since the 60s, the Muslim presence in Spain can be considered of four different kinds in a chronological order.

First of all, the non-economic immigrants who came to this country as students enroling in the universities and a high percentage of whom went back to their places of origin. These people came mostly from the Middle East, Syria, Lebanon, Palestine and Egypt. The political circumstances peculiar to some of these countries induced some of them to remain in Spain, where they settled as members of the learned professions or tradesmen. They founded mixed families and adopted the Spanish nationality.[2] These Arab-Muslims, some of them Christians belonging to various confessions, I have called somewhere else "invisible Muslims." Even though they preserve their religious practice and their tongue, they are wholly integrated and are not subject to any kind of rejection by the Spanish population. However, they often express their feelings as victims of the Spaniards' profound ignorance regarding the Arab World and Islam.

The second group of Muslims, chronologically speaking, is that made up of an active and visible though small population core, consisting of converts, or, as they are sometimes called, "neo-Muslims". The phenomenon of conversions has not yet been sufficiently researched by sociologists. In principle, the issue seems to have been researched rather by the Arabists.[3] The approach made by an Arabist to the matter lacks knowledge of sociological analysis techniques. However, it must be noted that a few Arabists have already published very interesting contributions that offer sociologists a valuable clue for further study of this human group.[4] The converted Muslims pose a number of questions within the social scope.[5] The non-Muslim population around them, knowing they are converts, looks at them suspiciously, regarding them as strange and transvestite elements. On the other hand, the practice of Islam gives birth to their demanding rights to exercise their religious freedom. These rights sometimes clash with the working, economic or structural domains of Spanish society which is not prepared, neither in its legislation nor as far as the general ideology is concerned, to take in a group of individuals who figure out the vital order in a different way.

The third great group of "visible Muslims" is made up of the recent economic immigrants, mostly coming from the Magreb countries.⁶ This group does not pose religious problems, at least upon arrival in Spain; these come later. Their main troubles concern their legal, labour or family situations. Regarding their legal standing, the measures for the residence permits' control and renewal are so strict that a vicious cycle begins from which these immigrants often find themselves unable to break on their own, given their low educational level or their ignorance of the Spanish norms or Spanish tongue.

Laborally speaking, there arises a serious problem because of the precariousness of the jobs they find, due to their lack of education or to the exploiting urge of the employers. Besides there is the notion perceived by the Spanish working population that sees them as an additional danger to the unemployment situation that the country is undergoing. Nevertheless, it can be statistically proven that the jobs accepted by the immigrants coming from the Magreb countries are very frequently those that have been rejected by the autochthonous population.

The labour marginalization leads many immigrants into smuggling or drug distribution networks, thus increasing their rejection by the indigenous population that sees them as potential criminals. The family domain is related to the question of housing. Many immigrants cannot find decent houses, forming shanty towns of the lowest kind for various reasons. On the one hand, the precariousness of employment and the rejection of the landlords towards hardly solvent tenants make them rather unwilling to lease. On the other, we must not forget that this is immigration of an economic nature, that is to say, the immigrants send their families in their places of origin as much of their income as they can afford. Another serious problem is family regrouping, which is virtually impossible given the iron-like procedures and demands. This fact increases the above mentioned problems in which the immigrants find themselves.

There is a fourth group of Muslims that is "visible" at times in certain areas of the country, but would nurture the mythical aspect of the Spanish understanding of Islam, without deprecatory connotations but definitely unreal. I am talking about the Arab sheiks from Saudi Arabia or the Arab Gulf Emirates who have acquired leisure properties or share in multinational companies in Spain. Their value as far as the Spanish society, politics or university are concerned is not significant at all, since it is nothing but an anecdotic fact to be found occasionally in the so-called gossip publications.

These Muslim groups, especially the recent immigrants, which are the most numerous and visible in the large cities, give to the presence of Muslims a look of marginalized proletarized classes, an easy prey to suspicion and contempt, and even violence and open xenophobia. This picture, together with the Islamic developments broadcasted by the media, adds to the scornful and suspicious[7] image the Spaniards create with regard to the Arab World and Islam.[8]

Social reality and religious reality

In order to approach the question why the Muslim presence is significant in Spain, we must start with a few preliminary assertions which although sufficiently known deserve always to be kept in mind.

First of all, it is widely known that Spain is a traditionally and mostly Catholic country. The declaration of the non-confessional state, including the total separation between the Church and the State, is a recent one that first appeared in the last Spanish Constitution; it is one of the first achievements of the Spanish democracy. Until very recent times, the presence in Spain of Spaniards belonging to Protestant confessions, Jews or Muslims was a fact that was not institutionally acknowledged. The individuals faithful to those confessions didn't have, despite being full-fledged citizens, the same legal treatment as those belonging to the Catholic Church, whether they were genuine believers or practitioners or not. As an organization, the Catholic Church enjoyed and still enjoys a number of privileges despite the signing in 1992 of an agreement between the State and the other confessions.

The advocates of the State's laicism themselves don't seem to be aware of the fact that, just as an example and albeit an anecdotic question, 90% of the holidays in Spain are at the same time religious feasts. Paradoxically, there are some municipalities controlled by left-wing parties or militant laicists that have submitted to the population the choice of a patron saint to declare a festivity day in the municipality, in order to cover the two local festivities the Law allows. These are the same laicists whose thundering voices deafen the sky when they refuse special treatment to the

Muslim workers in Ramadan, for example, alleging that Spain is a non-confessional and lay State. The same phenomenon can be observed in the face of another anecdotic fact: nobody raises their voice for the nuns to give up their habits and wimples while they cry out and are shocked by a Muslim woman wearing a veil. Some voices are already asking whether reducing Religion to the strictly private sphere is a progressive approach. I find this is an interesting point, specially when recent sociological studies indicate a deinstitutionalization of the religious aspect rather than a fall into unbelief of the Spanish society.[9]

In my opinion, the Spanish religious scene is still lacking study and definition, and more importantly, reflection on this matter could greatly clarify the real incidence in potential conflicts or fruitful exchanges of the various religious beliefs of the Spaniards or of the Spanish residents.

Secondly, Spain has lived through a long period of isolation that has started to open up within this last twenty years. Spain has been traditionally a country exporting economic and intellectual emigrants. Very recently it has turned into an immigration receiving country.[10] The diversity of races, languages and cultures, beyond the Spanish regional diversity, is not the usual landscape of the country. Until very recently the internal differences were kept hidden under an imposed layer of uniformity, so that the presence of coloured people or people talking other tongues and practising different habits and religions -the occasional tourist aside- is a new fact, as it is a new fact to have these people settling in Spanish territory.

That is to say, the existence of Spaniards, born in Spain or nationalized, who might be different from the standard type has been hidden for a long time. Now that it is impossible or undesirable to hide the difference, there are not only Spaniards who are different, but there are also human groups coming from abroad that are different. All this still is part of the above dialectic between the real and the mythical. The identity signs of the Spanish character are in the process of change, both in imagery and in reality. To this we must add the new ways of relating to the non-Spanish.

The religious as an identity sign

For the majority of the Spaniards, the religious aspect only constitutes a secondary identity sign. Accordingly, their perplexity in the face of the

Muslim communities adopts various forms of expression depending on the groups of Muslims with which they are in contact. The Muslims, on their part - and also depending on their relationship to Spain - declare 'Islamity' as an identity sign in several different ways. The group of "invisible Muslims" perceive a kind of ignorance among the Spanish born about their religion but especially, and more importantly to them, about their culture. Their complaints refer to the scant treatment the Arab-Islamic culture is given in the text books comparing, for example, to the classical culture of Greece and Rome or to the scarce information the Spanish children are given in school about the present and recent history of the Arab World and of the geography or civilization of the various areas of the world of Muslim majority. It is hard for them to understand that in Al-Andalus less attention is payed to the Muslim civilization than to the romanizing or the Catholic Kings. They regret that every time an issue related to the Arab world is discussed, their children will be asked what it is they do and how they are really like. They equally regret the fact that despite speaking proper Spanish and having no external features capable of distinguishing them from most Spanish people, they are asked every time why their names are so strange.

Lately, after the signing of the agreements between the State and the Muslim Communities,[11] they are claiming the right to religious education in school, in order not to feel discriminated toward the Catholic children, who can receive this kind of education in public schools. The agreements that contemplate this question,[12] are based on the agreements with the Catholic Church. Nevertheless, the Ministry of Education has recently implemented an education reform whereby - while the teaching of Catholicism in the schools is not totally given up - another choice in the teaching of History of Religions, is offered. Its contents is still to be defined. Neither Catholicism nor History of Religions are subject to evaluation in the pupil's *curriculum*. This reform is being widely contested by the Parents' Associations (APAs), both Catholics and non-Catholics. Several protests have reached the courts with various results. The Spanish Muslims are shocked by the fact that, given the traditional good relations between Spain and the Arab World and the proximity of the Mediterranean, the Spaniards are more aware of other cultures or are more influenced by the trends and opinions of Americans than by a better and more fluent communication with the peoples of the Southern Mediterranean shore.[13] However, it must be pointed out that these "invisible Muslims" do not make a fundamental identity sign out of religion. For them, their original tongue and culture which they try to preserve and transmit to their children are more important.

The newly converted are a special group deserving particular treatment for different reasons. First of all, this special treatment is necessary due to the fact that Islam is almost their only identity sign, together with living in closed neighbourhoods, wearing clothes they see as "more Muslim-like" and, in some cases, claiming a repressed Islam preserved all through History. That is to say, they regard themselves as descending from the Spanish Muslims and, sometimes, raise political alternatives to rescue a very peculiar Al-Andalus.[14]

Many Spaniards coexisting with these communities see them as somewhat strange. Paradoxically, these people however have become involved with Christian or other citizen associations for the social struggle and attention to the immigrants.[15] From among these groups of newly converted Muslims, there are many who receive a higher education provided by the University departments of Arabic in order to improve their knowledge of their religion and of Arabic. The new Muslims, together with the immigrants, have claimed prayer-rooms in public buildings and firms. They are claiming also their own burying places,[16] as well as consideration in the labour field to their feasts and eating habits. The recent immigrants, however, are too overwhelmed by their legal, family, labour and economic situation to feel spiritual matters as something prioritary.

Political response to the presence of Muslims

The political field distinguishes two clearly differentiated levels which we could call "major policy" and "minor policy", based on the nomenclature employed by Carlos Celaya in a recent article published in the magazine *Awraq*.[17]

The major policy would include the reflection, documentation, study and projection within the electoral programs of the political parties on the issue of immigration, its control, developments and corresponding regulations, as well as the analysis of the autochthonous population responses.

As far as this level is concerned, it must be said that the political parties seem to get busy with this issue only when elections are at hand. In my opinion, the legislation that has been implemented, its frequency, and its real degree of implementation, as well as the administrative difficulties that it brings about, should also be included within the "major policy." Another aspect that would fall within this chapter would be the European communitarian policy regarding emigration and the relationships with "the other", including the resulting repercussions on the Spanish legal developments.

To the sphere of the "minor policy" would belong a number of initiatives wherein the civil society, organized in associations, institutions, neighbourhood-, small town-, or regional groups, intervenes directly, either taking the place of the State or substituting it.[18] The "minor policy" would also include those aspects related to the performance of the local, regional or autonomous administrations of the several Spanish regions, each having competences in the fields of citizen security, or managing those matters related to the social welfare, such as education, health or housing.[19]

The political parties' ideology also affects the performance of this "minor policy." Generally speaking, as it is only natural, left-wing parties pay greater attention and seem to advocate a clear option as regards concepts such as integration or inter-culturality, opposite to the right-wing parties that talk of eradicating xenophobia, racism and ghettos, but watching it all from a negative stance as if it were a public order problem. Curiously enough, it must be pointed out that the generally conservative nationalist parties, at least those who are taking part in the government of their respective regions, -CiU (Convergencia i Unió) in Catalonia, PNV (Basque Nationalist Party) in the Basque provinces, or PA (Andalusian Party) in Andalusia-, see quite clearly the question of inter-culturality, integration, etc. This is specially evident in Catalonia, historically a place of internal immigration and during these past few years a place of a very strong economic immigration from abroad. There, the institutions of whatever rank can be found to be deeply interested in all these issues. Very likely it is the search of their own national identity, opposite to the State, the claiming of their particular idiosyncrasy, the defense of their language (Catalan, Basque, Galician), that has caused these communities to be more perceptive to the phenomenon of "difference." The social programs unfolded by these communities are much more progressive, numerous and advanced than those developed by the State in the hands of a socialist party.[20]

Nevertheless, the State government has paid a great deal of attention to those issues related to immigration, developing a whole legal corpus since 1990, which refers to the border control, to the immigrants' integration and civil rights, and the legalizing of their situation in the country, etc.

When implementing the approved legal texts the following can be observed: first of all, there exists a clear interference between the competences of several concerned ministries, such as Social Affairs, Labour, Justice and Internal Policy, and Foreign Affairs. The coordination groups created have not succeeded in their endeavours.[21] Secondly, there is a clash between the EC regulation and the Spanish reality, whose policy must be that of stopping or restraining immigration even when the number of immigrants is not a serious problem. Thirdly, the complexity of the norms regulating the acquisition of permits and other rights causes problems rather than solving them, creating in itself illegal situations undesired by the immigrants.

The political actions distinguish between Muslim immigrants and Muslims with Spanish nationality, be it acquired or native. The relationship with the nationals is difficult in so far as these Muslims have neither group awareness nor interest in vindicative associationism except in very particular cases. There are several aspects of the State-confessions Agreements, which have not been implemented due to internal disagreements within the Muslim community that must cope with, among other things, interests of class or country of origin. The immigrants, however, are more prone to contact those organizations able to channel their rights and meet of their needs. The current political situation, driven by other priorities, leaves much to be desired in improving the relations with the Muslims, whether they are nationalized or immigrants, as is shown by the letter submitted by a representation of the trade union, social, and immigrants' organizations to the President of the Government in April 1995, pointing to the legislation's problematic points and its effects, as well as laying out the immigrants' claims.[22]

Conclusion

The social and political reactions to the presence of the "different" in the linguistic, cultural, religious and national fields respond to extremely complex mechanisms, the study of which demands the cooperation of different scientific spheres, such as sociology, psychology, history, philology and religious sciences. To date, the academic approaches to this issue have not had the benefit of the necessary interdisciplinary coordination. The works appear in disarray and the gathering of the necessary material is very complicated. Nevertheless, there is in almost all degrees of academic, political and social responsibility a marked interest in this question. The general scene, approached from any of the possible standpoints, appears scattered and blurred, but marked indeed by a real will of unity and definition, which, no doubt, will take some time to rectify itself in effective actions.

Notes

[1]   From a literary point of view and from the outlook of contemporary Arab authors, the 'mythical al-Andalus' does also exist. From this stance it is essential (Martínez Montávez 1992).

[2]   It is to be pointed out that in the 60s a certain bibliography developed referring specifically to the mixed couples' problems. For example, Vega 1979; García Hernando 1975; Borrmans 1974; Mohr 1978. Almost all these texts emerged upon the Catholic Church's initiative and are of a pastoral nature, so that they cannot be regarded as historical or sociological surveys properly, but they nevertheless reveal the fact that a number of mixed couples were forming then constituting a genuine novelty in the Spanish social scene.

[3]   Valencia, in Abumalham (ed.) 1995: 175-188.

[4]   Valencia 1995: 239 and following.

[5]   Valencia 1995: 239 and following.

[6]   There are now some specific studies, some of them of a quantitative nature, drawn up by university researchers or by organisms of the State Administration, the Trade Unions or the Catholic Church regarding this kind of immigration. For instance, B. López (*Awraq* 1993: 127-257) coordinates a number of articles on immigration preceded by a note, where some other publications on this issue are mentioned. See also López 1993 or the ones gathered in Abumalham 1995. There are a few doctoral dissertations, some in progress, others completed, concerning various aspects related to immigration, inter-culturality or the image of "the other," such as, for example, Pumares Fernández 1994. On the other hand, we have daily instances in the Spanish newspapers, such as articles, pieces of news and comments about immigration and other related issues: borders' closing, legal problems, delinquency, housing, family regrouping and so on.

[7]   Nevertheless, the CIS (Sociological Research Center ascribed to the Presidency Ministry) recently carried out an opinion poll, a summary of which was published in the newspaper *El País* (27-3-1995), whose results showed a significant decrease in the xenophobia percentage figures.

[8]   The Spanish press has often published articles regarding fundamentalism and Islam which could have explained many a question, but have gone unnoticed; see those gathered in Martínez Montávez 1995.

Political parties have also encouraged work on this question with uneven success, for example: Fundación Cánovas del Castillo 1992, gathering the contributions to a discussion organized by this conservative foundation where José Mª Aznar, President of the Popular Party, Salvador López de la Torre, editorialist of *ABC*, Bernd M. Weischer, of the German Institute of the East in Hamburg, and Reiner Glagow, deputy of the Hanns Seidel Foundation in Spain, participated among others.

[9]   Mardones 1994; Tornos 1995.

[10]   See Aragón in Abumalham, M. (ed.) 1995.

[11]   Ministry of Justice 1992: 37-48. It must be shown that the Islamic Commission of Spain is not comprised of numerous associations of Muslims, whether nationalized, new converts or immigrants. These non-integrated associations do no feel bound for such accords in many cases, and follow their own initiatives. The Islamic Commission of Spain, on its part, does not intend any association with the groups that have not joined.

[12]   Ministry of Justice 1992: art. 10 and ff.

[13]   Lately it can be observed in Spain an increasing interest in the Mediterranean as an important factor of political and cultural projection. This interest stems from the Gulf War, and there are already a few publications mirroring it. Just as an example, (Mira 1991) featuring a debate between Eduard Mira, Luis Racionero, and Eugenio Trías.

[14]   Valencia, in Abumalham (ed.) 1995: 180-181 & 183.

[15]   Valencia 1995: 239 and following.

[16]   Valencia 1995: 239 and following.

[17]   Celaya 1993: 227-250.

[18]   Cáritas Española, the first of the associations to get involved, has been taking care of the immigration problem, and periodically publishes diverse documentation or organizes specific programs on this issue. One of the last documents, Cáritas Española 1995, is divided into the following chapters: Presentación, Introducción: La inmigración responde a causas estructurales.- Importancia del éxito o fracaso del proceso de integración, Procesos de Integración I.- Marco político: elementos para una política global de inmigración; 1. El consenso, 2. La previsión, 3. El Pacto Institucional, 4. El estatuto de residente permanente, 5. El reconocimiento del papel de las ONGs, 6. El marco europeo, II El marco legal: A. Ley de "Derechos y libertades de los extranjeros en España"; 1. Entradas y visados, 2. Permisos de trabajo, 3. Permisos de residencia, 4. Tramitaciones, 5. Expulsiones, B. Ley de "El derecho de asilo y la condición de refugiado", III El marco social; A. Trabajo; 1. Contratación, 2. Permisos de trabajo, 3. Medidas de fomento del empleo y capacitación laboral, 4. Política de contingentes, B. Sanidad; 1. Situación actual, 2. Sanidad integral para todos, C. Vivienda, D. Formación; 1. Alfabetización de inmigrantes adultos, 2. Promoción de las mujeres inmigrantes, 3. Educación de la segunda generación, 4. Formación pre-profesional y promoción laboral, IV Las actitudes; A. La sociedad civil, 1. Las ONGs y otras fuerzas sociales, 2. Los medios de comunicación, 3. Los inmigrantes, B. Los poderes públicos; 1. El Gobierno Central del Estado, 2. Las Administraciones Autonómicas, 3. La Institución del Defensor del Pueblo.

[19] The newspaper *El País* (28-3-1995) published a brief news item under this headline: *Los inmigrantes argelinos de Valencia no deberán volver a su país para obtener visado.* With a disposition of the regional authorities, applicable only under their jurisdiction and not in other autonomous communities, a regulation entered into force for protection of immigrants in exceptional situations, that was not being applied in a widespread manner.

[20] As early as 1991 (first semester) we have a monographical issue of 318 pages (Departament de Treball de la Generalitat de Catalunya 1991) devoted to the matter of the *Treballadors estrangers immigrants a Catalunya.* In 1993 there is a 137-pages report (Barcelona Town Hall 1993) with plentiful bibliography on *Immigració estrangera a Barcelona,* drawn up by the Comissionat de l'Alcaldia per a la defensa dels drets civils. The Social Welfare Department published a document (Departament de Benestar Social 1994) that in chapter III, 7 contemplates the advise and proposals to the central administration on immigration (p. 26). The Barcelona Town Hall, in its Consejo de Bienestar Social, created a working group made up of some forty people coming from the administration, trade unions, the university, several political parties, and representatives from the private organizations devoted to immigration. This group has also drafted documents containing proposals for organization that involve the national politics, issuing their recommendations around some questions such as border control, immigrants' regularization, inter-ministerial coordination, refuge, the immigration Forum, quotas, as well as their advise to the regional administration. This document saw the light in September 1994.

[21] The most clear instance is that of the Comisión Interministerial de Extranjería created by virtue of Royal Decree 511/1992 of May 14th (*Boletín Oficial del Estado* 1992).

[22] Published in a separate sheet by the *Asociación de Solidaridad con los Trabajadores Inmigrantes,* Madrid. This letter to the president specially insists the need of operation Royal Decree 511/1992 of May 14th.

5

Dutch Political Views
on the Multicultural Society

Wasif Shadid & Sjoerd van Koningsveld

Recent developments in various parts of the world show that the stability of multi-ethnic and multicultural societies is continuously under severe pressure. During the past decade, conflicts between ethnic and religious groups have increased considerably in number and intensity. These conflicts vary from armed struggles in countries such as Somalia, the former Soviet Union, Yugoslavia and Ireland to serious calls for separation and autonomy in Belgium and Canada. Although on a smaller scale, a similar process of ethnic rejection is also to be perceived with respect to the integration of minority groups in West European societies. The rapid expansion of extreme right-winged movements, as well as the tone and contents of the ongoing discussions in the so-called 'public debate on minorities', demonstrate a considerable decrease in tolerance towards other cultures and ways of life. In other words, the margins of the multi-cultural society have become increasingly narrow. Some central issues in this ongoing public debate are the (in)compatibility of Islamic and Western cultures, the limits of cultural relativism and the (im)possibility for Muslims to integrate while preserving their cultural identities.

The present contribution attempts to analyze the different views held by Dutch politics concerning issues of importance to the position of ethnic minorities, and of Muslims in the Netherlands in particular. The analysis will be based on the views on these issues, of the larger political parties as reflected in the reports of their scientific research bureaus, in statements of their prominent members and in their national election programmes of 1994 (See Verkiezingsprogramma's 1994).

The multicultural society

In the Netherlands, discussions on the meaning and dimensions of the multicultural society are rife. Some authors consider it a special form of pluralist society based on a democratic model. This implies a society which consists of various social groups each with their own distinct cultural traditions and based on certain accepted moral values, such as freedom, equality and tolerance. (See Tennekes and Musschenga 1984, 114 ff.).

In accordance with Gordon (1978), Procee (1991,1993), in this context, makes a distinction between corporate pluralism and liberal pluralism. The former concerns societies made up of various groups having distinct cultural identities and private, almost autonomous, institutional facilities such as schools, hospitals, media and labour unions. The emphasis here falls on the groups, which are more or less obliged to participate in their private institutions. Liberal pluralism characterizes societies in which the emphasis is laid on the individual as a member of a group. The various groups participate in and use public facilities while having sufficient freedom of action to fill-up and preserve their cultural identities. The individual is free to choose between the facilities available.

With respect to the presence of (non-Christian) ethnic and cultural minorities in contemporary West European countries, a multicultural society should be a society in which these groups and their cultures have been accepted as component parts of such a pluralist society, and in which this acceptance is reflected in official government policy, both in theory and in practice. This implies a society where minorities have the same chances and opportunities for a vertical social mobility and the preservation of their cultures and identities as the indigenous religious groups have.

Dutch political parties on the multicultural society

A closer examination of the documents produced by Dutch political parties on the position of minorities in the Netherlands, i.e., the extent to which these groups are considered an integral part of the Dutch multicultural society, reveals that all parties involved pay considerable attention to three central issues.

The first issue concerns *immigration and remigration*. In this regard attention is paid to the possibilities political parties are willing to create for immigration, especially for family reunions, and to their ideas on remigration.

The second issue is that of *cultural contact and cultural identity*. Here, considerable attention is paid to the relation between minority cultures and those of society, as well as to the opportunities and facilities that may be offered to preserve the identities of migrants. This also includes the attitude of the political parties towards lessons in languages and cultures of origin, Islamic schools and other religious activities.

Finally, the issue of the *emancipation of minorities in the socio-economic structure of society* is dealt with. In this regard attention is paid to the causes of the deprivation of these groups and the possibilities to create or guarantee certain basic conditions enabling them to correct this situation and to catch up.

The documents and statements analyzed reveal that in Dutch politics five perspectives on the multicultural society may be distinguished. These may be labelled as the perspectives of (1) *rejection* and (2) *discouragement*, on the one hand, and those of (3) *selective*, (4) *corporate* and (5) *liberal pluralism*, on the other.

The perspective of rejection

A rejection of the permanent presence of minorities in the Netherlands, in combination with an emphasis on the incompatibility of their cultures with Western cultures, is found mainly in extreme right-winged circles. In the election programme of the Centrum Democrats (CD, extreme-right party) for example, it is clearly stated that the Netherlands is full, and that the integration of minorities as well as the influence of foreign cultures should be stopped. This can be realized by stopping immigration and by enforcing remigration of unemployed foreign workers in particular, to their countries of origin, six months after their last employment. As to the elimination of the influence of foreign cultures, the CD plead, among others, for the dissolution of intercultural marriages. In its election programme, this party states that, in its unreflected policy, the government has confronted Dutch youth with irresponsible options for the selection of their life partners. This policy has resulted in multicultural marriages for which the government should bear full responsibility. Therefore, the government is obliged to facilitate the dissolution of such marriages on the request of the Dutch partners and the removal of the foreign partners back to their countries of origin as soon as possible.

Furthermore, the CD plead for ceasing subsidies to stimulate foreign cultures and for dissolving their institutions already established. In this context, they above all refer to lessons in the languages and cultures of origin, which should be provided only in the light of remigration and based on a contract to be signed by the person involved and the government of his country of origin.

The rejection of a multicultural society, in which Muslims and Muslim cultures are integrated, is most obvious in the note of the 'Nederlands Blok' of 1994. This party is of the opinion (p. 34-35) that, due to his religion, the average Muslim has got many psychosocial characteristics making him unsuitable for functioning in a modern Western society. [...]. Therefore, the incorporation of Muslims will confront Western societies with huge, and possibly unsolvable, problems, which should be prevented through an active remigration policy.

The rejection perspective sees the weak socio-economic position of minorities merely in terms of deprivation, essentially caused by their culture and religion. According to the note of the 'Nederlands Blok', "the isolation and marginalization of Muslims in the Netherlands are not due to discrimination, intolerance or unequal opportunities. They are mainly caused by their insufficient education, aversion to the Western way of life and by their Islamic upbringing" (p. 28).

Furthermore, these parties reject the rights which minorities have already acquired in society. The CD, for example, plead for the abolition of affirmative action measures taken in favour of the groups concerned and for the prohibition of their using of social security facilities. At the same time, they stress the need for the promotion of Dutch culture and for measures of positive discrimination in favour of 'real' Dutch citizens. In their election programme, they write that "discrimination against Dutch workers in favour of minorities, whether or not of the Dutch nationality, should be penalized." Besides, The "Reformatorische Politieke Federatie" (RPF, a Protestant Christian party) feels that the right already granted to foreigners to participate in municipal elections should be withdrawn.

The perspective of discouragement

A second view regarding the multicultural society is labelled the perspective of discouragement. Its central features are ethnocentrism, cultural antagonism and the desire for compelled assimilation. Roughly speaking, the perspectives of rejection and discouragement show great similarities. The major differences between the two are not primarily to be found in their views on the multicultural society as such, but rather in the kind of measures advocated to prevent such a society. The discouragement perspective views Islamic culture as underdeveloped, creating an unbridgeable gap between this culture and Western culture. Consequently, supporters of this perspective stress the importance of discouraging minority groups, and Muslims in particular, to preserve their cultural identities and encourage them to remigrate to their countries of origin. However, they do not go so far as to plead for their expulsion from the Netherlands, as long as they adapt themselves to the Dutch culture and way of life.

With respect to adjustments, supporters of the discouragement perspective handle a double morality standard. They quietly tolerate the deviations from the social norm of the native Dutch groups while, on the other hand, those of Muslims are considered to be totally unacceptable and are used as evidence of the incompatibility of Islamic and Western cultures. The discouragers clearly illustrate the way the classical categorization principle works, where similarities within the ingroups and the differences between them and the outgroups are exaggerated. Such a perspective is repeatedly expressed in the political discourse of the People's Party for Freedom and Democracy (VVD, right-winged liberals). In public speeches and in the media, Bolkestein, leader of the VVD in the Lower House, has criticised Islam, the Muslim world and the future of Muslim minorities in Western Europe. He has also warned against the danger threatening Western Europe because of the influx of refugees and immigrants, from Muslim countries especially. Furthermore, he has highlighted the antagonism between their religion and Western culture and considered the discussion on the integration of Muslim minorities as being a power conflict. In this regard, he said that, "if integration is to be declared an official government policy, then which cultural values will have to dominate: those of the non-Muslim majority or those of the Muslim minority?". The leader of the VVD, as well as the unofficial viewpoints of his political party, moreover, questioned cultural relativism and emphasized the universality of certain Western values. In this regard, they mentioned separation of Church and State, freedom of speech, tolerance and anti-discrimination. According to Bolkestein, these values have been engendered by the liberal philosophy and are lacking in Islam. To prove the assumption that Muslim immigrants do not subscribe to these values, the leader of the VVD referred to the situation in the immigrants' countries of origin. Consequently, he rejected any kind of compromise on these essential matters.

A similar ethnocentric attitude is also to be found in the political working paper of the VVD with respect to the affairs of minorities. Its author argues that, "if we are not allowed to hold up our Western values as a model for other cultures, we will be condemned to a moral laissez-faire attitude and to moral paralysis." According to him, such a situation should be prevented by making it clear to the Muslim minority that it is out of the question to haggle about certain political principles, not even a little bit. (Van der List 1992, p. 13).

However, ethnocentrism is not just to be found in VVD circles. Left-winged political parties also stress the incompatibility of Islam with Western culture. According to the Socialist Party's (SP) note, 'Gastarbeid en Kapitaal', differences in culture and development make it difficult for the Dutch to work or live with their foreign colleagues, especially those originating from Muslim countries. It quotes with approval that "Muslims have a different style of reasoning and a cyclical and repetitive attitude." The SP suggests, so-called in favour of the groups concerned and of the Dutch, that after two years minorities should either naturalize or remigrate to their countries of origin. Those who decide to stay should be obliged to take special courses in Dutch language, culture and way of life (see also Shadid and van Koningsveld 1995).

The most obvious ethnocentric attitude is to be found in the election programme of the "Staatkundig Gereformeerde Partij" (SGP, a Protestant-

Christian party). This party states that, as Dutch culture is largely based on (Protestant) Christianity, it should not be equalized with other cultures. Consequently, the government should not be permitted to contribute, neither financially nor in any other way, to the spread of anti-Christian beliefs. Subsidizing mosques must be rejected."

In the previous paragraphs, we have illustrated the ethnocentric attitude of some political parties as well as their assumptions concerning the incompatibility of Islam with Western culture. It is also of great importance to pay attention to their ideas about the necessity of and their readiness to take concrete measures with regard to migration and immigrants. Both VVD and SGP plead for the reduction of the number of immigrants, because the Netherlands is not an immigration country. The former party believes that a considerable increase in immigration will jeopardize the effectiveness of the integration measures already taken. It is of great importance to prevent such a situation both by constraining immigration and by increasing the attractiveness of remigration through the introduction of a remigration-option. The SGP attempts to limit the number of immigrants tightening up the admittance requirements, so that family reunions will be permitted only for family members in the first degree and the spouse.

Moreover, supporters of the discouragement perspective plead for a policy of discouragement where facilities for preserving the cultural identity of minorities are concerned. In its election programme, the VVD states that "though the government, in observing the constitutional right to found private organizations, cannot prevent eventual pillarization, it should, nevertheless, apply a discouragement policy in this regard". Such an attitude can readily be explained because, in the view of the VVD, minorities are not primarily regarded as cultural groups but rather as a kind of economic asset, which must be developed to have it play a vital role in creating an economic basis in the Netherlands. The aforementioned examples clearly illustrate that both the unofficial views of the VVD as expressed in their working paper and by Bolkestein, as well as its official views, assume a relation of tension between minorities retaining their cultural identities and their integration in the host society.

The discouragement policy can also be deduced from the negative attitude of some political parties with respect to lessons in the languages and cultures of origin, Islamic schools and other religious activities. The VVD argues that preserving one's cultural identity should be the responsibility of the groups concerned. Therefore, the government should refrain from subsidizing lessons in the languages and cultures of origin and should delete such education from the regular curriculum. Also the RPF feels that providing subsidies for such lessons, for prayer halls and for other religious activities should be stopped.

The perspectives of discouragement and rejection also differ in their explanation of the weak socio-economic position of minorities in the Netherlands. The former perspective attributes the causes of this weak position only partially to the culture of the groups concerned. Other factors, such as the insufficient educational qualifications of the individual members of these groups and the decrease in the demand of unskilled labour in society, are also mentioned as possible causes. Therefore, the VVD has expressed the opinion that, besides being entitled to help in the course of the integration process, minorities should also be under the obligation to improve their educational level and schooling in order to increase their chances of achieving a respectable position in society. This may be realized by introducing the so-called 'basic-education duty' or 'settling down contracts'. Strikingly, in its election programme the VVD does not refer in any way to the Bill for the improvement of the proportional labour participation of minorities. By this Bill, submitted by the political parties of the VVD, Green Left and Democrats '66, employers are obliged to report annually on the number of minority groups employed in their companies.

The perspective of selective pluralism

This perspective consists of a mixture of ethnocentric and cultural-relativistic attitudes. On the one hand, cultural pluralism is considered to be an enrichment to society while, on the other hand, the right to preserve one's own cultural identity is only conditionally accepted. In their election programmes, the Labour Party (PvdA) and Democrats '66 (D'66) explicitly mention that the Netherlands has always been open to foreigners and has in fact become an immigration country with various ethnic groups and religions. Especially the PvdA considers immigration to be advantageous, as it provides a stimulus for the prosperity and development of society. Both parties oppose the idea of forced remigration, considering this as a signal indicating the decline of society. Simultaneously, however, they fervently plead for the limitation of immigration to the Netherlands. PvdA is satisfied to mention the fact that over the past years, labour immigration has been practically stopped, and additional conditions with regard to the right to family reunion and family formation have been formulated. Therefore, compared to other European countries, the number of immigrants into the Netherlands has remained limited to 5.5% of the total population only.

With respect to the cultural integration of immigrants, the election programme of the PvdA also highlights some aspects of cultural relativism. It states that it is impossible for a democratic state to determine the meaning of cultural progress or to judge it as to its value. The state, therefore, should remain neutral in these matters, as well as protect pluralism. Moreover, in a special paper of the same party (*Kansen geven en kansen grijpen.* Den Haag 1992), cultural integration is viewed as a mutual process. On the one hand, immigrants should get acquainted with the norms, values and customs of the host society and, on the other hand, society should incorporate their cultures. However, such an incorporation reflects a double attitude, conditioned by the extent to which the observance of certain norms and values of minorities affects the basic rights of others (p. 15). The underlying assumption is that some norms and customs, especially of first generation Muslims, not only collide with those of the host society, but also provoke generation conflicts within the groups concerned. In this context, reference is made above all to practices such as arranged marriages, authoritarian parent-child relationships, and the position of women. The PvdA says that such norms and practices should be adjusted. However, adjustments should not be enforced, but must be carried out within these communities themselves and based on their spiritual and cultural heritages. The social democrats show a double attitude because, "on the one hand, they consider Western values superior ... and the starting-point for their policy on minorities policy but, on the other hand, they reject the assimilatory consequences of their universalism" (Fermin, 1994, p. 59). A similar double attitude is perceptible in the election programme of D'66. Respect for and appreciation of the cultures of immigrants are emphasized, but at the same time, it is argued, that these cultural heritages should neither conflict with human rights nor raise any obstacles which might result in their isolation.

The election programmes and working papers of the parties concerned also include conditions with regard to other aspects of identity preservation, including lessons in the languages and cultures of origin and Islamic schools. As for the former, the aforementioned note of the PvdA mentions the necessity and advantages of such an education. Knowledge of the language of origin is often linked to that of the original culture and basically contributes to the second-language acquisition. According to the PvdA, the government should offer these facilities, and ensure that no gaps will occur in the regular educational programme of the pupils. Besides, preference is given to lessons in the mother tongue instead of in the official language of the country of origin. Teachers who are educated in the Netherlands are therefore to be preferred. In this regard, D'66 argues that such an education should be well integrated in the school as a whole.

With regard to Islamic schools, supporters of selective pluralism take a paternalistic attitude. PvdA mentions in its note that the phenomenon of Islamic schools is inspired by Dutch tradition, and doubts whether it is supported by the majority of the Muslim community. This party prefers 'normal' schools and urges the question to be taken into consideration of how these schools can meet the religious needs of pupils having various cultural backgrounds. D'66 pleads for enough scope for these communities to teach at their own schools in accordance with their religious convictions, but also prefers schools where Dutch children and those of minority groups can meet on a basis of mutual respect. Moreover, the party believes that the confessional schools should justify the way they express their identity to the government. If they refuse, they should lose their subsidies.

From the perspective of selective pluralism, minorities are not really seen as cultural groups, but rather as social groups in which the individual plays a central role. In this respect, it has a focus similar to that of liberal pluralism. Within the framework of integration, members of minority groups have to participate individually in the general facilities of society. According to the previously mentioned paper of the PvdA, real social integration is a matter of full access to the main sectors of society, such as the labour market, education and health care. The existing diversity of ideologies, religions and cultural backgrounds should at the same time be reflected in these sectors. Therefore, these sectors should tune their organization and staff to the pluriformity of society (p.14).

In this perspective, the weak socio-economic position of minorities is considered to be the result of a deprivation caused by the low educational qualifications of the individual members of the groups concerned, and of discrimination as well. According to D'66, discrimination on the labour market is a real problem and its impact should be diminished through the introduction of the previously mentioned Bill for the promotion of the proportional labour participation of minorities.

The perspective of corporate pluralism

In Dutch politics, not only the above mentioned perspectives, but also the view on the multicultural society as a form of corporate pluralism can be distinguished, especially in circles of the Christian Democrats. The main idea in the election programme of the "Christen Democratisch Appel" (CDA, Christian Democrats) emphasizes spiritual or religious freedom, which demands pluriformity and diversity. This party prefers a society consisting of a cultural mosaic, i.e., of integrated cultural (religious) groups which, at the same time, have retained their cultural identity. The CDA considers integration to be the capacity to (1) participate in the labour process, (2) to obtain an income, and (3) to develop a cultural identity of one's own within societal networks chosen by the groups themselves. In other words, participation and emancipation in society should be realised from within these networks and through private institutions. Societal networks including the core family, relatives, friends and various other private organizations are considered to be the institutions par excellence, to guarantee the security of the individual and save him from loneliness and from hanging back. This means that in the perspective of corporate pluralism, neither the individual nor the group is considered to be the only focal point of action. It is the responsible person as part of a social network, consisting of groups and organizational frameworks, which underlies the basic ideas on society of the Christian Democrats. (See

Salemink 1993, 492). This train of thought typifies the way in which Dutch society had been organized since the introduction of the so-called pillarization system, at the end of the nineteenth century as a result of an ideological struggle between Catholics and Protestants.

In regard to the integration of non-Christian minorities, supporters of the pillarization system refer to the valuable contributions which this system made to the emancipation of Catholics and Calvinists in the Netherlands. They urge Muslims to create their own pillar in order to achieve such an integration and emancipation in Dutch society. It is, however, remarkable that the pillarization strategy nowadays is introduced in order to improve the weak socio-economic position of Muslims in the Netherlands. Contrary to this, the traditional pillarization in the Netherlands was not really meant to diminish the deprivation of the groups concerned but primarily to guarantee the preservation of their specific identities. Thurlings (1978, 37) argues that if Catholics (of that time) had considered their problems a matter of social deprivation, they would not have needed the pillarization system at all, because in that case it would have been more effective for them to continue their cooperation with the liberals.

As to maintaining the cultural identity of the groups concerned, corporate pluralism stresses the principle of equality. With respect to education, for example, the CDA chooses in its election programme for a fully subsidized national educational system consisting of both public and confessional schools. Within this system, every person, *irrespective of his origin or income*, should be entitled to equal claims to education of the same quality. However, this party also holds the view that other necessities needed to preserve a cultural identity, such as education in language and culture of origin, should be provided outside of school hours, and that parents should contribute to them financially.

Due to several factors inherent to the nature of the groups concerned, as well as to society at large, the advocated pillarization system will not be effective in realising the socio-economic emancipation of Muslims in the Netherlands. First of all, and in contrast with Dutch Catholics and Protestants, these groups are ethnically, culturally, as well as religiously heterogeneous. They originate from different countries and belong to different cultures and streams of religion, which is the reason why they are incapable of formulating a common objective or of founding a communal pillar. In addition, they have to do without a broad social framework in society because employers and sufficiently skilled staff belonging to their confession are lacking.

Furthermore, the Christian Democrats primarily define the weak position of minorities in terms of deprivation. Contrary to other previously mentioned perspectives, they do not attribute such a deprivation to differences in culture, but essentially to structural factors inherent to the groups concerned, such as a lack of education and schooling. Consequently, they urge the government to assist them in order to reduce the impact of these obstacles.

The preceding viewpoints justify the conclusion that in their policy on minorities, the Christian Democrats concentrate on the emancipation of these groups in Dutch society from within their own social and religious institutional frameworks, while at the same time maintaining their cultural identity. The great emphasis which the Christian democrats put on culture and religion as fundamental pillars of society will, however, also have a negative effect on the position of minorities in the long run. In a working paper of the scientific research bureau of the CDA, a distinction is made between nation and state. The former is defined as "a community of people usually sharing historic events, a common language, culture, religion and national consciousness." The state, on the other hand, has a public function with respect to all the citizens of a country. (Salemink 1993). Since the Christian Democrats explicitly emphasize a common religion as a substantial feature of a nation, non-Christian groups are denied the opportunity to become part of the Dutch nation, even in the long run. Consequently, it is obvious that within the perspective of corporate pluralism, a real integration of religious minorities in the nation is out of the question.

The perspective of liberal pluralism

Compared to other political parties, Green Left (GroenLinks) holds different and extreme views on the multicultural society and chooses in its working paper on minorities (see GroenLinks 1993) for a liberal pluralistic perspective. The features of this perspective are clearly expressed in the ideas of this party on immigration, on the cultural position of immigrants and on their emancipation in Dutch society.

With respect to immigration, Green Left and Minister Pronk (see Pronk 1994, 200), Minister of Development Aid and a member of the PvdA, argue that the Netherlands should be willing to admit more foreigners, at least as long as the international causes for immigration have not been taken away. This, according to Green Left, is not only desirable but, without any great difficulty, also possible. Holland by now has become an immigration country. In this regard, the party even pleads for legalizing illegal foreigners for whom social premiums have already been paid or who have resided in the country for more than two years, as well as for extending family reunion rules so as to include marriage and non-marriage relations.

It is remarkable that the plea for more foreigners, at least to some extend, is inspired by the assumed positive effects of immigration on Dutch society. In the party's election programme, several positive effects, such as "a well-balanced age distribution of the population, the emergence of new kinds of business activities, a better occupation of the labour market and the enrichment of Dutch culture," are explicitly mentioned. According to Pronk (PvdA), the most positive impact of immigration should be looked for in the need for Dutch society to be dynamic and to renew itself. This can only be realized through a confrontation of cultures within the boundaries of one's own country, leading to an increase in mutual understanding and shared information. Admittance of foreigners to the Netherlands should, therefore, not only be based on economic, juridical and ethic criteria, but on socio-cultural considerations as will.

With regard to the cultures of immigrants and the preservation of their cultural identities, Green Left, in its previously mentioned paper, rejects both rigid universalism and ideological cultural relativism. According to this party, cultures are not static but are changing constantly and it is therefore erroneous to pin people down on their original cultural traditions. Besides, culture does not have the same meaning to every individual and it is difficult to trace where one culture begins and another culture ends (p. 40).

However, this party does not consider minorities as cultural but rather as socio-economic entities. In its previously mentioned working paper,

Green Left points out that an adequate policy on minorities should concentrate on the reinforcement of the social position of minorities rather than on the preservation of their cultural identities (p.51). Consequently, this liberal pluralistic view has the disadvantage of implying a form of hidden assimilation, especially in a society with great power differences. Green Left is aware of this fact but accepts it nevertheless because, according to them, the strategy of liberal pluralism is the best way to promote interaction between the various groups concerned. Therefore, willingness to interact should be the only criterion for the hierarchic classification of cultures. Those cultures who want to learn from others should be more highly.

Nevertheless, Green Left considers the cultures of minorities as subcultures within a general Dutch culture and at the same time pleads for a complete freedom of education and religion. Consequently, this party argues that general cultural activities should be aimed at every individual in society, irrespective of his origin or ethnicity. This, for example, means that in the curricula of primary and secondary schools it should be possible to include optional subjects on languages and cultures of Surinamers, Turks and Moroccans for all of the pupils. This party also criticizes the contents and methods of lessons in the languages and cultures of origin. With their consent it quotes several researchers who question the scientific basis of the assumptions regarding the positive effects of this kind of education.

The liberal pluralistic view defines the weak position of minorities in the Netherlands essentially in terms of discrimination. It considers intentional and unintentional discrimination against minorities, as well as their unequal legal status, to be the crucial causes of their deprivation. To reduce the influence of these constraints, Green Left advocates the introduction of the Bill for equal opportunities mentioned in the previous sections. In its election programme, this party goes even further and pleads for more effective measures, such as contract compliance. This means that government subsidies for and contracts with employers should be subject to conditions regarding the readiness of employers to employ more members from minority groups. In addition, this party stresses the importance of equal political rights for the sake of emancipation, and pleads for the extension to all levels of the passive and active franchise for foreigners who have been residing in the Netherlands for more than two years.

The liberal pluralistic views as formulated by Green Left can best be compared to the American traditional ideology of amalgamation, launched as a reaction to the assimilation ideology. This ideology assumed that, in the long run, the various groups in society would take what was best of each culture, which would ultimately result in one single culture in which all of the groups could recognize themselves.

Despite its idealistic objectives, the perspective of liberal pluralism has nevertheless a certain driving force. It stresses the explicit recognition that immigration is not only favourable to the migrants themselves, but to Dutch society as well. Furthermore, this view counterbalances and challenges the rejection perspective in which slogans such as 'the country is full' and 'our own people first' are heard more and more frequently.

Discussion and conclusions

The aforegoing analysis has dealt with the views of Dutch political parties on various items regarding the multicultural society. The analysis clearly shows that, even though these parties share similar views on certain aspects, such as immigration, it is justified to distinguish between various perspectives concerning their ideas on both the socio-economic and cultural position of minorities in the Netherlands.

Firstly, where immigration and remigration are concerned, a continuum can be seen, ranging from 'the country is full', on the one hand, to 'the country is not full', on the other, as defended by the rejectionists and liberal pluralists, respectively. In between, one can find those claiming the Netherlands 'is not an immigration country', and those who are of the opinion that de facto it 'has become an immigration country', as defended by the discouragers and by supporters of selective and corporate pluralism, respectively. Except for the liberal pluralists, however, the perspectives distinguished stress the importance of reducing immigration to the number stipulated by international treaties and national regulations. In other words, these perspectives do not differ fundamentally but gradually on the issue of immigration: immigration to the Netherlands should be restricted, but the manner according to which this should be realized differs.

As regards the desirability of pluralism and the outcome of cultural contacts, hardly any differences exist between the perspectives distinguished. However, except for the corporative pluralists who prefer a cultural mosaic, they in fact all defend a monocultural society model.

A similar consensus can be found regarding their ideas on improving the weak socio-economic position of minorities. It is interesting to mention that, with the exception of the liberal pluralists, all perspectives comprise elements of 'blaming the victim'. This pattern of thought explains the main causes of the situation from within the groups concerned, i.e., by attributing them to their culture and to a lack in the conditions necessary for their emancipation, such as insufficient education and schooling. Only the liberal pluralists primarily 'blame the system' and stress the fact that deprivation is mainly due to direct and indirect forms of discrimination against the groups concerned.

Secondly, the analysis reveals that where Muslim minorities are concerned, the Dutch political parties act as if Dutch society has become multicultural only after the immigration of these groups to the Netherlands. Besides, they also act as if the slogan 'integration while retaining one's own cultural identity' has been launched especially for these groups. Most modern societies, however, are composed of various cultural, ethnic, religious and ideological groups which at the same time share and subscribe to certain fundamental values needed for society to function. In practice, these groups may have fundamental differences of opinion about certain values, but simultaneously accept and respect the opinions of the majority on these relevant matters. In democratic states, the majority, however, is composed of cross-sections of these groups. The Dutch constitution, for example, has been based on such a principle since the introduction of the pillarization system at the end of the 19th century. In other words, modern and democratic societies do not essentially differ as to the cultural or religious composition of the population, but rather with respect to the space minorities are allowed to practice their culture, and experience and shape their identity.

Furthermore, the questions and doubts raised about the integration of Muslims in Dutch society as expressed in the election programmes and working papers of the political parties are not primarily juridical, but rather social-normative in character. Religious freedom, freedom of speech and the equality of all individuals, irrespective of their ethnicity, religion or gender, are after all the foundations on which the Dutch Constitution is based. Therefore, these questions and doubts reflect first of all the unreadiness of society at large to offer opportunities to Muslims to participate in the socio-economic, cultural and ideological cross-sections of society, while at the same time preserving their (religious) identity, if they should so prefer. The social and political resistance against some distinct wishes of Muslims, including the wearing of head-scarves, Islamic schools and the founding of prayer-halls and mosques, clearly indicates that such opportunities are not optimally present in the Netherlands. As far as Islamic schools are concerned, it is clear that despite the constitutional freedom of religion and education their foundation does not proceed smoothly and is the subject of heated discussions. Generally speaking, two main objections have been raised against the foundation of Islamic schools. These objections can be characterized as paternalistic and figurative and are easy to refute. First of all, it has been argued that such schools would constrain the integration of the groups concerned, because contacts between children from different ethnic backgrounds would be minimalized. This argument does not carry much weight as one can observe that the phenomenon of the so-called 'black' and 'white' schools has become a reality within the sector of public schools over the past decades. In fact, one fifth of the primary schools in the four major cities in the Netherlands include more than 70% of pupils from minority groups. These figures clearly indicate that ethnically separated education has been a fact for a long time. The second objection concerns the assumption that this type of school is outdated because the Netherlands is already depillarized. But it is also a fact that at present 60% of the primary schools in the country (5,000 schools) belong to the confessional type and that the thirty Islamic schools make up only a fraction of this total. The aforementioned clearly indicates that the juridical integration of Muslims in the Netherlands, i.e., the opportunities laid down in the constitution, develops at a greater pace than the social acceptance of the pluralistic aspects of that constitution.

Thirdly, the analysis presented in the previous sections reveals that only those cultural aspects of the Dutch multicultural society are rejected which concern Islam and certain Muslim groups. Other immigrants, such as Surinamers, Antillians and Indonesians, are often absent in the discussion. In the course of the past decade, the debate on ethnic minorities sofar has resulted in the division of society into two broad categories: 'ingroups' against 'outgroups'. Both, tone and content of the discussion imply that the outgroups mainly consist of Turks and Moroccans to whom a uniform Islam is ascribed as their religion and as the sole ingredient of their cultural background. Their socio-economic and intra-Islamic diversity, as well as other aspects of their cultures are hardly taken into consideration.

Furthermore, the criticism of Islam and Muslims has an axiomatic character and has mainly become aimed at (1) certain theoretical aspects of this religion, (2) the behaviour of some of its adherents and (3) the way it is practised in the Muslim world. Nonetheless, statements of politicians and views of political parties on this religion are put in generalized terms where Islam as a religious system and its adherents are concerned. Such opponents, however, overlook certain substantial facts. They overlook the fact that the majority of Muslim countries concerned have no Islamic political system. The lack of freedom of speech as envisaged in these countries should therefore not be ascribed to Islam, as supporters of the discouragement perspectives do, but rather to the non-Islamic political systems prevalent in these countries. In addition, such opponents mistakenly assume that the majority of the Muslim migrants in the Netherlands support the way freedom of speech is interfered with their countries of origin. On the contrary, the vast majority considers Western democracy as an example to be followed.

As far as the notion of cultural antagonism between Islam and the West is concerned, not only politicians but also scholars get stuck in certain sensational examples of Islamic behaviour related to such issues as the position of women, sexual morality, and the authority of the father. These assumptions have also an axiomatic character because they never indicate to what extent such behavioral aspects are accepted and applied by the groups concerned. According to some scholars (see as an example Tennekes and Musschage 1984, p. 125), the abovementioned antagonism is however not part and parcel of the practice itself. After all, such behaviour can also be found with autochthonous groups. It is rather embedded in the norms and values of the minority groups and in their perspective on reality. With this opinion, the authors assume that this kind of behaviour forms an essential part of the views of Turks and Moroccans on reality. It is surprising that the authors do not attempt to substantiate this assumption by offering some empirical evidence. When trying to explain this kind of behaviour, they only state that these communities have not taken their distance from the dominance of men, the authority of the father, and the views on men and women on which these are based.

From all that procedes we have to draw the conclusion that the alleged cultural antagonism is not based primarily on empirical research but largely on ascribed attitudes and identities. Such identities are artificial images and are derived from the comparison of two ideal types of view: those of the predominantly secular Dutch society, on the one hand, and of certain conservative thoughts in Islam, on the other. In addition, the generalization of such thoughts and the divergent behaviour of some Muslims play a central role in the construction of these artificially constructed identities. Apparently, researchers and scientists in this field do not succeed in making the diversity in cultural perspectives and behaviour of Muslims clear. Unfortunately, they do not succeed in making clear that also within these communities a distinction should be made between the ideal and the actual, and between theory and practice. A closer examination will reveal that, in practice, the vast majority of these groups, for example, attaches equal importance to an education for both boys and girls, recognizes the equivalence of both men and women, organizes the relations with their children on the basis of a dialogue, and the like. Those who do not live up to these social norms should therefore be considered the exceptions and not the rule.

In this context, both scientists and politicians who participate in the societal debate on minorities in the Netherlands have neglected the crucial question why society indeed tolerates the deviant behaviour of autochthonous groups while adamantly rejecting that of Muslims. There are autochthonous groups who discriminate against homosexuals and ethnic minorities, who reject women's passive right to vote, who refuse preventive vaccination or oppose the incorporation of the evolution theory as a key part of the final examination at schools. In their election programmes, GPV, RPF and SGP (Christian parties) even plead for the abolition of the Act on equal treatment because it is supposed to infringe upon certain inalienable fundamental rights, such as freedom of religion and education. The latter party also explicitly advocates the withdrawal of the Acts on euthanasia and abortion and rejects all kinds of artificial conception. Consequently, the crucial question is here: Why is it so difficult to tolerate certain cultural utterances made by some Muslims as comparable deviations?

The answer to this question should be sought in the rejection of Muslims as fellow citizens by society. It is a factual refusal to accept the idea that Holland has become an immigration country and that, nowadays, a considerable number of people in that society do not only have a different appearance and culture but at the same time also wish to identify themselves with that society. The ongoing discussion between politicians, scholars and journalists on the incompatibility of Islam with Western culture, therefore, should be considered as a preserve to retain the mono-cultural and mono-ethnic composition of Dutch society.

Consequently, unless the government applies a diversified policy comprising society as a whole, a Dutch multicultural society in which Muslims and Islam play a considerable role will remain a utopia. Such a policy should entail more than the obligation of members of minority groups to acquire cognitive skills, such as a knowledge of the Dutch language and culture. The ultimate objective of the immigration policy should focus on the acquisition of mental skills required to learn to accept and to tolerate, and should not only be aimed at minority groups but also at society as a whole. As far as the former is concerned, such a policy should be meant to increase their sense of belonging, i.e., their feeling of being at home in the Netherlands and their readiness to accept the country as their second fatherland. Regarding the latter, it should contribute to increasing the readiness of the original population to accept minorities as fellow citizens with equal rights and duties.

In conclusion, an adequate policy for achieving a multicultural society should focus on challenging the assumption that the Netherlands is only meant for the originally Dutch population; on improving the socio-economic position of minority groups; on emphasizing cultural similarities; on tolerating cultural differences, intensifying intercultural dialogues and tabooing the exploitation of negative sentiments in society for demagogic reasons. In this context, prominent politicians, communication media, parents and schools could play a crucial role.

6

The Politics of Integration
in the Netherlands

Ruben Gowricharn & Bim Mungra[1]

At the end of 1991 the leader of the Dutch 'liberals', Frits Bolkenstein, launched the statement that, in order to integrate, Muslims in the Netherlands should adjust themselves to Dutch customs. Soon after this statement was made the Prime Minister at that time, Ruud Lubbers, countered that Muslims should build a pillar)[2] of their own to achieve their goals. Surprisingly, it was not Bolkensteins statement which caught public attention, but that of the Prime Minister. During the next months there was a heated debate in the national newspapers on this issue in which journalists and social scientists dominated. The central issue was whether the pillar-model could be resorted to in order to alleviate the problems of migrants)[3] in general and those of the Muslims in particular.

The issue was fiercely debated. That was due chiefly to the context in which the statement was made. Two aspects of this context seem to be important. One concerns the attitude towards Muslims. A number of events in the last couple of years have produced hostility towards the Islam which is associated with religious fanaticism and, subsequently, with a threat to Dutch civil order. The behaviour of Islamic people is allegedly not in line with Dutch customs and, therefore, they are not considered integrated. In this view integration comes down to 'Dutchification' which is supposedly incompatible with Islamic life styles.

The second aspect regards the socially retarded position of ethnic minorities. Since the end of the Eighties there is an increasing feeling that integration policy has failed. This is deducted from the request of the Dutch government to the Scientific Council for Government Policy for new advise on this matter. The suggestion that Dutch society failed to incorporate its migrants and that an 'ethnic-pillar' might be a better avenue to social integration, is probably felt as an official certificate of failure.

Apart from the context we consider it likely that the debate was partly an ideological clash. In the past, the leaders of the pillars, especially the Catholic one, have been criticized for using the specificities of their people such as their religion, regional concentration and life style. In other words, they should have exploited their 'particularisms'. This criticism was raised by those advocating both left and right wing variations of universal ideologies like liberalism and socialism. Hence the plea for a 'migrant pillar' sparks off an old conflict between adherents of different philosophical orientations among the Dutch.

In this paper we intend to review the debate on the basis of a selected number of articles.[4] At first we will briefly discuss the concept of pillarization. Since the historical circumstances have changed significantly, we rule out the possibility that the same institutional and cultural constellation can be reproduced. We will therefore review the pillar model in terms of the *functions* it fulfilled and pinpoint some of the relevant preconditions. The arguments in the debate will then be summarized. This is followed by a discussion involving the very existence of a 'migrant-pillar'.[5] Here a comparison between the 'migrant-pillar' and the traditional pillar is made in terms of functions rather than of similarities. Finally, we will comment on the integration model of those in favour of and those against the pillar system.

Pillars and cultural plurality

The issue of pillarization has attracted a great deal of attention, especially among political scientists and historians. In spite of the vast amount of literature, there is no agreement on the historical periodization, functions, or even concepts regarding pillarization. In spite of these controversies Lijpharts well known *The politics of accommodation: pluralism and democracy in the Netherlands* features as the most authoritative study on this topic. We will not try to discuss the different positions, but will utilize that study as our point of departure.

The Pillar system

There is a broad consensus that pillarization - in its Dutch form - is based on different life styles. People from different backgrounds - Catholics, protestants, liberals and socialists - were regionally concentrated and lived in different social compartments. The institutional composition of the pillars was different. Generally speaking, every pillar had its own schools, shops, youth organizations, recreation facilities, churches (only the religious pillars), radio and television broadcasting corporations, newspapers, literature, trade unions, employer organizations, political parties, even universities. Most of the time, this vertical organization exceeded (horizontal) class contradictions thanks to, or in spite of, the unequal development of classes in the different pillars (Stuurman 1983).

The origin of this societal organization dates back to the previous century. Most authors agree that pillarization originated in the period between 1870-1920. Since then and until the 1960's, pillars were considered a characteristic feature of Dutch society. The period thereafter until today is marked by a process of de-pillarization. Stuurman (1983: 12-3) argues that this classification is too static. During all the periods both pillarizing as well as de-pillarizing forces were operating. It is also widely accepted that in the period after 1960 de-pillarizing forces were dominant, although this position is qualified as exaggerated (Thurlings 1978; Middendorp 1979).

The forces leading to pillarization are ascribed to the emancipation of Catholics and of small traders, craftsmen, farmers and labourers of protestant descent, called *kleine luyden*. These people belonged to the minorities of that time and had a less prosperous position. The strategy to improve their position was to withdraw themselves, to build up institutions of their own and, using these as there base, to compete with the established groups. There are two major issues linked with the emancipation-through-pillarization model: the right to have own schools and universal suffrage. Historically spoken, the battle was settled in favour of the minorities. This resulted, among other things, in the constitutional right for minorities to have their own life styles and religion. The Social Democrats adopted a similar strategy, with the important difference however, that they never resorted to isolation. They built their own institutions in confrontation with the established groups. But they too, produced their own subculture and organizations, thus constituting a separate pillar.

The different pillars hardly mixed, in fact there was a mutual latent hostility. There was a strong identification with one's own pillar. At the same time it was the rule to respect the life styles of other groups or ignore them. People from one pillar did not try to convince those from other pillars. Competition was contained while commodity and labour markets were segmented. This pattern of 'peaceful coexistence' marks Dutch culture, a feature which is often confused with the celebrated Dutch tolerance (Van Doorn 1985[b]).

The political functions of this constellation were obvious. One major function was its power to control. Elite-formation was crucial for pillarization since it was a 'mobilization-model from above'. The pillar required strong leadership, discipline and social control, as well as the containment of internal opposition. Due to this power base the leaders of the pillar could develop an extensive network with elites of other pillars, deal effectively with them and contain conflicts between pillars.[6] The pillar system has built-in tendencies towards social and political stability, both vertically and horizontally. No wonder that the system was also labelled a system of *pacification*. Pacification and stability required compromises, a practice which enabled the minorities to acquire equal rights. *Pacification* thus enables *democratization* and, hence, *emancipation*: these were three important outcomes, or rather functions, of pillarization (Lijphart 1968).

From the Sixties onwards this system has eroded. A higher level of welfare, urbanization, changing life styles and individualization struck at the roots of the pillar system. As one author puts it, "the introduction of the bicycle struck the roots of pillarization" (Fortuyn 1995: 38). Indeed, there are definite changes in the realm of life styles, recreation, marriage, etc. The borderlines between the pillars lost their rigidity, and ideological or religious affiliation are presently less emphasized. Dutch society became increasingly secular and subjected to universal ideologies. These changes did not go unnoticed, prompting many publicists to announce 'the end of the pillar system'. One could argue, however, that in this view the presence of many pillar-features is neglected. The pillars are still recognizable in its institutional forms, although reduced in size and significance. Political parties, trade unions, schools, hospitals, media, universities - to mention the most influential institutions - are still organized along lines of the traditional pillars.

The functions of the system are also still there. It is true that democratization is hardly an issue, but the pacification and the emancipation-function seems still relevant, albeit in a different form. Due to the loss of electoral support, for example, the religious political parties fused and became one christian-democratic bloc. Although they seldom use religious arguments to rationalize political decisions, religious world views are present in their politics: the Christian Democrats' position on crime, family, abortion, etc. are a case in point. And even within the Christian Democratic party there are occasionally outburst with regard to the representation of power along Catholic and protestant lines. Similarly, the Social Democratic pillar still maintains its rank and file in a traditional manner; old issues like wages, labour conditions and employment, which shaped their agenda during the peak of the emancipation process, still feature high on the Social Democratic agenda. It would therefore be quite exaggerating to relegate the pillar system to the past.

The debate about an 'immigrants'-Pillar'

The responses to the statement of the prime minister who, by the way, changed his position at a later date, can be classified in: a) a small group in favour of the pillar-model of emancipation and b) a majority against it. The arguments in favour of pillarization were:
- Catholics and other groups did achieve upward mobility through self-organization. While it was recognized that the historical and social conditions have changed and some degree of de-pillarization is not denied, the principle idea is considered useful. It was suggested that religious rather than ethnic background may at present serve as the common denominator for pillarization (Andeweg, Zijderveld).
- Since freedom of religious and educational organization are constitutionally guaranteed, there is no valid reason to deny migrants this right. However, this right should not be imposed on them by the Dutch (Zijderveld, Lijphart).
- Emancipation through pillarization is subject to stages. During the stage of de-pillarization the communities may suffer from severe internal

conflicts in the attempt to liberate themselves. Nevertheless, the gains exceed the losses and one should not be deterred by some unintended effects (Andeweg, Chavannes, see also Wassink).

- If the migrants are denied the right to build a pillar of their own, this may result in a loss of political control. Since large segments of minorities are excluded from the labour market and driven into low-quality quarters of the housing market, the emerging of ghettos and hence social disorder may be likely outcomes. Pillarization may serve as a useful political instrument to control this section of the population (Zijderveld).

The main arguments against the pillar-model were:

- Minorities are too small to constitute a political group of any significance. Worse, they are internally divided. So the potential to become a pressure group is minimal to non-existent. This is evident especially since minorities do not have powerful organizations such as trade unions, employer organizations and the like (Van den Broek and Gruisen, Fennema).

- The (traditional) pillar encompassed the total life of individuals, a pillar was a 'holistic whole'. This situation does not exist any more, not in the least because geographical and social mobility did diminish the regional concentration of members of the same pillar. In contrast, migrants constitute predominantly an urban problem and they are very mobile (Andeweg, In 't Veld, Chavannes).

- Pillarization presupposes segregation at the bottom and integration at the top. If and when pillarization is fostered, this may not serve the integration of migrants in Dutch society. Pillarization may boil down to segregation which is considered synonymous with non-integration (Fennema, In 't Veld).

- Referring to the islam and the increasing secularization therein, it was emphasized that for many Muslims this is an identity rather than a religion. A pillar based on this identity may contribute to the 'cultural emancipation' of minorities but it is unlikely that it will have effects on their social and economic position (Shadid).

The discussion was marked by a few elements. Present-day problems were hardly discussed. Most participants in the debate were implicitly concerned with the question whether the historical process of pillarization can be replicated. This issue was explicitly discussed and came also prominently in the newspapers headlines. In other words, the participants in the discussion referred to the *historical* conception of pillarization and, more specifically, to the social structure underlying the concept. Consequently, the functions of the pillar system were bypassed. There also was hardly any reference to the present-day migrant institutions, nor could the question be raised whether the constellation of migrant institutions can produce similar functions as the pillar system did. The debate, however, comes up with an important question. Given the constitutional right to establish own institutions, why is it that the idea of a 'migrant-pillar' is resented? To answer this question it may be useful to look more concretely at a case. We single out the attempt to establish a Hinduschool in The Hague.

Case: Hindu school

To Surinamese Hindu's the idea of a separate school was not new. Surinam has a long history of Catholic, protestant and public schools, proceeded by the establishment of so-called *coolie-schools* in colonial times (Ramsoed en Bloemberg 1995). In 1960 the Hindus managed to establish their first secondary junior high school, the *Sri Vishnu mulo school*. One of the major motives to start such an enterprise was that many Hindustani pupils, especially those from the rural areas, could not fit in the urban schoolsystem which was dominated by 'westernized' creoles. Bad assessments of Hindustani pupils and large numbers of drop outs, together with the desire to maintain their own identity, led to the establishment of a Hindustani junior high school in the capital city of Paramaribo.

From the outset the Sri Vishnu school had a hard time maintaining itself. In the late-colonial Surinamese society there was a status-hierarchy of schools: the christian schools were allegedly the best, followed by the public schools and, way behind them, the Sri Vishnuschool. Since it was a public conviction that the Sri Vishnuschool represented the lowest quality of education, it attracted many drop-outs (from different ethnic background) from other secondary junior schools, thus enforcing the reputation of being a low-quality school. The majority of the pupils were

Hindustani's from the rural districts, however, who did not master the Dutch language as well as their urban school mates. These two circumstances exerted a downward pressure on the educational level, indeed. In spite of these set-backs, the results of the school turned out to be excellent. By the end of the Sixtees the Sri Vishnu school had established the reputation of being one of the best secondary junior high schools in Surinam. This is concluded from the performance of its former students in high school-, college- and university-education. It is our estimation that eighty to ninety percent of the first generation Hindostani's with an university degree have attended the Sri Vishnu school.

Given this experience with education in a culturally plural society it seems natural that similar problems in the Netherlands evoked similar initiatives. In The Hague, the city with the largest concentration of Hindustani's, the performance of Hindustani pupils in Dutch primary schools was far from satisfactory (Mungra 1990). In many cases the pupils felt uneasy at school. A group of parents and teachers consulted several educational experts in the field and concluded that a special Hindu school may countervail many of the problems they were facing (Bloemberg en Nijhuis 1993: 37). The main arguments put forward to justify the foundation of a Hindu school were: (1) the small upward mobility of the pupils to higher forms of education; (2) the identity of the Hindustani pupils was not preserved, on the contrary; strengthening their cultural or religious identity will increase their ability to compete in Dutch society; (3) a Hindu school will create the possibility to attend classes in their own language; and/or; (4) improve the communication between the school and the parents; (5) the Dutch school system did not fit in the cultural background of the pupils; (6) due to cultural misjudgments, especially alleged language-problems, many pupils were wrongly referred to lower-level schools.

Of course, educational motives were not the only driving forces which constituted the foundation of a Hindu primary school. Non-educational considerations, such as the desire to preserve their cultural and religious identity and life styles, for example, also had a stake in the pattern of motives.

In 1987 the Foundation Hindu Education in the Netherlands (Stichting Hindoe Onderwijs Nederland, SHON) was established. The SHON collected the required fifty signatures from parents who desired a Hindu school and submitted a request to the municipality of The Hague. The request was met with mixed feelings both at the council, as well as in the educational field. As before, when the foundation of islamic schools was discussed, local politicians felt that their policy had failed. The most dismissive reaction came from the liberal spokesman who argued that the Hindus were creating another pillar. The Social Democrats were reluctant, although they, like the liberals, recognized the constitutional right of the Hindus to have their own schools. Only the Christian Democrats were in support of the request. Feelings were also mixed in the educational field. There were headmasters who regretted the idea of a separate school for Hindu pupils, pointing at the lost of a potential 'market'. Others endorsed the desire of the Hindu's and offered their cooperation. In the end, the request was granted. In august of 1988 the first Hindu primary school in The Hague started, named after its successful example in Surinam, the Sri Vishnuschool.[7] In the next year a Hindu school was founded in Amsterdam; Rotterdam followed in 1990.

The schools started with relatively small numbers of pupils but these numbers increased rapidly, as the table indicates.

Number of pupils attending Hindu schools, 1988-1993		
	start	*1993*
The Hague	80	160
Amsterdam	24	110
Rotterdam	47	140

Source: Bloemberg and Nijhuis, 1993; 37.

This development contradicts a major argument against Hindu schools in public discussions, namely that the number of the pupils would be too small for a separate school. Considering the rapid increase of pupils, more schools may be needed to satisfy the Hindustani community (cf. Mungra 1993). Another argument raised referred to the low quality of the school.

It is argued that the level of education is low and will block pupils from moving upward and thus enhance their isolation in Dutch society. Bloemberg and Nijhuis (1993) looked into this argument. According to their report the teaching material is not selected on the basis of Hindu principles; christian holidays are celebrated, there are hardly any religious behaviourial rules, the medium of instruction is Dutch and the schools are strongly oriented on Dutch society. Moreover, the transfer of knowledge is eased by the smaller gap between the school and the 'home culture'.[8] In spite of the fact that most pupils of these schools stem from lower milieus, half of the pupils of grade eight of the Sri Vishnu school move up to higher forms of education. In short, there is hardly any evidence to support the low quality argument, or the idea of social isolation for that matter. A similar conclusion is drawn by Shadid and Koningsveld (1988) in their discussion on islamic schools.

Immigrant pillar

The constitutional right to establish their own school is not contested, yet there was an unmistakeable *reluctance* to grant the Hindu's a school of their own. Several reasons may account for this. First of all, there is a general reluctance which stems, as we hinted before in the introduction, from universal philosophical orientations.[9] Secondly, there is the notion that separate institutions may enhance the social isolation of immigrants rather than integrate them in Dutch society. According to the reports there is hardly any evidence for this position. Thirdly, there is the interest of local politicians who viewed these initiatives as failures. And finally, the established schools saw the 'market' of pupils diminished with the advent of this type of schools. Thus ideological and institutional interests can be held responsible for the reluctance of supporting minorities with their constitutionally backed claims.

The question remains however, whether the constellation of immigrant institutions constitute a pillar and serve emancipation purposes. In the past fifteen years immigrants have gradually established numerous companies, mosques and temples, sports organizations, schools, welfare institutions, etc. They made a significant inroad into the media (radio, television, newspapers), political parties, trade unions, municipality councils and national parliament. We call this development an *external* differentiation because these organizations were founded outside the established pillars. Within existing Dutch institutions, such as trade unions, political parties and christian churches, there are special work groups for migrants, often staffed by members of these groups. This development may be seen as an *internal* differentiation within existing pillars. People from the external and internal different segments interact: they consult and support each other, either formally or informally. A similar process was utilized by for example the women movement.[10] They created their own institutions (magazines, publishers, pubs, bookstores, welfare institutions, professorships, etc.) and at the same time were represented separately in the established quarters like trade unions, universities and political parties. This process of internal and external differentiation may be labelled as a form of *re-pillarization* (cf. Zahn 1991: 179).

In spite of their relatively small numbers (about six percent at the national level and twenty or more percent in the major cities), the internal and external differentiation - and the subsequent social stratification - of the migrants is not without relevance. They constitute a loosely organized, though influential group in Dutch society. There is no distinct political or economic elite as in the traditional pillar. The pacification-function, therefore, does not materialize in its traditional vein. Because of its 'riot-potential' there is a continuing necessity to maintain social peace. At present the pacification of migrants is not achieved through union politics but through special programs (affirmative action, subsidies, migrant welfare institutions) which are advocated by both the migrants themselves, and by their 'representatives' within the established institutions.

The whole of immigrants' institutions also contributes to democratization and emancipation. As far as the democratization-function is concerned, one can point at the formal and informal stake migrants have in de decision making process. Although their influence may be considered to be insufficient, a degree of democratization can not be denied. The fear for race riots (political pressure), together with their increasing electoral significance buttressed this position. The emancipation function can be read from the employment the immigrants' institutions generates. Due to the rise of these institutions a significant number of jobs was created. Not to mention the emergence of a class of ethnic entrepreneurs which is increasing in size and has rising to respectable standards.

The relevance of an up-to-date 'immigrants'-pillar' as described above lies not only in the social, economic and political functions as is usually emphasized in Dutch social science. The whole of institutions and representations also constitutes an environment producing cultural and psychological effects. It enables, for example, the supply of culture-specific commodities and services - ranging from food to religious services -, thus contributing to their cultural reproduction (Gowricharn 1987). The surrounding world becomes recognizable and their degree of 'feeling at home' rises. These are important effects which may increase their desire to integrate in the host society. In this sense the 'immigrants'-pillar' displays another similarity with the traditional pillar, the provision of cultural and psychological security. A similar argument is brought forward by Hira (1994).

The similarities in organization and functions may be plentiful, but there are also important differences. Two of these seems relevant for our arguments. The first being that the migrants do not constitute a holistic whole. Migrants in Dutch cities are dispersed, socially and geographically, and are not confined to certain quarters. In view of their ramified activities, the relatively openness of Dutch society and their participation in several domains, it is save to assume that they have *multiple identities*. Even the most devoted Muslim or Hindu buys in different shops and does not care whether his general practitioner is white or coloured. So there is no - intended - 'isolation at the base'. This fact preempts an important argument against pillarization of minorities: in the sense that it will increase their isolation. The second difference is that migrants do not constitute an organic whole as in the traditional pillar system. There is a vast diversity among the Muslims, for example, and significant numbers of them socialize predominantly in Dutch circles while others are strongly integrated in the Muslim community. While the social structure, as well as the form of (re)pillarization has changed dramatically, the *functions* of present-day migrant communities are strikingly similar to those of the traditional pillars.

Two perspectives on integration

The relatively small size of the migrant population nor the relative openness of Dutch society prevent migrants to establish their own institutions or increase their representation in existing institutions. What we have to conclude from the foregoing is that the *institutional representation* of migrants is different from the traditional pillar system. Perhaps more important are the similarities between the migrant and the traditional pillar. In spite of the changed historical circumstances the importance of this representation - judged in terms of emancipation, democratization and pacification - is still relevant. The question whether the historical experience of an 'emancipation through pillarization' can be replicated is therefore misdirected. Rather, the question addressed should be in what form and to what extent these functions are fulfilled in their re-pillarized forms.

In practice the Dutch government allowed the formation of an 'immigrants'-pillar'. For example, laws were adjusted to enable Hindu's and Muslims to practice their own religion. The finances for most provisions were supplied by the government. In other words, institutions initiated by migrants were regulated rather than sabotaged. The official attitude towards 'migrant-pillars' can therefore be labelled as *ambiguous*. On the one hand, there is the recognition that migrants are entitled to have their own provisions and life styles; on the other hand there is a reluctance to stimulate those initiatives. Probably this has to do with the connotations the concept of pillarization evokes. The leaders of the Catholics and of the *kleine luyden* consciously chose the pillarization-strategy and devoted much energy in shaping the pillar. This strategy is associated with 'social separatism' and a weakening of the social cohesion, an idea which collides with the present-day conception of integration.

Pillarization transforms people from policy objects to social subjects. That is to say, people take their own initiatives and do not depend on government incentives. This is in line with the desire of the Dutch government that citizens take more responsibility and also corresponds with the idea that some degree of self-organization is a precondition for emancipation. The *spontaneous* growth of migrant institutions therefore corresponds with the official Dutch position. The conscious attempt to develop a pillar, however, is resented. This *ambiguity* prompts the question how the Dutch preferably will like to integrate migrants.

Official integration policy in the Netherlands is almost synonymous with the economic independence of ethnic minorities. This will be achieved when migrants are employed and earn their own living. Of all domains of social life, employment is considered the most important, though not the sole, indicator of integration. The emphasis within integration-policy is therefore on employment and education. Present employment policy (including vocational training) represents a short term solution. It is expected however, that the future chances for employment will depend on educational achievements. So it seems safe to say that this concern with education reflects a long-term perspective on the same issue. The major instrument of employment policy consists of education and or training: the 'ethnic unemployed' should be enabled to compete with other job seekers. The underlying assumption of this policy is that given unfettered competition and a (economically) rational selection by personnel officers, the market will allocate the right man to the right job. It is often reported, however, that the market is subject to rigidifies such as racial discrimination and that the manner in which migrants apply for jobs requires improvement. Thus additional measures are taken to remove these obstacles and misjudgments. The belief that the labour market is intrinsically rational and just in its operation is, however, unquestioned.

This official market-led-integration model is based on a number of assumptions. One is that it takes the individual as the unit of action (and analysis). These individuals are supposed to be unrelated to each other which makes each of them an atomized actor. Secondly, non of these individuals are suppose to be able to influence the outcome of market processes. The market allegedly consists of a large number of individuals, both at the demand and the supply side. The market is said, therefore, to be impersonal and universal in its operation. The level of integration, then, depends on the size of the number of individuals who acquire a job. Thirdly, since the market supposedly clears on the basis of economic rationality, the social and cultural features of the job seekers (or of the personnel officers for that matter) is considered irrelevant. Or even worse, in many cases the culture of immigrants is considered to be an obstacle to integration, while the (labour) market is presented as its solution (Gowricharn 1993).

Conceptually there are interesting differences between the market and the pillar model of integration. Whereas the first takes the individual as its unit of action, in the pillar model it is the group which is 'acting'. The market is an economic domain while the pillar model is built on political power. The market claims to be impersonal, the pillar is based on cultural specificities, and so on. A closer look at this dichotomy is less sharp than it seems. It can be defended that the labour market consists of numerous sub-markets, each with its own subculture, while the pillars - whether traditional or in its latest forms - do contain labour markets.

For instance, the internal section of the 'immigrants'-pillar' represents a segment of the labour market with high quality jobs. The growth of the internal 'migrant pillar' enlarges the number of jobs in so-called primary markets. These markets are also encountered in the external segment: the firms, welfare institutions, schools, etc. The assertion that the external segment of the pillar contains secondary jobs requires not only empirical justification, but also misses the point. The issue is that the two models of integration, the market and the pillar model, are not mutually exclusive. The point can hardly be over-emphasized. Both the external and the internal segments of the 'immigrants'-pillar' are at the same time part of the labour market: the growth of the pillar is positively related to the job market.)[11] The overlap between pillars and labour market can be reformulated as a segmentation of the latter along cultural lines. The expansion of this market segment does not contradict the desire to build an 'immigrants' pillar'. Framing the discussion in terms of *oppositions* - markets versus pillars - bypasses the 'emancipation-effect' of the pillars, even in terms of official government policy. The reason for missing this point is that most participants were referring to a historical concept of pillars or to established legal rights.

Summarizing our argument: in terms of concept and social structure the pillar model can be seen as a historical phenomenon. Viewed in terms of the functions it fulfilled, however, the pillar model still has some relevance. Although the migrant communities are loosely organized and do not exhibit all features of the traditional pillar system, there are tendencies which can be conceptualized as forms of re-pillarization. This process does not contradict the desire of the Dutch government to integrate immigrants through markets. On the contrary, due to the expansion of the 'immigrants'-pillar' the number of jobs increases. It is highly probable that migrants will have more access to the jobs in these segments of the labour market. Hence the encouragement of pillarization will expand the labour market and improve the position of migrants. It is a model worth trying.

Notes

[1] We are grateful to Cees Bronsveld for some useful comments on an earlier draft of this paper.

[2] The pillar system (Dutch: *zuilenstelsel*) is a vertical societal organization, thus dividing a population in different segments. The concept will be outlined in section two below.

[3] For convenience sake, throughout this paper we will use the term 'migrant' synonymously with 'ethnic minority'.

[4] The articles used are among others: Andeweg, R.B.: Is verzuiling instrument voor integratie minderheden? *Trouw*, 31-10-1991. Zijderveld, A.C.: Minderheden in Nederland meest gebaat bij verzuiling; *NRC* 23-12-91. Chavannes, M.: De prijs der verzuiling (2); *NRC*, 4-1-92. Shadid, W.A.: Een islamitische zuil is onhaalbaar; *NRC* 6-1-92. In 't Veld, R.: Nieuwe zuil waarschijnlijk geen bijdrage aan integratie; *NRC* 9-1-92. Lijphart, A.: Tegen gedwongen zuilvorming; *NRC*, 9-1-92. Fennema, M.: Verzuilingsmodel niet toepasbaar op immigranten; *Volkskrant*, 11-1-1992. Broek, A. van den en B. Gruisen: Zeepbel van de islamitische zuil; *NRC*, 25-1-92.

[5] This concept of a migrant-pillar is used for want of a better term. It refers to the whole of economic, social and cultural provisions migrants have established and which marks there identities and life styles. There is no analytical claim involved in using this term.

[6] The term 'elite-cartel democracy' is also used for this system. The model is widely applied to countries like Surinam and South Africa, see: Lijphart (1968) and Dew (1978).

[7] This project was predominantly led by Brahmins, belonging to the largest Hindu 'current', the Sanatham Dharm. A few years later conflicts with the Arya Samadj - the second largest Hindu 'current' among the Surinamese Hindus - centered around the position of the Brahmins, appeared to be unmanageable. This resulted in the foundation of a second Hindu school in The Hague. For an account from this perspective, see Schwenke (1994).

[8] For an extensive discussion on the functions of the school, see Teunissen (1990).

[9] This includes the social sciences as well since they are imbedded in the Enlightenment. Van Doorn (1985a) discussed this issue as a clash between (sub)cultures and reformulated the pillarization process as the formation of a plurality of cultures.

[10] Wassink (1992) suggests that the 'gay-movement' also managed to create its own pillar.

[11] The reverse, however, does not hold: the job market (especially in the private sector) may expand without having a significant impetus on the 'migrant-pillar'.

7

Islam, Hinduism and the Limited Secularity in India

A Model for Muslim-European Relations in the Age of Migration?

Bassam Tibi

In our age of globalization massive migration from poor countries to those with real or perceived prosperity has become a major phenomenon.[1] In particular, migration from the Islamic part of the Southern and Eastern Mediterranean, but also from South Asia to Western Europe, has contributed to the creation of a sizable, ever-growing Muslim minority.[2] The result is an ever-changing composition of the population of the recipient countries. Multiculturalism and ethnic conflict are equally related to this recent phenomenon. Islamic scarves in French schools[3] as a source of conflict is a case in point.

The debate on the future of Islamic minorities in Western Europe revolves around the issue whether the integration of Islam or the creation of a distinct Islamic community within the secular European culture is to be preferred. One of the results of massive migration from the World of Islam to Europe has been the fact that "'Western' and 'Islamic' can no longer strictly be identified with particular geographic regions ... Muslim immigration ... suggests that we may soon be forced to speak not simply of Islam and, but of Islam in, the West",[4] as John Kelsay argues. The question that arises in this regard is whether Muslims will become European citizens or whether they will form "a sort of sectarian enclave in the context of a larger, Western culture, in the West, but not of it"?[5]

The alternatives are: Integration of Muslims in Europe, or the creation of a distinct, but consistently alien, Islamic community. In my book *Im Schatten Allahs. Der Islam und die Menschenrechte*[6] I identify the alternatives with a focus on Islam in Europe as Euro-Islam, i.e. an institutionally binding interpretation along the lines of secular Western constitutions, or a Ghetto-Islam, a communitarian Islam in its own right with deep tensions affected by the surrounding European secular social environment. In order to answer the question *communitarianism or integration of Muslims living in Europe as European citizens* I want to draw on the case of India. This country is a constitutionally secular state that, nevertheless, grants the Muslim community the practice of a "Muslim Personal Law" based on the *shari'a*. In my opinion, the question is whether this case provides a model for the future of Islam in Europe. The following case study establishes the ground for giving a profound answer to this question.

The Secular Nation-State and its citizens: communitarianism or citizenship

The processes of globalization resulted in re-shaping all political entities in our world along the lines of the European model of the nation-state. However, the globalization of the secular nation-state[7] does not necessarily imply the spread of the political culture of this institution worldwide. One of the paradoxes of the current nation-state system, as revealed since the end of the bipolar world of the Cold War, is the fact that "people are ostentatiously both very international and very parochial", as Robin Jeffrey has observed in his book *What is happening to India*.[8] To draw a line between the country at issue and Europe Jeffrey argues that there is a similarity between the war-ridden Balkan and India. Orthodox Serbs and Muslims co-existed in peace in Southeast Europe for many centuries,[9] but they are currently waging a bloody war: "In outward forms they are globalized, in themselves, they are prepared to die for identities as local as a Balkan valley was to its inhabitants"[10] in earlier centuries.

In my book *Krieg der Zivilisationen/The War of Civilizations*[11] I draw a parallel between the current scenario in the Balkans and a possible future scenario in India, if Hindu-fundamentalists of the Bharatiya Janata Party and other movements like Shiv Sena were to grow as strong as the orthodox Serb fundamentalists are in the Balkans. Does this scenario matter for Europe?

In relating the addressed issue to Western Europe several questions pertaining to Muslim-European relations rise to the fore. In recalling European history of religious wars and the fact of how the secular state succeeded in ending that era, this study aims at drawing a comparison between the Muslim-Hindu relations in the secular nation-state of India and Muslim-European relations under the conditions of communitarian multiculturalism.

At issue is the status of the Muslim minority as a community in India after the partition of the Indian subcontinent in 1947. The pertinence of this status for the study of the Muslim minorities in Western Europe in the age of migration lies at the centre of the inquiry. The essential question to be answered focuses on whether the special status of the Muslim minority in India could serve as a model for Western Europe to emulate, or does it, rather, serve as a warning of a conflict-erupting pattern. In other words: Could the secular state accommodate ethnic non-secular communities as collectivities, or, reversely, do these communities undermine the secular character of the state and its citizenship?

Defining the scope of inquiry: does the model of India matter for Europe?

Hinduism and Islam in India are significant for Europe in comparative terms as an object of study with regard to their capability to coexist peacefully in a political culture defined by the modern secular nation-state. Unlike the Western nation-states the Indian state does not impose its secularity on religious minorities. It is true that the constitution of India in its article 44 rules the elaboration of a secular *common civil code* for all Indians, regardless of their religious affiliations. This code has never come into being. Political realities as well as articles 26, 27, and 28 of the Indian Constitution grant minorities the right as communities to manage their own religious affairs. The result is the legal reality of *Muslim Personal Law*, as based on the *shari'a*. To be sure, shari'a has two meanings: traditionally, shari'a is not a political issue insofar as it focuses on civil law affairs as marriage, inheritance, and other personal affairs. Muslim Personal Law in India is based on this understanding of the shari'a.[12] The other meaning of the shari'a is the one developed by contemporary Muslim fundamentalists who interpret the shari'a as a political-legal body essential for their concept of the Islamic state.[13] Indian Muslims insist on their practice of the shari'a as civil law, but have no political claims related to a Muslim state.

Relating the communitarian rights of Indian Muslims to the immigration issue in Europe evokes the question whether it is recommendable to grant non-Western minorities - evolving as a result of immigration to Western Europe - a status similar to the one given to Indian Muslims. Despite the fact that the latter are not immigrants, their identity revolves around the issue whether it is related to the polity of India or to the *Umma*, i.e. to the worldwide Islamic community. The answer to this question depends not only on how India's identity is being determined, but also on the image which Indian Muslims have of themselves. Muslims living in European states are exposed to a similar challenge. Are Muslim immigrants willing to identify themselves as European citizens?

If India is able to dissociate its polity from Hindu culture and then rigorously be shaped along the lines of political culture of the secular nation-state, why then cannot Muslims unequivocally feel like citizens of India? Could Indian Muslims practice the shari'a and - in this line - link themselves to the universalism of the Islamic *Umma* and at the same time continue to be true citizens of India? The essential concept underlying this question is the idea of citizenship.

In looking comparatively at classical America, the ideal model of a melting pot suggests that every person could become, on the grounds of equality, an American citizen, regardless of religion, colour, gender, and ethnicity. In the course of a newly evolving culture of multicultural and feminist preferences, this classical model is being called into question. The result has been "The Disuniting of America".[14]

Unlike America, and despite some rare exceptions, Europe was not - until recently - a continent for immigration of people coming from non-European civilizations. By the late 20th century European realities are changing radically in this regard. In view of this change, contemporary Europe is being faced with two exclusive alternatives: either to emulate with the classical model of the colour, religion, and ethnicity blind concept of American citizenship, or to comply with fashionable demands for communitarian multiculturalism leading to a virtual segregation in the name of honouring ethno-religious identities. With regard to the latter an examination of the Muslim-Hindu relations in the secular state of India seems to bear great relevance in the search for choices for determining the future of Europe. This inquiry promises to provide fruitful results for developing and recommending policies for dealing with the ongoing changes in the composition of European populations.

At the hub of the issue lies the fact that India is a secular nation-state only in a limited sense. It is true that the Indian constitution promises in article 44 a "uniform civil code" for all citizens. However, this promise remains behind the realities and the accomplishments of Indian secularism. This article is also in conflict with articles 26 to 28 in the same constitution. In questioning the relevance of the nominal Indian nation-state for Western Europe while determining the relation of the European majority to the Muslim minority of immigrants, we implicitly are virtually evaluating the Indian case. Is the limited and incomplete secularity in India an expression of a flawed nation-state or can this case serve as a model for Europe in the age of Muslim immigration to this continent?

To begin with, institutional secularity is based on a legal concept that divorces law[15] from religion. In this sense the modern nation-state is based on a legally secular body politic, both on the institutional and normative level. In acknowledging the link between legal norms and culture, communitarian multiculturalism must consequentially lead to a reconsideration of the secularity of admitting alien legal traditions, regardless of their secular or religious character. In this sense it is possible to view India as a true multicultural society. But then the questions have to be asked: Does this multiculturalism work? Could it also serve as a model for others? To be sure, cultural pluralism is one thing, but communitarian multiculturalism is another!

Despite the already mentioned article 44 in the Indian constitution, it is clear that the "continuance of traditional ideas alongside of those of the new secular ... democracy"[16] prevails. Nevertheless, the *dharma*,[17] the legal concept of Indian civilization, reflects such diverse accounts that it cannot serve as the grounds for a civil code.

Unlike the Islamic *shari'a*, the *dharma* refers to a diversity of customs rather than to truly legal concepts. The formation of the modern nation-state in India confronted Hinduism with the challenge of accommodating the *dharma*/righteousness to the new conditions. As the expert on Hindu law D. M. Derrett states, "Hindus were unable to rise to these challenges. Hindu law was old, but prolix, confused, and incapable of self-renewal unaided".[18] Thus, it remained the privilege of the Muslim minority in the new secular state of India to employ the *shari'a* as its own religious legal body to be the foundation for a *Muslim Personal Law*. Indian Muslims[19] who subscribe to the shari'a insist on the implementation of the very same shari'a to be part and parcel of their constructed Islamic identity. Consequently, they view any effort pursued along the lines of article 44 of the constitution to develop a uniform civil code which would also be applicable to the Muslim minority to be an assault on their cultural identity. The inability of the Indian nation-state to frame a uniform civil law for all Indians, while allowing Muslim Indians to conduct their affairs in compliance with the *shari'a*, paralleled by government interference with Hindu practices, has been a source of conflict. These conditions have created a situation that "feeds the feeling that Indian secularism is increasingly being directed against Hinduism"[20], as the Hindu scholar Arvind Sharma rightly states.

Along lines similar to the Indian case, some segments of the Muslim minorities in Europe are now demanding the recognition of the normative body of the Islamic shari'a, purportedly to be consequential to the admission of their cultural identity within a multicultural setup. The al-Azhar sheykh Muhammad Abdullah al-Samman[21] rejects the integration of Muslims living in Europe as an effort at their 'Christianization'. The stereotype of a *salibiyya*/crusader mentality crops up again, however, in a new shape.

The call for the formation of a Muslim community in Europe underlines the relevance for Western Europe of the Indian case of the relations of Islam and Hinduism in the age of massive Muslim immigration.

The pendulum between secularity and the divine State

Hindu-nationalists resent the practice of the shari'a by the Muslim minority of their country. They extend this attitude to a resentment of the secular state in India. The result is an erupting conflict.[22] As the Indian scholar Kuldeep Mathur argues in a paper presented to an international conference on democratization in Asia, "secularism becoming a source of danger to Hindus emanates from state actions to protect minority rights".[23] In other words, in the understanding of the leaders of the Hindi community in India, secularity has a specific meaning: it serves as a cover for the practice of non-secular laws, i.e. the *shari'a*.

Aware of the fact of being a minority, Indian Muslims understand that "the concept of the Islamic state/*nizam Islami* (regulation of polity according to Islam) cannot be achieved in present circumstances in India".[24] Thus, they confine themselves to the demand of a recognition of the *shari'a* by the state. The secular Indian state complies with this demand. In return, Muslims accept the secular character of India only in the limited sense that the state separates politics from religion on general grounds. However, the state must operate without interfering in the application of shari'a law by Muslims. Muslim Personal Law is the legal device for managing the affairs of the Muslims within their own community. Despite this non-fundamentalist view which is overly accepted by Indian Muslims, one cannot overlook the fact that also in India there is a variety of Islamic fundamentalism.[25]

Conversely, Hindus view this limited secularity as an exclusive privilege for minorities and as an assault upon their own cultural lifestyle. Hindus resent secularity, and view it as an obstacle for them, being the majority, to shape the state along the lines of their own civilization, i.e. Hinduism. In the end, this resentment has lead to the rise of Hindu fundamentalism which is splitting the polity of India.[26]

The conflict between the Hindu majority and the Muslim minority touches on two *pivotal issues*:

- The flawed secularity of the Indian state leads to deepening the existing trenches between the diverse religious and ethnic groups in the very same society. In this sense the Muslim minority creates a ghetto with its own rights. It rebuffs any policy to subject Indian Muslims to the common civil code valid for the entire society, as ruled by article 44 of the constitution of India.

- On the other hand, this kind of minority rights leads to a resentment by the majority, amounting to a whole-sale rejection of secularity. In this context Hindu nationalists politicize Hinduism in an effort to subdue

Hindu diversity to an integrist interpretation, which amounts to religious fundamentalism.[27]

Hindu fundamentalism has been viewed as an arbitrary effort to apply an overall scripturalism to the diverse Hindu precepts and teachings of the *Vedas*. The result is the new introduction of a one-dimensional interpretation of Hinduism. Along these lines the *dharma* resembles a fundamentalist design of the *shari'a*. In this context the Hindu religious claim of *hindutva*/Indianness becomes the identity of an exclusive India in which there is no place for Muslims and other non-Hindus. As the prominent Indian sociologist T. K. Oommen argues, this interpretation is faulted on many counts, the most important of which is the fact that the real state of India is not compatible with the claim of territorialization of Hindu civilization.[28] Underlying this is the simple fact that the nation-state of India - despite a Hindu majority (be it 65 or 85% - the determination of the figure is a political, not a statistical, question) - is virtually a multi-cultural and multi-religious state. Viewed from this angle, the granting of the practice of shari'a for the Muslim minority and the response to this privilege of an ever-growing Hindu fundamentalism seem to create a threat to the inner peace of India which could lead to the crumbling of the nation-state. In my already quoted book *Krieg der Zivilisationen/The War of Civilizations* I express the misgiving that this clash between a politicized Islam and an equally politicized Hinduism in India could lead to a similar, albeit in the consequences more dramatic, showdown between the two civilizations as the ongoing tragic conflict between Islam and Serb-Orthodox Christianity in Bosnia.

On these grounds I want to present the hypothesis that the Indian case of the relations between Islam and Hinduism does not provide a model[29] for Western Europe to emulate in the age of migration from Muslim countries. In comparing the anti-Islamic attitudes of Hindu fundamentalists with European right-wing xenophobia directed against Muslim immigrants, I am inclined to expand this hypothesis. The underlying argument is that any overriding of secular, i.e. religion and ethnicity blind, citizenship through communitarian minority preferences or rights would bolster xenophobia in Europe in a similar way as the practice of the *shari'a* in India strengthens anti-Islamic attitudes of Hindu fundamentalists. In order to examine this hypothesis, I want, in a summary fashion, to review the historical background of Islam and Hinduism on the Indian subcontinent from the Islamic invasion through the partition of India. This historical review serves as an effort to trace back the roots of conflict.

Hinduism and Islam in an historical perspective

In classical Islamic doctrine the call for Islam/Da'wa and the geographical enhancement of *Dar al-Islam* as the geographical territoriality of Islamic civilization, even though completed through minority means, is not considered by Muslims to be an act of war/*harb*. They rather view it as futuhat/opening for the extension of *Dar al-Islam*, or House of Peace, against the non-Islamic territoriality, or *Dar al-Harb*/House of War.[30] Despite this image of one's self, the Islamic invasion of India, as a *jihad*, was clearly an act of war and violence. As the historian of civilizations Fernand Braudel puts it, the establishment of Muslim India in 1206-1757, beginning with the founding of the Sultanate of Delhi, could only be "successful ... in wholesale military occupation", and, he adds, Muslim invaders "could not rule the country except by systematic terror ... there were forced conversions. If ever there were an uprising, it was instantly and savagely repressed; houses were burned, the countryside was laid waste, men were slaughtered and women were taken as slaves".[31] Despite this forceful method for the partial Islamization of India, Islam has become, next to Hinduism, an element of the cultural heritage of that South-Asian subcontinent.

The Empire of the Great Mogul, which lasted more than three centuries, is essentially comprised of equal measures of Indian and Islamic great imperial history. Babur, the founder of the Mogul Empire in 1526, continues to be a symbol of the cultural greatness of Indian history in its period of Islamic-Hindu civilization. He represents a kind of symbiosis between Islam and Hinduism. However, the emperor Babur equally stands for the origin of the tensions between Islam and Hinduism. The Babri Mesjid, the Mosque of Babur, which allegedly was established on the very spot of the Hindu Rama Temple, is among the ideological symbols for the articulation of the rift between Muslims and Hindus in contemporary

India.[32] In other words, the history of Islam and Hinduism accommodates equally the peaceful coexistence and the rivalry between the two civilizations.

Unlike the Muslim minorities in Western Europe (about 15 million, expected to grow to 40 million in the year 2025), the Indian Muslims are natives, not immigrants. Basically, they are Hindus of lower casts who converted to Islam. The reference of the quoted historian Braudel to forced conversions notwithstanding, it is true that lower cast Hindus converted to Islam at free will to escape their minor status. In this regard Indian Muslims are comparable with the Bosniaks of the Balkan,[33] who, as former Christian Bogomiles, freely converted to Islam ensuing the Turk-Muslim invasion of the Balkan. For this reason the attitude of Hindu radicals vis-à-vis Indian Muslims is comparable to that of the orthodox Serbs vis-à-vis Bosnian Muslims. In both cases Muslims are despised as "renegades". This anti-Islamic attitude oscillates between the Nazi-like aspiration of "ethnic cleansing", such as recently practised in the Balkan, and - as in India - an effort at the re-Hinduization of Indian Muslims.

The destruction of the Babri Mesjid in Ayodhya by Hindu-fundamentalists of the Bharatiya Janata Party/BJP on December 6, 1992 was an exceptional expression of the dreadful Hindu fundamentalism. Like Serbian atrocities against Muslims it was an attempt to extinguish Islam on the Indian subcontinent. The former vice president of India, K. R. Narayanan, an untouchable by caste, commented on the Ayodhya assault, "The attack on the mosque was the greatest tragedy since the assassination of Mahatma Gandhi in 1948".[34] The leading editorialist of the *Frankfurter Allgemeine Zeitung*, Klaus Natorp, rightly expressed the misgiving that not "only the stability of India is at stake, but also the relations of India to all other Muslim states ... This event is paralleled by the genocide of the Bosnian Muslims by the Serbs".[35]

Given the fact that the Muslim minority in India amounts to circa 130 million (ca. 12% of the population) and that India is surrounded by two Muslim states - Pakistan and Bangladesh - with a population of about 200 million, a possible Balkanization of Hindu-Muslim-relations ensuing the assault on the Mosque in Ayodhya could leave the tragedy of Bosnia looking comparatively like a minor event. For this reason the de-escalation of the tensions between Islam and Hinduism on the subcontinent, as well as a search for ways for peaceful coexistence, must be considered as a contribution for world peace.

In relating these issues to Europe, I want to argue that the relations between Islam and Hinduism in India provide rather a warning to precaution than a model for European countries in the age of immigration. The creation of Muslim communitarian ghettos in Europe with possible preferential minority rights could lead to similar explosive effects as the one described in this study on India.

To be sure, the reservations articulated in this article against communitarianism with regard to the Islamic presence in Western Europe are a plea for integration, but not for assimilation. By integration I am basically addressing political issues; in the main, a needed consensus on secularity, constitutional individual human rights in the Western sense, and religious pluralism. With regard to the latter, Muslims would be required to give up on the Islamic concept that non-Muslims are *dhimmis*. Integration of Muslim immigrants in Europe requires their consent to the political culture of Western civilization, but not their assimilation into it. This distinction between political and economic integration, on the one hand, and cultural and religious assimilation, on the other, allows Muslim immigrants to couple their Islamic identity with Western citizenship with the result that they can become European citizens while maintaining parts of their Islamic identity.

Conclusions

Historically, the introduction of Islam to India was related to war and violence. Nevertheless, it resulted in an indigenization of the introduced patterns. The result has been Indo-Islam. Despite the atrocities of Islamic invasion, Muslims and Hindus managed to live together peacefully, and they equally contributed to a new Hindu-Islamic civilization that ended with the British colonial invasion.

The decolonization of India could have resulted in some way in a continuation of the earlier Muslim-Hindu symbiosis, had Indian Muslims not claimed the partition of India in 1947. They initiated the partition of the subcontinent in an Islamic state, Pakistan, and a secular state, India. This Islamic conduct has been the beginning of the politicization of both major religions on the Indian subcontinent. Gandhi did not lead the anti-colonial struggle on religious grounds, as his Muslim rivals did. Gandhi, even though guided by the ethics of Hinduism, aimed at continuing a Hindu-Muslim symbiosis in an independent secular nation-state of India. Muslim leaders did not share this approach, and the result was the partition of India in 1947. Despite all the odds, India[36] has managed from the outset much better than Pakistan, but it is now in a looming crisis haunted by fundamentalism.[37]

In defining religious fundamentalism as an expression of the politicization of religion[38], I contend that Islamic fundamentalism has been the very first variety of this global phenomenon on the Indian subcontinent. It is true, the founders of Pakistan and the leaders of the All-India Muslim League, like Mohammed Ali Jinnah (1867-1948), were not fundamentalists, but rather ethno-religious nationalists. However, the very first real fundamentalist movement on the subcontinent has been an Islamic one: the Jama'at-i-Islami. The spokesman of Muslim fundamentalists in India and also one of the most influential precursors of current worldwide Islamic fundamentalism, Abu al-A'la al-Maududi (1903-1979) established the mentioned movement of Jama'at-i-Islami[39] in 1941. Maududi was the major spearhead, not only of the partition of India, but also of the intensification of Islamic-Hindu tensions. After the partition the Indian branch of that movement created its own organization with the new name Jama'at-i-Islami Hind (i.e. Jama'at- Islami of India). While dispensing with the demand for an Islamic state, as referred to earlier, the renamed movement insisted that the Islamic *shari'a* should be binding for all Indian Muslims.

It is wrong to simply reduce the rise of Hindu fundamentalism to a reaction to Islamic fundamentalism. Nevertheless, the study of Hindu fundamentalism clearly shows how this ideology is an expression of the politicization of Hinduism along lines similar to those of Islamic fundamentalism as a political Islam. The interpretation of the truly diverse *dharma* as a coherent legal system can be viewed as an effort to emulate the political interpretation of the Islamic *shari'a*. When a similar progression is followed, the collections of the vedas are considered by Hindu fundamentalists to be a monotheistic revelation looked up to in a very scripturalist manner. Politicised and selective scripturalism is one of the basic features of religious fundamentalism.[40] It is not so much the text that matters, but rather the ways the text is instrumentally employed in a clearly political context. Religious Hindu fundamentalism results in the construction of an anti-Islamic neo-Hinduism that implicitly emulated the well-rooted Islamic fundamentalism. It would be superfluous to mention how strong the anti-Hinduistic sentiment of political Islam in India is.

Both varieties of religious fundamentalism, the Islamic and the Hindu types, are based on several similar foundations: the politicization of religion, selective and arbitrary scripturalism, the demonization of the other, and, above all, the call for a religious state based on divine order, be this the *shari'a* or the *dharma sastra.* By igniting the tensions between Islam and Hinduism, by determining that Hindu and Muslim communities are exclusive "imagined communities",[41] and by "inventing" a respectively anti-Islamic or anti-Hindu "tradition",[42] both Islamic and Hindu fundamentalism promote the Balkanization of India in the process called "After the nation-state"[43] as a beginning of a new dreadful era of "global disorder".

In order to meet the fundamentalist challenge and to save the nation-state in India from crumbling, it is imperative to materialize article 44 of the constitution by developing a common civil code which would deprive the Muslim minority from practising the *shari'a,* and which would thus disarm the Hindu fundamentalists' arguments against secularity in India.

In relating the Indian context to Western Europe in our age of globalization and world time, the Indian lesson helps provide an answer to the call for a multicultural communitarianism for granting Muslim immigrants collective minority rights.[44] The answer can be stated in this precise and succinct manner: the inner peace of Western Europe requires a clear "no" to the communitarian call for the Islamic shari'a for Muslim minorities. The Indian experience provides a timely warning.

The problems of integrating Islam into European societies come not only from Muslims, but also from European right-wing extremism. In order to deal with the emerging "negative attitude of large sectors of European societies toward ... the religion of Islam",[45] it is important to provide democratic solutions for taking the issues out of the hands of extremists. Otherwise, these political forces would be able to "attract significant percentages of voters in local and national elections", as Van

Koningsveld rightly argues. In my view, communitarianism is not the democratic solution needed. I share Van Koningsvelds' view that "the dramatic events in South-Eastern Europe have created fears about the survival of freedom, democracy, and equality in regard to Europe's Islam." We need to take these fears seriously and avoid the kind of multicultural communitarianism that may strongly feed them.

Notes

[1]   See the contributions in Cornelius et al. (1994).
[2]   See Gerholm and Lithman (1988).
[3]   See Ross 1993, pp. 4-9.
[4]   Kelsay 1993, p.118.
[5]   Ibid.
[6]   Tibi 1994[a], chapter 12.
[7]   The best account for this in Giddens 1987, in particular, chapter 10, on the globalization of the nation-state, pp. 255-293.
[8]   Jeffery 1994, p. xxiii.
[9]   See Malcolm 1994 and Tibi 1994[b].
[10]   Jeffrey, 1994, p. xxiii.
[11]   Tibi 1995[a], in particular, pp. 25f, 122f, 165f.
[12]   The authoritative work on this subject is Schacht 1964.
[13]   See the chapter on shari'a in Tibi 1994[a], pp. 194-216, and chapter 10 on the fundamentalist interpretation of the shari'a.
[14]   Schlesinger 1992.
[15]   For more details, see Hart 1961. For a discussion of the Islamic shari'a from this point of view, see Tibi 1990, chapter 5, pp. 59-75.
[16]   Derrett et al. 1979, p.107.
[17]   See Badrinath 1993.
[18]   Derrett, et al. 1979, p. 107.
[19]   For a survey on Islam in India, see the chapter by S. Shahabuddin and Th.P. Wright in: Esposito 1987, pp.152-176.
[20]   Sharma 1993 (ed.), pp.1-67 (on Hinduism by Sharma), p.55.
[21]   Samman 1987.
[22]   See Pulsfort 1993.
[23]   K. Mahur, *Hindu Assertion, Casteism and Indian Democracy*. Paper presented at the international conference on Democracy and Democratization in Asia, May 30 - June 1, 1994/Center for Asian Studies, Université Catholique de Louvaine, p. 14.
[24]   Shahabuddin and Wright in Esposito 1987, p. 172.
[25]   Agwani 1986.
[26]   On Hindu fundamentalism, see the best account by Gold 1991, p. 531-593.
[27]   See the references in notes 20, 22, 23, and 26. See also Pulsfort 1991 and the chapter on India by Voll in T. Meyer (ed.) 1989.
[28]   Oomen 1994.
[29]   Tibi, 1995[b].
[30]   See Tibi 1996 (forthcoming) and Tibi 1995[a], chapter 4, pp. 191ff.

[31] Braudel 1994, p. 232. On the history of India, see also Kulke and Rothermund 1982, pp. 181ff.
[32] On this, see Gold 1991, pp. 531-32. See also Sharma 1993 and Pulsfort 1993.
[33] Balic 1992, chapter 1992, pp. 80ff.
[34] Quoted by Jeffrey 1994, p. xxi.
[35] Klaus Natorp, in: *Frankfurter Allgemeine Zeitung*, December 8, 1992.
[36] See the special issue "Another India" of *Daedalus* (Fall 1989).
[37] On the rivalry between Islamic and Hindu fundamentalism in India, see Voll 1989.
[38] Tibi 1995^c. See also chapter 7 on India.
[39] On Jama'at-i-Islami and fundamentalism in Pakistan, see Ahmad 1991.
[40] See the introduction and the concluding chapter by Marty and Appleby 1991.
[41] Anderson 1991.
[42] See the introduction "Inventing traditions" by Hobsbawm in Hobsbawn and Ranger 1983.
[43] Horsman and Marshall 1994.
[44] For this debate in Germany, see Tibi 1994^a, pp. 337-351.
[45] The following quotes are from P.S. van Koningsveld 1995.

8

Muslims as Dhimmis

The Emancipation of Muslim Immigrants in Europe: The Case of Switzerland

Jacques Waardenburg

The title of this paper should not, of course, be taken literally. Present-day Europe is organized not according to religious communities but according to national states largely brought together in the European Union. Observing the rule of separation between church and state, European governments keep the various religious communities in their countries at a distance and as far as I can see, the development is towards an equal treatment of these communities. Consequently, in Europe there cannot be dhimmîs in the juridical sense of the word.[1]

Yet, taken metaphorically, the title may characterize a situation common to immigrants in Europe, among them Muslims and Hindus, at least as long as they have not obtained the nationality of the country where they have settled, and sometimes even afterwards. The official status of "dhimmîs" has prevented Christian and Jewish inhabitants of the Islamic caliphate, later empires and present-day Islamic states based on the Sharî'a such as Saudi Arabia and Iran, from enjoying effective political power and equal rights with Muslims, even when they have the same nationality. In actual fact the Muslim and Hindu "foreigners" in Europe nowadays have relatively little political power effectively to defend their community rights or themselves individually from discrimination in European societies, although the situation is different in different countries, Sweden being somewhere at the top and France somewhere at the bottom of the scale.

Besides the relative lack of political power, the social and economic structure of European societies and countries also tends to relegate the great masses of non-European immigrants to a situation of marginality. For some ninety percent of them there can be little hope of arriving at full participation in the social and economic life of society. Very few indeed can even achieve social mobility to improve the situation, if not of themselves, then at least of their children and grandchildren.

The difficulties surrounding the political, social and economic emancipation of immigrants from outside Europe are numerous and need not be enumerated here; there are also difficulties for migrants inside Europe but we will not consider them here. As far as the political situation of Muslim immigrants are concerned, nearly all of them come from countries which cannot be called democratic in any European sense of the word and which have hardly provided them with any education in democracy. On the contrary, numerous Muslim countries try to keep those of their citizens living in Europe dependent on them and subjected to political and other control - not without success. Such pockets of Muslim communities are liable to secrete forms of authoritarian leadership and manipulation which, in conjunction with the largely collective and emotional ways of behaving of their members, present a serious obstacle to the development of personal and civic responsibility as presupposed in democratic procedures which, unfortunately, are usually not explained to them.

As to their economic and social situation, apparently little can be done for it in a time of economic hardship and rising xenophobia and racism in European societies. The immigrants' educational and cultural situation is hardly more encouraging, though some countries are quite willing to face the problems of dual culture.

The question, then, which initiatives have been taken, in particular by Muslim groups and bodies supporting them, with a view to effective emancipation, is an urgent one. Which role can the formation of locally active Muslim communities play in such an emancipation process, politically and otherwise?

We shall take here the Swiss situation as our point of departure. We shall signal some reorientations occurring among Muslims here, in particular in the French speaking part of Switzerland. On the basis of the Swiss case we shall then try to identify some contextual factors which obstruct or are helpful to community formation with reference to Islam. Finally we shall ask how the formation of Muslim communities may be able to promote the emancipation of Muslim minorities in Europe, while closing with some considerations of a more general nature.

Muslims in Switzerland[2]

According to the official census figures there were in Switzerland:

in 1970: 29,400 Muslims (0.05% of the population)

in 1980: 56,000 Muslims (0.89% of the population)

in 1990: 152,217 Muslims (2.1% of the total population). Of them, 7 735 (5.08%) had Swiss nationality, 61 454 had a permanent resident status, and 23 064 (15%) were refugees or asylum seekers.

Consequently, 59 964 Muslims were here on a temporary permit, the large majority of them wanting to stay. It is remarkable that only 23% of the Muslims in Switzerland are living in the ten largest towns of the country; most Muslims live in smaller towns or in the countryside.

In 1990 the country had 65 149 Muslims of Turkish nationality and 55 453 Muslims of ex-Yugoslav nationality. These two groups together constituted 79,22% of the total Muslim population in Switzerland, most of them living in German speaking Switzerland. In 1990 there were moreover 8 172 Muslims of various Middle Eastern nationalities, 5 605 from North Africa, 4 611 from Asian countries other than the Middle East, and 1 431 from Africa south of the Sahara.

Of the 152 217 Muslims living in Switzerland in 1990, 117 411 were living in German, 13 509 in Italian and 21 297 in French speaking Switzerland. The latter represent 15% of the total number of Muslims living in Switzerland. Of them, 30% come from ex- Yugoslavia, 24% from Turkey and 18% from North Africa. According to a rough estimate, there are about 250 Islamic centres in the country, including mosques, prayerhalls, and Muslim associations.

Political culture in Switzerland has grown from below; the country never had a central authority able to impose itself on the autonomous cantons. In order to arrive at decisions, political or otherwise, elaborate negotiations take place between the interested parties, in search of some kind of consensus. In this art of negotiation the parties concerned tend not to define their positions exhaustively in advance, refraining from open conflicts or sometimes even from acknowledging that conflicts exist.

Another aspect of Swiss political culture is a basic respect for Swiss minority groups and their particularisms, with a conscious policy to do justice to given differences. There is no common ideology which could homogenize Swiss society and the very basis of nationhood is a subject of ongoing discussion. The tendency in German speaking Switzerland is to stress ethnic and cultural entities as constitutive of the nation, which is conceived here primarily as a sort of contract between the cantons. The French speaking part of the country tends to develop a more political concept of the state, which is conceived here primarily as a common political project of the cantons.

This political culture largely determines the views held of immigration. Of all European countries, Switzerland probably has the most restrictive immigration policy. With the exception of a liberal policy for admitting refugees and asylum seekers, which lasted until 1995, and apart from marriage with a Swiss citizen and the special status of people working in international organizations, foreigners can only obtain a permanent resident permit if clear Swiss interests are involved and if the local commune agrees.

Still, of the total population of Switzerland, at present some 18% are foreigners. Whereas European immigrants are held to be able to assimilate to Swiss society, non-European immigrants, who are more severely screened, are recognized as constituting their own communities with their own cultural identity. Official policies at central government level are rather open to the particular cultural expressions and needs of these communities, but in various ways keep an eye on their activities.

New Muslim orientations in Switzerland

In a recent French language publication, Patrick Haenni, who has done much research on Islam in Switzerland and to whom we owe a great deal of our information (Haenni 1994), contends that since the early 1990s a new kind of Muslim associations has arisen in Switzerland, as had happened already earlier in other European countries.[3]

In a first phase, that of the first generation of immigrants, Muslim associations mainly took care of the social needs of their members, offering them a meeting place while keeping up their cultural traditions and encouraging their religious practice. At the time, these associations had relatively little contact with the larger society; they even had a protective function in so far as they were building up more or less closed communities pursuing their own goals in their own circle. Such organizations appealed to communal and ecclesiastical authorities for assistance, in particular permission to establish prayerhalls, Quran schools and other facilities needed for social life and religious practice. Felice Dassetto calls them "associations préventives" (Haenni 1994, 188) and sees them in the context of a still provisional presence of foreign workers who for the most part cherish the idea of going back to their Muslim countries of origin. Within the Swiss social setting, such associations acquired a rather inverted character, often avoiding anything that would draw public attention to them. In this way they carried on their work practically undisturbed.

A new phase started in the early 1990s with a second generation and the rise of some new associations. They addressed Swiss society by appealing explicitly to two of its prominent values, the right to be different and the right to cultural autonomy. This developed on the one hand into communal claims explicitly referring to Islam, which were addressed to the authorities and society at large. On the other hand it led to forms of community building which were no longer simply apart from society. Rather, they made an effort consciously to distinguish themselves from society by actively offering an alternative to it, using an Islamic discourse. Instead of the older passive attitude there now arises an attitude of active self-awareness, which seeks to obtain the best possible conditions for the community's position in society, with a public recognition of its presence and its "Islamic" character and activities. In Felice Dassetto's terminology, this is the phase of "contre-socialization défensive" (Haenni 1994, 188); he sees a direct link between the rise of this kind of associations and the fact that the Muslim workers have now become settled and abandon the goal of an eventual return to their countries of origin, settling down as residents for good in their new country.

In the Swiss context this self-affirmation by Muslim associations leads not so much to conflictuous confrontation as to a process of ongoing negotiations with different kinds of official and private bodies and authorities, in order to arrive at long-term arrangements on which all parties agree. The issues concerned are those of the second generation of immigrants, just as the leadership of this new type of movements is in the hands of relatively young people who have obtained a certain integrated place in society and who respond to demands from other second generation immigrants, their peers.

This transition had taken place already earlier in other European countries but the Swiss scene, by being much less politicized than that of its large neighbours, offers a unique opportunity for close observation. Even if the new orientations in the French speaking part of Switzerland have been stimulated by similar orientations in France, the contexts and styles of looking for solutions in both countries are quite different and so are the fruits.

Following Patrick Haenni (1994, 187) we can also distinguish a new kind of Islamic discourse in this new type of self-affirmative Muslim associations, which are also much more open to international Islamic networks. This discourse is distinguished by its social aspects and its prescriptive nature, adapted to the overall context of the immigrants' life. According to Haenni, the religious aspects recede, but this may be contested in view of the fact that constant reference is made to Scripture; Quran and Sunna remain the basis of the Islamic discourse.

The discourse of these self-affirmative associations apparently largely serves to articulate and guide the immigrants' search for a social identity which corresponds to their new situation. It suggests a solution to the evident loss of both material and symbolic control of the situations in which the immigrants happen to find themselves in their new country of residence. Most important, this discourse gives an acceptable interpretation of the palpable difference between the situation of the Muslim immigrant communities and the largely secular European societies in which these communities have to live. One way of doing this is by giving an essentialist turn to the differences perceived between Islam and the West and considering the two as opposed to each other. The Islamic discourse, in the words of Denis-Constant Martin, obtains an ideological dimension by offering a theoretical explanation of the difference between minority and majority (Haenni 1994, 187,197 Note 5).

Such a discourse, of course, is itself conditioned by these Muslim immigrants' lack of integration in their new societies. However much difficulty Western readers may have in appreciating its contents, this kind of Islamic discourse has important functions for Muslim immigrants in Europe. It helps these immigrants to identify themselves as Muslim and fosters a new kind of communal togetherness, in which Islam is constantly referred to. It develops a common code of behaviour, with the help of Islam understood as a prescriptive system. And last but not least, it expresses a social and spiritual link with the countries of origin and the Muslim world at large where the same discourse is held, stressing common Islamic values transmitted from the past.

According to Haenni, in contrast to earlier Islamic discourses, this new discourse addresses not only members of the Muslim associations themselves but also non-Muslims and society at large. If this is true, as it seems to be, his following hypothesis is worth pondering. Through this Islamic discourse, Muslim associations of the new type look for an interaction with society and the authorities in order to obtain a legitimate and recognized place in society, and, we would add, in the public sphere at large. This opening up of a relationship of dialogue with the majority society implies new strategies which were unthought of in the more or less self-contained and protective associations of the first phase. These strategies imply social and political action as part of the community's self-affirmation. They presuppose that the associations concerned have acquired a certain status, representing sizable Muslim communities, with a leadership that has become familiar with the political and administrative system of government in the country of residence. All of this presupposes a certain degree of integration, and in certain sectors assimilation, in the country concerned, and it may strengthen such an integration.

Another important element in the new orientation of Muslim associations is the acceptance of the principle of intercultural dialogue in the Swiss context (Haenni 1994, 188-9). Such a dialogue allows one to affirm one's identity and to enter in contact with people beyond one's own community, and eventually, through the media, with the public at large. It is the formula of dialogue which makes it possible for Muslim minority groups, or at least its leadership, to meet the majority and the authorities of the society concerned.

Another element is the title under which the dialogue takes place. There is a significant shift when Muslim immigrants want to engage in dialogue not under the label of "immigrants" but under that of "the Muslim community", explicitly referring to Islam as a religion. It is this Islam that provides a cultural and religious specificity and enables members of this

Muslim community to claim a special recognized status. In other words, Islam as a recognized world religion and personal religious faith offers a unique possibility for immigrants to enter into dialogue so to speak on a higher than merely material level. What immigration officers may call the problem of the presence of a group of non-European immigrants, is, in these terms of the people concerned, the presence of Islam as represented by a group of people belonging to the world-wide Muslim community.

Like other European countries, Switzerland has experienced affirmative action in favour of Islam through various incidents. An interesting case was the plan to stage Voltaire's play *Mahomet ou le fanatisme* for the bicentennial of the author's birth in Geneva in 1994. Some young, active "second generation" Muslims organized a campaign against it. They not only succeeded in having the play cancelled but also took the opportunity, through the media, to insist on dialogue so that the various communities could get to know each other better. Then there have been on a more popular level, like elsewhere, protests against headscarfs being forbidden on identification photos and against mixed swimming of school classes.

Interestingly enough, the local courts, concerned with integration on a local level, have mostly rejected such affirmations of Islamic specificity. The federal court, however, which has a broader and more open concept of integration, respecting cultural particularism and freedom of religion, pronounced itself in favour of the Muslim demands. Consequently, it is more on the local level than on that of the higher policy-making bodies that the presence of Muslims, and immigrants in general, is felt to have negative implications. As elsewhere, the media play an important role in engaging a more general social and political debate on these matters.

The present-day Swiss situation with regard to Muslim immigrants and Islam can now be summarized as follows:
1) Neither the Swiss authorities on the local (communal and cantonal) and the federal level, nor the Muslim organizations have taken up clearly defined positions in advance as to the forms which Islam can take in the country in the future. There is no question of violent debates (or rather non-debates, in fact monologues) between government officials and Muslim representatives such as one can find, for instance, in France.
2) There is a clear self-affirmation, with continuous reference to Islam, on the part of a number of Muslim groups and their representatives. Appar-

ently, institutionally and otherwise, they are looking for more direct relationships with the authorities. Even if such self-affirmations start on the individual level with personal demands, the latter are taken over by Muslim associations and put into the form of communal demands with reference to Islam as a religion.

3) As far as the state is concerned, its officials and official bodies on various levels have recognized the continued presence of Islam and Muslims in the country. On the one hand, true to the attractive principles of Swiss political culture, the state respects cultural diversity and religious plurality, including freedom of religion. This shows up, certainly at the higher levels, in a conciliatory attitude to Islamic claims and a willingness for dialogue. On the other hand, however, along Swiss lines of discipline, the state applies an increasingly restrictive immigration policy as far as non-Europeans are concerned, and increasingly direct and indirect police checks on immigrants, so that in a number of cases fundamental human rights are at stake. In Switzerland, as elsewhere, the state has a vested interest in keeping immigrant communities under supervision, which constitutes one reason for pressing them to have institutional representatives. Along the lines of Swiss political culture, however, the state tries to avoid conflicts in politically sensitive areas. It tries, for instance, to neutralize their political contents by institutionalizing possible opposition forces on a cultural rather than a political level. This favours a certain institutionalization of Islam in the country but rather cleverly suppresses any direct political expressions referring to Islam that might infringe on security.

Immigrants' Islam

Looking at the data concerning the development of Islam in Switzerland during the last eight years, I would propose the following interpretation, which may also apply to certain developments elsewhere in Europe.

To begin with, "Islam" is a tricky word, used by Muslims and the western public, including the media, in very different ways and with different meanings. And when we analyze some newer, more creative interpretations of Islam, such as those contained in the newer Islamic discourse which Patrick Haenni describes, the conceptual situation only becomes more confused. Any scholar of Islam, whether Muslim or non-Muslim himself, will have to recognize that the Islam of the new Islamic discourse is not the same as the Islam of which the medieval *fuqahâ* and *ᶜulamâ'* made their rational systematizations. Nor is it the spiritual religion of inner experience of which the Sufis speak. We are dealing here with some interesting new constructs of Islam which arise in the communities of Muslim immigrants in Europe and which, in the Swiss context, do not appear to be dominated by political forces either Swiss or coming from abroad.

The Islam of immigrants should not be considered as just a product imported ready made from Muslim countries for consumption here. It is neither a simple revival of an Islam of the past, nor a spiritual religiosity conveyed in age-old forms. The more creative versions of Islam developed here represent both a collective and an individual effort to respond to specific problems with which Muslim immigrants in the diaspora have to cope.

Patrick Haenni (1994, 194) aptly characterizes what happens: as a religion, Islam establishes and prescribes particular ritual patterns of behaviour in its *'ibâdât*. This common ritual behaviour weaves a certain web of relations between the people who, by participating, constitute a new community. And this in turn creates a specific collective consciousness, responsive to the problems with which the Muslims concerned are confronted. One such problem is the fact that they have no direct access to what is meaningful in Swiss society or to the way in which social life in a Swiss commune or canton is structured. The Islamic discourse provides people then with a new system to interpret their ordinary every-day experiences, including those of friction with a foreign, Swiss world that is practically closed to them as newcomers, if only because of the language barrier. Their own new system gives coherence and meaning to their life experience and offers in fact a kind of alternative to the rather foreign Swiss system and Swiss interpretation of life and the world. The ways in which Islam is constituted, or, as we prefer to call it, is constructed in Switzerland and elsewhere in Europe are directly linked to the immigrants' experiences in their country of residence.

I also subscribe to Patrick Haenni's further elaboration. He contends that, at least in Switzerland, the communities which build themselves up with reference to Islam are not just a replica of those communities existing in the countries of origin. Their function is not so much to conserve and transmit a heritage from the past, although this may have been the main function of the older protective associations, but rather to act as agents of integration. These more recent and more open communities allow marginalized immigrants of all sorts, who happen to be Muslims, to rediscover those features of their culture and values of their religion which are significant to them in their new situation. In this way, by resorting to Islam and its community institutions, people are also enabled to come to terms, at least symbolically, with situations of great deprivation.

After all, Islam appears to be the only common denominator on a social and spiritual level between very different individuals who happen to be immigrants coming from Muslim societies. As a consequence, this Islam acquires a kind of new value in the immigrant situation: beyond its religious aspects it is a reality bringing these individuals closer to each other, by focusing on something from which they derive their identity and which gives them a sense of togetherness supported by deeper feelings and emotions.

The interesting point is that this common construct of Islam is made in response to a context which is largely inaccessible and practically unknown to them. It gives them an identity and symbolic status which has a social value, that of being Muslims, and it allows them to develop their own common discourse which enables them to make sense of their new situation and live and act meaningfully. In other words, by constantly referring to Islam Muslim immigrants construct a meaningful world of their own, in response to the Swiss world. With the help of their code of behaviour, developed with constant reference to Islam, they can find answers to problems encountered in the Swiss context. And precisely in the present economic crisis, which has not spared Switzerland, and the accompanying social hardship of frightening xenophobia and loathsome racism on the part of some Europeans, Muslims in Europe can recenter their cultural and communal life, giving it a spiritual foundation. As a result they are able to face others and society with a sense of human dignity proper to the Islamic faith. No wonder that Islam, in such a context, stakes more claims and can offer more than it did when the first immigrants arrived a generation earlier.

Contextual factors

On the basis of the Swiss case we are in a position to identify some factors in the context of the life of Muslim immigrants in Europe, that influence the ways in which they articulate their Islam. In the context of the theme of this conference we are particularly attentive to the rise of any self-affirmation and political mobilization of the Muslim community which refers to Islam. The following five factors can be deduced immediately from the Swiss experience:

1. A timespan of at least two generations appears to be required for building up any continuing and durable communities able to impinge on public awareness. In Switzerland it was only in the early nineties that Muslims made public claims with reference to Islam.

2. A centralized government which coordinates and takes all major decisions about Muslim immigrants seems to lead to stronger self-affirmation and political action among the Muslim communities than a political system where the relevant decisions are taken by autonomous bodies. In Switzerland, which has a very decentralized system of government and immigration policy, Muslim immigrants are spread over the whole country, including the countryside. As a consequence, Islam has a very "local" character and cannot be mobilized easily for concerted self-affirmation and political action by the Muslim community as a whole.

3. The variety of origins of Muslim immigrants hampers the self-affirmation and political action of the Muslim community. In Switzerland, the Muslim immigrants from Turkey and ex-Yugoslavia are not only linguistically but also culturally distinct from those coming from North Africa and the Middle East. Of different origins, both groups happen moreover to be concentrated in two different parts of the country. It requires special efforts to bring together Muslims of different origins around a project accepted by all. In the newer, active Muslim associations too, different Islamic networks can be distinguished which are closely connected with the origins of the associations' leadership.

4. The presence of a common cause, such as the protest against *The Satanic Verses* by Salman Rushdie, helps a Muslim community to engage in common expressions of protest and action. In Switzerland there have been hardly any *causes célèbres* to further the penetration of international

Islamic networks among Muslim immigrants or bring about a wholesale mobilization of all Muslim groups, as did the Rushdie affair in Britain. Because Switzerland is relatively isolated, its Muslim community, too, is at a certain distance from international protest movements appealing to Islam. Swiss political culture, moreover, discourages protest movements which have serious political implications.

5. The experience of a common threat, such as attacks on Turkish people in Germany, leads Muslim immigrants to unite to cope with it, for instance by demonstrating or offering open resistance. In Switzerland any visible threat to Muslim immigrants, once they have been admitted, is absent. Politically, the authorities manifest a preparedness to dialogue and there is at the moment no strong extreme right-wing political group that could constitute a political danger. Ideologically, although Islam is not well-known and is mostly feared for its possible political implications, radical secularism has only a limited impact here. The Churches proclaim dialogue with Islam, and the idea of pluralism, propagated to promote tolerance in Swiss society which is itself religiously very heterogeneous, can be usefully applied to the presence of religions other than Christianity as well.

There are of course many other contextual factors which influence the articulation of Islam among Muslim immigrants in European societies, such as laws regulating religious organizations as well as explicit government policies to promote emancipation and economic and social integration. On the one hand, unemployment and discrimination against foreign Muslim workers may lead to presentations of Islam as a religion of brotherhood and social justice, opposed to the inhuman and ungodly character of secular western society. On the other hand, any officially propagated ideology of a religious or secular nature which is felt to be hostile to Islam will constitute a focus of Muslim reactions of protest.

In this connection attention must be drawn to those findings and private opinions of western experts on Islamic matters, which have not only an academic but also a social relevance in the current western discourse on Islam to which Muslims are sensitive. At the present time, scholarship on these matters has a special responsibility, in so far as it may form another "contextual factor" of the development of Islam in Europe. In the sensitive area of religion, unfounded opinions should be replaced either by knowledge or by an honest acknowledgment of ignorance.

Emancipation and Muslim community building

We have shown the transition from an older, more passive type of Muslim cultural and religious organizations to a new type intent on active community building, politically conscious, and in interaction with society and the authorities. The new organizations, in so far as they stress their Islamic identity, distinguish themselves by their conscious self-affirmation and their willingness to take action to defend their rights, if necessary in the courts. We have also seen that in this new type of organization new constructs of Islam are developed which offer a meaningful ideology to a minority living in a precarious position in many respects. When these groups engage in dialogue with the majority or with the authorities, they refer explicitly to Islam, and in particular in the form of quotations of Quranic verses. Finally, starting with the Swiss experience, we have enumerated some contextual factors, which influence the way in which Islam is articulated by Muslim immigrants in Europe; these factors could easily be differentiated and augmented.

We have intentionally abstained from referring to generalizing concepts such as Muslim fundamentalism, "intégrisme" and so on, preferring to remain as close to human realities as possible and not to distort them by giving them labels implying western political views and concepts. For these do not lead to true knowledge but on the contrary veil reality, by imposing particular western interpretations on it. We have not discussed either the many internal factors which obviously play a role in the articulation of Islam by Muslim immigrants in Europe, such as the motivations and aims of those who have positions of political and/or religious leadership of Muslim associations in Europe; the many different influences coming from Muslim countries and international Islamic networks; centres of ideological manipulation and propaganda through cheap Islamic literature, cassettes, videotapes, etc.; and last but not least the complex role of all those who claim to "know" Islam, from the simple *imâm*, or the authoritarian *shaykh* to the intellectual *'âlim*. What strikes any observer of Islamic developments in Europe over the last thirty years is the communal character of all Muslim orientations and movements, and the proclivity of building up Muslim communities from the grass-roots among Muslim immigrants, all parties referring to Islam as their common religion. The process of Muslim community building in Europe, implying the institutionalization of Islam as a religion, has religious, social, and also political aspects which deserve careful study in the years to come. In this community building, it seems to me, lies the heart of the possibilities for the emancipation of Muslim immigrants in Europe.

In this connection I would like to make a few general observations further to the title and subtitle of this paper.

The concept of emancipation, as applied to Muslims, has been used in very different senses over the last hundred years. For Snouck Hurgronje, it meant liberating Muslims from the chains of the system of prescriptions and doctrines developed in the medieval period and the weight of traditional society, which impeded intellectual inquiry and personal development. For feminists, emancipation in the first place means the liberation of women, and in particular Muslim women, from traditional male authority, and encouraging them to take their destiny into their own hands. For secularists, emancipating Muslims primarily means freeing them from subjection to their religion and to things irrational in general, or at least bringing them to consider religion as a private affair independent of any religious authority or social control. Most defenders of emancipation stress the need for self-emancipation: outsiders can only create favourable conditions for a process of emancipation which depends finally on the will and initiative of the people concerned.

As I see it, the emancipation of Muslims in European societies is at the moment basically a social and political affair, essentially of transcending the abject state of marginality and passivity in which many Muslim immigrants find themselves in these societies. Obtaining full political, economic and social rights and participating as equal partners in western societies is just the opposite of the *dhimmî* status referred to at the beginning of this paper. And just as in most Muslim countries Christians and Jews emancipated themselves and participated in the movements of independence and nation-building, Muslims in Europe should emancipate themselves and participate in building a new Europe.

At this point, however, the parallel stops, because the situations are different.

First of all, any emancipation of Muslim immigrants in Europe, like that of European immigrants in the USA, implies naturalization and thus, if not a full severing, then at least a loosening of links with the country of origin. It is saddening to see how much Muslim immigrants in Europe are still manipulated by not only political and social forces at work in European societies, but also those political forces from their countries of origin that want to keep them under their sway. Turkish and Moroccan immigrants in the Netherlands, for instance, can participate actively in the political process on the level of the municipal councils with the right to vote and stand for election, but they still submit to the dictates of the Turkish and Moroccan governments as regards the Turkicization of Kurds or the infallible authority, religious and political, of the King.

Second, whatever current ideas may prevail among Muslim immigrants and the European public alike, supported by certain media and political interests, it should be affirmed again and again that there is a fundamental difference between the status of an immigrant and that of a Muslim. Immigrant status is a legal matter and has gradations, so that one moves up, so to speak, from a tourist visa to having a visiting, working, or permanent residence permit, and finally obtaining the nationality of the new country. The status of Muslim is a matter of belonging to a specific socio-religious community in Europe, comprising not only Muslim immigrants who may become naturalized but also European Muslims. Confusion arises when the categories of "immigrants" and "Muslims" are used interchangeably. A number of so-called "Muslim" problems in Europe are in fact "migrant" problems and confront both Muslim and non-Muslim immigrants from outside Europe, whose number tends to be restricted by European governments. While Muslim migrants may look for Muslim solutions for the problems they face as immigrants in Europe, these problems are the same for all immigrants from outside Europe. Muslim immigrants may develop their own ideas and practices of Islam as a religion in Europe, but such religious issues should be carefully distinguished from immigrant problems.

Thirdly, the desire of European governments for adequate representation of the Muslims living in their countries is not only an administrative problem. The new orientations and developments of Islam in Europe to which we have alluded suggest that a sizable number of Muslim immigrants will emancipate themselves from dependency on current Islamic authorities abroad. In a pluralistic Europe there should be room for different interpretations, orientations and practices in different groups within the various religions, including Islam. Personal responsibility, more than obedience to human authority, is a typical feature of Islam and the freedom involved may be a key factor in the long-term development of Islam in Europe. Just as political forces from outside should influence the Muslim communities as little as possible, no political straight-jacket should be imposed on them from inside. If the Muslim communities of a given country are not free to choose their own representatives and form of representation but somehow have them imposed from above, this can only lead to a politization of Islam in Europe, for which certain European governments, for instance the French one, must be held responsible. This should be avoided, and the freedom of Muslims, Jews and Christians to develop their own institutions and ideas, should be respected as part of the freedom of religion.

Summary and Conclusion

In the preceding pages we have identified the relative lack of political and other forms of power exercised by Muslim and other immigrants living in Europe, as a handicap for improving their situation in European societies. In order to promote their integration in these societies conditions have to be created favourable to their economic and political, social and cultural emancipation. The thesis submitted here is that Muslim organizations have a potential to further such emancipation processes which is still largely unexploited.

There have been interesting experiences in Switzerland, which has a tradition of recognizing particularities of minority groups. We refer here to a publication in French by P. Haenni. On the federal level there has been a certain openness to demands connected with Muslim culture and relig-ion. Since the early 90s certain new orientations have been observed in Muslim associations here, such as playing a growing role in society, developing a new Islamic discourse about society so as to offer an alterna-tive model of meaningful social life, and taking initiatives in intercultural dialogue. All of this testifies to a growing willingness, on the part of both

Swiss and Muslims, to negotiate about the future of the Muslim community in Switzerland.

This opens a field of research, the present-day Islam of immigrants in Switzerland, seen as a response to the situation in which these immigrants find themselves, developing constructs of Islam that are different both from the classical and traditional ones and from those obtaining in Muslim countries today. Some contextual factors of European societies can be identified which have an immediate influence on the Muslim articulation of Islam. I contend that for those immigrants who identify themselves as practising Muslims, the new orientations of Muslim associations show that, directly or indirectly, they have a potential for furthering emancipation and can function as agents of integration.

Muslim communities entering into interaction with European societies will demand free expression for Islam as a religion and insist that Islam offers the right code of human behaviour and the right social order. Such claims may be new to European societies, with their own norms and values, and their sometimes rather closed traditions. Negotiations, however, should take place between Muslim associations and other interested parties, on a democratic basis; these should be pursued pragmatically, with an open attitude to requests that are justifiable and without ideological hangups. In the long term, all concerned will be called to engage in a common struggle, step by step and without utopian blueprints, against current forms of injustice which Muslims and non-Muslims alike recognize. In this domain, both groups can arrive at common action, political and otherwise through dialogue, furthering much-needed emancipation.

Notes

[1]   *Dhimmîs* were non-Muslims living in Muslim territory and beneficiaries of the *dhimma* ("protection"), "...the term used to designate the sort of indefinitely renewed contract through which the Muslim community accords hospitality and protection to members of other revealed religions, on condition of their acknowledging the domination of Islam" (Enc. of Islam, 2nd ed., s.v. *Dhimma*, Vol. II, p. 227).
Originally only Christians and Jews could be *dhimmîs*; the term was then also applied to Zoroastrians and incidentally other faiths as well. *Dhimma* indicates consequently the status of a "recognized minority" in Islamic law. But it designates not the citizens of a nation state but the members of a religious community. Rules about *dhimmîs* were abolished with the establishment of nation states with modern law systems. The *dhimmî* system presupposed the inequality between Muslims and non-Muslims. The

idea of *dhimma* offered a solution to the problem of religious minorities but at the price of giving them only a secondary status both legally and socially. What was "protection" in Muslim eyes, was "discrimination" in modern terms. The same ambiguity exists in the term "protectorate" applied to French rule over Tunisia and Morocco. The "protected" countries found themselves in fact under French domination!

2   We have used here in particular, besides an article with appendix of Patrick Haenni (Haenni 1994), an as yet unpublished paper by Jean-Claude Basset, "Rapport sur l'islam en Suisse et les études universitaires" (Geneva, 15 April 1994). We could not consult the *mémoire* of Patrick Haenni, *L'islam suisse désamorcé* (Paris, Institut d'Etudes Politiques, 1993). We do not mention here journalists' publications with the exception of Christophe Büchi, "Morgenland Romandie", *Die Weltwoche* Nr. 22 (1. Juni 1995), p. 49-55.
The official census, which is carried out among the Swiss population every ten years, includes the religion people adhere to. From 1970 onwards the figures for Muslims in Switzerland have become significant. The official census reports published by the Federal Office of Statistics give detailed lists of the Christian, Jewish, Muslim and other communities according to the age, sex, country of origin, canton and commune of residence. See Office Fédéral de la Statistique (1990).

3   We leave aside here developments in other European countries and the extensive literature existing on the subject. See, for instance, Albert Bastenier and Felice Dassetto, "Hypothèses pour une analyse des stratégies religieuses au sein du monde migratoire en Europe", *Social Compass* 1979, Nr. 1. Observations on the development of Muslim communities and Islam in the Swiss context can be useful for comparative purposes and for interpreting their development in the European context as a whole.

9

Dialogues at Different Institutional Levels Among Authorities and Muslims in Belgium

Johan Leman & Monique Renaerts

The Belgian State and its religions

The Belgian constitution guarantees freedom of worship, the free practice of religion, as well as the freedom of expression on all topics. In accordance with the Constitution, the State has no right to concern itself with the appointment or designation of ministers of religion, or to interfere in religious internal affairs. The founders of Belgium opted for a separation of church and state.

In Belgium, there is neither a concordat nor absolute laicization. Relations between the state and religion are rather neutral: the state considers religion to be part of the country's institutional framework. All religions may find a place in this system, but it is the responsibility of the legislator to decide whether a religion may, in addition, be officially recognized. In making this decision, he is guided by the question of determining whether the religion in question meets the needs of the population, or a sufficiently large portion of the population. The fact that Islam was officially recognized in 1974 by the Belgian public authorities has had the effect, among other things, that Islamic religion may be taught during official education - which actually began the following year - and that the payment of salaries and pensions to ministers of the Islamic religion is theoretically incumbent upon the state -- which has not yet come about, because it has not yet been possible to create a recognized authority to administer this, and other, temporal aspects of the Islamic religion (Leman, Renaerts and Van den Bulck, 1992; Leman 1992).

Theoretically, the status of the Islamic religion in Belgium is identical to that of the Catholic, Protestant, Anglican, Jewish, and Orthodox religions, but in practice, a number of implications of this recognition have not yet materialized, although recent progress seems to have been made in this regard. In fact, the institutional dealings of Muslims in Belgium have been constantly disturbed by the problem of the legitimacy of their representation. Whenever one seeks to outline the dialogue which has begun on several levels in Belgium between the authorities and the Muslims, the essential aspect of the problem involves attempts intended, through the formation and abandonment of all sorts of new positions and alliances, to reinforce social representativity and to clarify the position of appointed spokesmen for the Islamic religion, while specifying the commitment of the authorities.

Prior to the "institutional presence" (before 1968)

Towards the end of the 1950s, the Islamic population of Belgium consisted principally of a few dozen students. At that time, Albanian refugees also sought asylum in our country. Under the influence of a few Islamic students and a few Albanians, a Committee was formed which later became the future Islamic Cultural Centre of Belgium (ICC). On 28 January 1962, during the month of Ramadan, the Committee filed a request with the Minister of Justice to permit the Oriental Pavilion of the Parc du Cinquentenaire in Brussels to be ceded to the Islamic community of Belgium. This building attracted the attention of the Committee because its architecture resembled that of a mosque. The building had not been opened for a quarter of a century, but as it was considered part of the Belgian historical heritage, it was hardly a matter of course that it should be ceded to the Islamic community, and thus other solutions were considered.

Starting in 1963, the management of the Committee, still a de-facto organization, passed into the hands of the embassies. The ICC, still active at the present time, was created in an embryonic form. Let us note the role played by the embassies in the management of the ICC. The Tunisian government provided the first Imam-Director, Mohammed Alaouini in 1966 -- 8 years before the official recognition of the Islamic religion in

Belgium. During the visit of the King of Saudi Arabia during the month of May 1967, just before the Six-Day War, King Baudouin is said to have presented the Oriental Pavilion to the Islamic community as a gift in return for donations given by the Saudi sovereign to the victims of the fire in the large Innovation department store in Brussels. There was a ceremony at the Saudi Arabian Embassy in which the Belgian Minister of Justice presented King Faisal with the symbolic keys of the Oriental Pavilion.[1] To gather the necessary funds for the repair and restoration of the building, the Embassy of Morocco took the initiative of drawing up articles of association. A general meeting was held on 7 March 1968. The articles of this international association were published in the annexes to the Belgian Monitor (B.M.) on 20 June 1968. The Centre was granted corporation status by the Royal Decree (R.D.) of 7 May 1968 (B.M. of 16 May 1968).

From institutional presence to initial objections (1968-1976)

The act of concession of the Pavilion, which was the property of the State of Belgium, was signed at a ceremony held on 13 July 1969. The Belgian government was represented by the Minister of Public Works; the executive committee of the ICC was represented by its chairman, the Ambassador of Saudi Arabia.[2] The ICC was very closely involved with two embassies - the Saudi and Moroccan - from the very outset. This has continued to be the case ever since.

Shortly thereafter, the idea arose of proceeding to recognize the Islamic religion, as stated in the introduction. The ICC played a crucial role in this process, which lasted several years, thanks to continual contacts between its Imam-Director and certain representatives of the Belgian political authorities. A draft law relating to the recognition of Islam was presented to the Deputies on 3 February 1971.

After several other unsuccessful draft laws, a draft was presented to the Senate on 2 May 1974 by Senators from the CVP (Flemish Christian Democrats); this draft included in extenso the text approved by the Commission of Justice, and was unanimously adopted on 20 June. Sent to the Chamber of Representatives, the draft was the object of a comparable vote on 17 July.

The adoption of the draft law by the Chamber and the Senate led to the promulgation of the law of 19 July 1974 relating to the recognition of administrative bodies responsible for managing the temporal affairs of the Islamic religion, thereby amending the law of 1870 on the temporal affairs of religious bodies, and adding an article 19bis to that law. It should be noted that this recognition, perhaps determined in part by considerations of international policy, was the first of its kind in the Western World.

In the 1975-76 school year, a circular from the Minister of National Education invited school administrations to organize courses of Islamic religion at the request of Islamic parents. This circular implicitly granted the ICC authority to submit nominations for teachers of Islamic religion to the Minister of Education. Before the federalization of education in Belgium (1968), teachers of religion were appointed by the Ministry of National Education for schools in the state system, and by the organizational authority for schools in the officially subsidized system. All teachers are paid by the Ministry of National Education. The monopoly enjoyed by the ICC of Belgium with regards to the Ministry of Justice and the Ministry of National Education at this time was, however, disputed, particularly since the Board of Directors consisted, in addition to the Imam-Director, of ambassadors. This objection led to the creation, in 1976, of a non-profit corporation called "Islamic Culture and Religion" (ICR) (B.M., 21 April 1977).

Many disputes involving concretely institutionalized Islam (1976-1985)

The existence of the ICR, apart from the appointment of a few professors of Islamic religion who, it was hoped, would form a counter-balance to those appointed by the ICC, and who would, it was thought, eventually be replaced, was more than ephemeral, not simply because of the poor skills of its members in cultural matters, but also due to the ambiguities which have characterized it since its creation. Some of its members are, in fact, supported by groups in the Belgian lay community, with the intention of proceeding with the consolidation of a lay segment in the Islamic centre. This instrumental procedure on the part of the Belgian lay community, which wished to introduce a lay segment into Islamic cultural organizations, rather than promoting a lay branch of Islamic culture within their own institutions, has continued through Islamic institutional history to the present day. It is clear that one of the major preoccupations of Belgian laicity is to prevent religion in general from acquiring too much weight in society. The struggle against an overly-pervasive Islamic religion, particularly in its strictest forms, was part of the more generalized struggle against the invasion of the public arena by religious authorities. Probably, in addition, there were fears of the rise of an overly zealous Islamic leadership among immigrant groups, harming the social and political progress which were considered to represent immigrants' true interests.

In any case, in February 1978, the laws of 29 March 1959 and 11 July 1973, referred to as the "Scholastic Pact", were amended. These henceforth granted official recognition to the teaching of the Islamic religion in Belgium, implicitly provided for in 1974. The law of 1974 was followed in 1978 by an R.D. relating to committees responsible for the temporal affairs of recognized Islamic communities. This decree, inspired by the director of the ICC, provided that Islamic communities might be recognized by R.D. for one or more provinces. Recognition of a community authorizes it to create a committee responsible for managing its own temporal affairs with regards to worship and representation in its relations with the civil authorities. According to the R.D., the ICC was responsible for determining the number of members to be elected upon the initial formation of the committee, and for organizing its first elections. The Centre, in which the influence of Saudi Arabia and Morocco, as well as that of the Islamic World League, is very real, hardly considered it urgent to hold elections, which might have led to the emergence of rival cultural centres. This decree was not followed up, since the Royal Decrees recognizing the Islamic communities for one or more Belgian provinces were never issued.

The law of 21 January 1981 regulates the question of salaries paid by the State to the ministers of Islamic Religion. It amends the law of 2 August 1974, which did not include Islamic religious practitioners among ministers of religion to be paid by the State. This law nevertheless remained a dead letter like the others, officially due to the absence of an authority considered a valid representative of Islamic communities.

It was, however, the question of teaching the Islamic religion which continued to occupy people's minds. In July 1984, the French-speaking Community's Consultative Council on Immigration declared that the function of teaching the Islamic religion appeared to contradict the objectives of intercultural education (Dassetto, F., 1991).

When Alaouini resigned in February 1986, Al Ahdal, who was then Vice-Director, was chosen as the new Imam-Director. Al Ahdal made attempts to normalize the status of the professors and employees.

On 3 July 1985, the Ministry of Justice submitted a draft decree to the Council of State aimed at creating a Superior Islamic Council in Belgium.[3] The opinion of the Council of State of 9 October 1985 was negative, since it considered that the draft R.D. - which went beyond the organization and functioning of the temporal affairs of religious communities by aiming at the creation of a Superior Islamic Council of Belgium, and even provided that the interlocutor of the State should be the chairman of this Superior Council - had no basis in the law of 4 March 1870, which regulated the "temporal affairs of religious communities" in Belgium. On 4 March 1986, the Ministry of Justice responded to the Senate that, since no Islamic community had been recognized based on the R.D. of 3 May 1978, the Director of the ICC was still, therefore, the most appropriate interlocutor.[4]

During the period between the mid-1980s and the early 1990s, the attitudes of political authorities became more rigid, due to the emergence of trends in Islamic communities in foreign countries which were perceived as unpredictable. A series of events, such as the demonstration in April 1986 against the American raid on Tripoli, the Rushdie affair, the problem of the Islamic head scarves in France and Brussels, the creation of the first Islamic school in Brussels, and the Gulf War, reinforced the concept of an Islam which was in danger of threatening the more or less precarious equilibrium achieved by Belgian society regarding relations between religion and public authority.

The problem of Islamic religious instruction gained renewed prominence in late 1985, drawing the attention of many politicians in 1986, particularly since events of a turbulent nature were simultaneously taking place in the Islamic states. In the eyes of certain politicians, who exploited the threat of Islam for propaganda purposes, teachers of Islam were, in fact, bearers of Islamic fundamentalism, the daily meat of the media. These fears are largely reflected in the press.

In most cases, during municipal council meetings, it was the PS councillors (French-speaking socialists) and PRL (French-speaking liberal reformers) who expressed the greatest fears of Islamic fundamentalism and the extreme clericalization of Islamic religious education. Nor did most of the other political parties, particularly in Brussels, hesitate to join in the recurrent expression of Islamophobic sentiments.[5]

On 20 April 1986, a demonstration was held against the American raids on the cities of Tripoli and Benghazi. The next day, the parties PRL, UDRT, and FDF took a position against demonstrators considered to be overly fundamentalist.

On 23 April 1986, a conference of mayors from the urban area of Brussels was held to modify the conditions of appointment of teachers of Islamic religion. Ch. Picqué, who chaired this conference, wrote to the Minister of Justice demanding an inquiry - perhaps even a commission of inquiry - to determine the "status, the nature of activities, directors, and location of the Islamic associative environment in the region of Brussels" (Dassetto and Bastenier 1986, 106).

At the beginning of May 1986, on the occasion of a question in Parliament relating to the demonstration of 20 April 1986, the Minister of Justice declared that, while he was disturbed, only the legal authorities, in his view, were entitled to decide whether there had been a violation of the law against racism and xenophobia, or the law protecting the heads of foreign states (1852).[6] During the same period, the conference of mayors of the Brussels urban area reached a decision as to the conditions of appointment of teachers of Islamic religion.

On 26 May 1986, Imam-Director Al Ahdal, during an interview with J.P. Colette, journalist from Le Soir, announced that he intended to create a recycling procedure for teachers of Islamic religion. His aim was to eradicate Islamic fundamentalism. This was the only official, or even semi-official, statement of this point of view ever taken by an Islamic spokesman in Belgium. As for the rest, there was complete silence, both on the part of the Islamic associations and embassies, etc....

A new regulation similar to that which had been requested by the municipalities was put together for the teachers of Islamic religion in May 1986. Its requirements were as follows: possession of Belgian nationality or five years' residence in Belgium; instruction in one of the two national languages; possession of a diploma "recognized" by the competent Ministry of National Education; foreign candidates would be subject to investigation by the "Office des Etrangers" (immigration authorities), and would be required to obtain a derogation of nationality. It is true that, until that time, due to the separation of church and state, there had never been any control over the qualifications of teachers of Islamic religion, and its quality often left much to be desired.

Despite the different objections in this regard, the ICC nevertheless continued to be the institution proposing candidate teachers.

In May 1986, elections were organized in a mosque in Brussels on the initiative of the Imam-Director of the ICC, Mr. Al Ahdal, with a view to electing four imams to participate in a Superior Islamic Council to consist of 13 members, including 5 ambassadors, three representatives from the Islamic World League, and one Belgian Muslim.

In September 1986, the Ministry of National Education sent school administrators a circular entitled "Derogation of Nationality".

With a view to preventing the diffusion of fundamentalist ideas, Ch. Piqué, as mayor of St. Gilles, in May 1987, issued a decree of execution prohibiting the sale of political, philosophical, and religious documents on the large Sunday market, well known all over Belgium, held on the Place Barra, the so-called "Marché du Midi".

All democratic political parties in the 1988 legislative electoral campaign took partly positions favouring the integration of Muslims and the rejection of Islamic fundamentalism.

On 29 March 1989, Imam-Director Abdullah Al Ahdal was assassinated, along with the librarian of the centre Salem El Behir, murders which remain unsolved to this day. A new Imam-Director of Saudi nationality, Sameer Radhi, was sent after the death of Al Adhal. This was the beginning of a new period.

Transition period: towards a new approach (1989-1994)

The Saudi imam, Sameer Radhi, who was rather ignorant of the Belgian Islamic community and political realities, arrived at a time when the situation was already explosive.[7] The problem of Islamic religious instruction in municipal schools was the order of the day. Sheikh Sameer Radhi was firmly convinced that that would be able to develop projects capable of restoring the prestige of the ICC of Brussels, badly tarnished by the many events which had shaken the Islamic community in past years. Inspired by certain individuals, he sincerely believed that the creation of an Islamic school would increase his popularity in the community. Other persons, particularly those belonging to associations which felt they had been pushed aside by the ICC, urged him to set up a Representative Islamic Council.

The opening of the Al Ghazali school (the first and, until this time, the only Islamic school in Brussels or anywhere in Belgium) might be counter-balanced against the refusal of two municipalities of Brussels to organize courses of Islamic religious instruction in their municipal establishments; but this argument was certainly not unique, since the concept of free religious education had already circulated for some time among certain persons close to the ICC. The daily newspaper Le Soir announced the opening of the Al Ghazali school in its edition of 24 August 1989. The ICC was said to have already filed a request for recognition and subsidies with the competent primary school authorities of the French community. This information drew a lot of comment from certain politicians.[8] The Islamic school opened its doors on 1 September 1989.

On 5 September, Ch. Picqué, who had in the meantime become chairman of the Region Brussels-Capital Executive, declared that he would take all steps to prevent the creation of the school. The ICC notified him that the school aimed at integration, and that its objective was to train good Muslims and good Belgian citizens. The majority declared that they were opposed to the creation of Islamic schools; others were more reserved, but declared that they could not prevent the exercise of a constitutional right. The *Vlaams Blok* accepted the creation of such a school with a view to returning citizens of extra-European origin to the land of their ancestors. It sent a circular to over 100 schools asking them to cease organizing courses of Islamic religion in their establishment.

In September 1989, following consultation between the Imam-Director of the ICC, still the official representative of the Islamic religion on a provisional basis, and the majority of groups culturally representative of the Islamic community, proceedings were begun to select a representative body from the community by election. On that date, a committee, consisting of 17 persons, was formed to prepare for the elections. The

Imam-Director also publicly stated that, in his view, the ICC of Brussels was not truly representative of Belgian Muslims. In the meantime, the "affair of the head scarves" exploded in a municipal technical school at Molenbeek. In November, several municipalities took preventive measures to prohibit the wearing of head scarves.

The Royal Commissariat on Immigrant Policy (RCIP), created on 1 March 1989, held several working meetings during the summer of 1989 in which several converted Muslims also participated; proposals were issued providing for the possibility of democratic elections in the Islamic community. In its first report of November 1989, the RCIP advised the government to create a "Superior Islamic Council" based on democratic elections in the Islamic community, intended to be the representative interlocutor of the Islamic communities. The methods proposed by the RCIP met with widely differing reactions, both in the world of Belgian politics and in Islamic lay cultural communities.

In December 1989, during the Interministerial Conference on Immigrant Policy, the government issued a decision to reject the electoral process, probably influenced by the climate of tension. In March 1990, the government, through the intervention of the Minister of Justice,[9] enjoined the Imam-Director to cease the electoral process. When the Imam-Director, very probably under the influence of certain converts, did not respond to the injunctions, the government discharged the ICC, following public disavowal, of its representativity and competence relating to the appointment of teachers of religion. The Council of Ministers, on 30 March 1990, decided to create a Provisional Council of Elders for the organization of Islamic worship. Three seats were allocated to representatives of the ICC, which barely answered the invitation. This Provisional Council of Elders was inaugurated on 2 July by the Ministry of Justice (R.D. of 24 November 1990).

This body, appointed by the Ministry of Justice, is responsible, on the one hand, for remitting proposals to the government relating to methods for the creation of a religious representative body, and, on the other hand, to deal with current affairs, teacher files, and the appointment of new teachers according to the requirements of scholastic establishments. In fact, no one in the Belgian political leaders or the Islamic community wanted to destroy Islamic religious instruction in official schools... it was therefore necessary to ensure that an organization could guarantee continuity in this sector.

Using its freedom to create consultative bodies in any field, the government did not contravene article 16 of the constitution, because the Provisional Council is not the official instance of representation of the Islamic community before the Belgian civil authorities, and in no way possesses the full role which would devolve upon the head of a religion. The composition of the Provisional Council of Elders is nevertheless unable to meet the aspirations of the Islamic communities. Most of the members have no competence or even religious practice, and simply reflect the Belgian equilibrium between political parties and Islamic communities, rather than representing the divergent doctrinal sensibilities of the Islamic communities.

The politico-ideological dissensions were very quickly aggravated by the random impulses of autonomy on the part of the Turks, who had close relations with the Turkish Directorate of Religious Affairs, and aspired to their own organization in order to keep their citizens exclusively within the sphere of the Turkish government, particularly through the appointment of Turkish teachers selected by them for Turkish children. Thus far, we have not mentioned the Turks, because, though they entered the Board of Directors of the ICC of Belgium in 1981, they never really made an active commitment with regards to the problems of the Centre, but rather carried on a policy of non-absence. It was only in 1989 that they became truly involved, against their will, in discussions of a "Belgian" Islam.

During this period, the Muslims went ahead with the electoral process initiated by Sheikh Sameer Radhi; this led to the election of the General Council of Belgian Muslims in February 1991, followed by internal elections to the Superior Council of Belgian Muslims. Turks close to the Turkish Directorate of Religious Affairs did not participate; their opponents from the Milli Görüs, on the other hand, participated fully, which distanced them from the Belgian authorities but brought them closer to militants who supported the electoral operation.

Faced with the two-fold reality of a Provisional Council of Elders on the one hand, which was entering a phase of complete immobility, and the Superior Council of Muslims, which was more dynamic but was not recognized by the Belgian state, and which, in addition, had to recognize that it lacked representativity, particularly among Turks, and that it was too Islamist, matters came to a dead-end. Nevertheless, in that view of unacceptability of the electoral process (Superior Council of Muslims) on the one hand, and the failure of the designation of persons not accepted by the community (Provisional Council of Elders) on the other hand, broad consultation was nevertheless begun for several months with groups representing different doctrinal and spiritual sensibilities. These discussions lasted several months, and involved groups representing different doctrinal and spiritual sensibilities as well as a variety of ethno-national components. It was still true that no one desired an impasse with regards to Islamic religious instruction. These negotiations finally led to the creation of a committee which presented the members of a new body, i.e., the Technical Committee, responsible for teacher files.

Regarding the educational files of the Islamic religion, the Flemish community, which became responsible for its own education upon the federalization of education in 1988, adopted a series of measures intended to increase the quality and professionalism of teachers without, however, affecting the content of the courses, on the grounds that this was the exclusive responsibility of a religious director. From that time, all teachers have been requested to follow a pedagogic training course accompanied by language instruction. Candidates for new appointments must possess a basic Dutch diploma or successfully pass a language examination organized by the State. While awaiting an initiative on the Federal level, the Flemish community seriously considered studying the possibility of creating a religious training institute for the Islamic community of Flanders, which could become an important point on the agenda for the new government recently installed in Flanders (1995).

Since the process which led to the creation of the Technical Committee had proven to be acceptable both to the Islamic communities and the authorities concerned, beginning in 1994 the same process was henceforth used to create a larger organization. And this leads us to a new stage in the process.

The new search for representative spokesmen

Encouraged by the relative success and pragmatism of the Technical Committee, in its restricted, but well defined and very real, areas of authority, the Minister of Justice took the decision, at the end of October 1994, to accept sixteen persons as interlocutors. Taken from a broad constituent assembly, this body, called the Belgian Muslim Executive, was created after long negotiations between the majority of existing tendencies in the Islamic communities. (The Milli Görüs tendency was not accepted by the Ministry of Justice).

This body, which provides for 17 seats, includes, for a probation period of one year, the powers relating to education granted to the Technical Committee, and was, in addition, granted authority to designate religious councillors to prisons and hospitals. The period of functioning, limited to one year, was to permit an evaluation of the effective representativity of the body, and to permit an examination of its orientation. This Executive met each month with the representatives of the Ministry of Justice, and recently requested (in May 1995) a slight increase in its powers, for example, management of the matter of Islamic cemeteries, and/or the recognition of official Islamic holidays. A seat remains to be occupied by a Turkish representative neither of the Milli Görüs tendency nor close to the Embassy.

In the meantime, events on the spot
In view of the above

The problems relating to the Executive confirm that there are different fields of allegiance.

First of all, there are certain Islamic groups, supported by international organizations, which belong, where the Turkish are concerned, to the Milli Görüs movement, and, among the Arabs, to the nebulous "Brother" movement. These tendencies, although a minority within the Islamic community, nevertheless tend to occupy the social and educational arena by offering dignity and personal value, as they see it, to young people.

The denunciations in the media of the "threat of Islamic fundamentalism" by the "cultural Muslims" belonging to the lay community, on the other hand, are only equalled by their inability to communicate with the religious community. Inspired by the composition of the Jewish consistory in Belgium, they nevertheless hope to find a position within a representative Islamic group.

A certain number of Moroccan and Turkish socio-cultural associations, using the same logic as the lay community of Islamic origin but for different reasons, demand direct participation in a religious body, or at least influence in the make up of such a body. Their weight as consumers of religious products cannot be ruled out, but their sphere of action lies elsewhere than in the strictly religious field. Some of their associations, moreover, lack sufficient basis in the community, and therefore represent only themselves and a group of sympathizers around these organizations; others maintain relations with foreign authorities, but the nature of these relationships is not clear to the Belgian authorities.

Diplomatic agents, although in a subtler manner, are not hesitant in attempting to influence the course of events to their advantage. They wish to inhibit the attempts of the Belgian authorities to establish a Belgian Islamic framework, either blocking it actively, infiltrating it in order to weaken the structure from within, or attempting to maintain certain key persons under their control.

The message that Belgium wishes to follow an Islam compatible with its own institutional framework in future must be stated more clearly by the Belgian authorities.

Independently of the above

In Belgium, the municipal elections of 9 October 1994 were marked by the election in several municipal councils of officials of extra-Community origin, more or less recently naturalized.

In the legislative elections on 21 May 1995, four candidates of extra-Community origin were elected to the Regional Council of Brussels. Most of them play an important role in the associational environment. How they intend to position themselves with regard to the religious demands of their community of origin, only the future can tell.

Local challenges involve, particularly, the installation of mosques, burial places, and authorizations for ritual slaughter. The obtaining of a building permit, compulsory for internal or external transformation of any building, is subject to a decision by the municipal political authorities. Through the granting of building permits and the inspection of safety standards relating to fire hazards, municipal authorities exert pressure on Islamic communities to restrict their visibility or presence in certain districts. In Belgium, certain municipalities granted Muslims a parcel in the municipal cemetery. In Liège, this concession dates back to 1971. In Antwerp, Muslims have just obtained satisfaction after negotiations lasting many years.

As far as elected officials of Islamic origin are concerned, it will be interesting to examine the role and position of these newly elected officials in the municipalities at the end of the present municipal legislative term. Will they confine themselves, or be confined, to representing persons of foreign origin; or will they, like other elected officials, represent the Nation, i.e, all citizens, as required by the Constitution? (Blaise, 1994.)

Conclusion

In Belgium, communication between the authorities and the Islamic communities began in the 1960s after the arrival of students - Albanian political refugees - who rapidly established contact with the embassies of Morocco and Saudi Arabia. The latter took the initiative in assuring themselves of support from the Islamic World League. The institution around which this action crystallized by the end of the 1960s was the ICC in Brussels. Turkish authorities have long adopted a distinct profile, extending to this very day, even though they have not been entirely absent from the ICC. It was in and around this ICC that the struggle for representation of the Islamic community took place between 1969 and 1989. It was only in 1989 that the Centre assumed - or was assigned - a less central position, partly on its own initiative, partly because its situation during the agitated period from 1986 to 1989 was no longer tenable, and partly because the Belgian authorities distanced themselves from it.

Given that Islamic religion instruction began to be given in official education immediately after the recognition of the Islamic religion, the debate on the representativity of the Islamic interlocutors has concerned, above all, competence relating to the appointment of Islamic religious teachers. Attention focused entirely on this question, with the result that other problems (for example, mosques, or the appointment and remuneration of imams) remained somewhat in the shade.

On the other hand, the permanent desire to respect the principle of equality with other recognized religions, and the dominant position of the Catholic Church in this context, has had the effect that the debate on the representativity was long reduced to seeking a moral and spiritual authority to represent all Islamic communities, leading to constant dead-ends.

It appears that a turning point was reached recently, when, in 1994, the idea of entrusting full powers to a spiritual authority was abandoned, and a more pragmatic formula was adopted, which consisted of uniting around a table representatives of Islamic tendencies who did not claim to be spiritual leaders, but simply acceptable, credible "technicians" who wished to ensure fulfilment by the Belgian authorities of a number of consequences and implications arising from recognition of the Islamic religion.

For 20 years, the focus upon the position of education, and the perpetual search for the most suitable spiritual leader, has marked relations between Belgian authorities and Islam. This explains, for example, why the associations of teachers of Islamic religion and the educational trade unions have always wished to occupy an important place in discussions on the orientation of the Islamic religion. The turning point reached in 1994 is still too recent to permit evaluation at this time.

New data has since come into the picture: since 1994, as well, elected officials of Islamic origin have made their entry into politics, even though through the traditional parties. This phenomenon is not, moreover, limited to Brussels.

It is clear that these two elements -- the presence of political leaders of Islamic origin in the various traditional parties and the pragmatization of relationships between the Belgian authorities and Islamic communities -- should normally mark a turning point constituting a counter-balance to the permanent interest of certain embassies and great foreign mosques of Islamic fundamentalist leanings in all the affairs of the Belgian Islamic community.

Notes

[1]   The Minister of Justice was Mr. P. Wigny.

[2]   The new ICC, also called the Grand Mosque of Brussels, was put in service on May 1977 and solemnly inaugurated on 9 May 1978 by King Khaled, during an official visit to Belgium, and King Baudouin.

Although the Islamic World League, with headquarters in Mecca, has always been represented on the ICC through the sending of religious emissaries and financial contributions, the ICC became officially dependent upon the Islamic World League in 1982 to obtain a stable working budget.

This was institutionalized in 1983 by an amendment to the statutes published in the annexes to the B.M. on 10.12.1992. The Executive Committee was henceforth composed of three representatives from the Islamic World League.

[3]   The Minister of Justice at this time was Mr. Gol.

[4]   Response to a question by the Senator Antheunis.

[5]   On 18 December 1985, a deputy of the UDRT (small right-wing party) Mr. Hendrick, raised a number of questions, including that of the total cost of financial interventions by the public authorities in favour of ministers and administrations of Islamic religion. On 5 February 1986, during a meeting of the Commission of Justice chaired by Mr. Moureaux (PS), the same Mr. Hendrick interrogated them on the risks of seeing the Islamic communities of Belgium infiltrated by fanatics of Islamic Jihad, agents of international terrorism.

J. Gol (PRL), Minister of Justice, declared that he would maintain surveillance of Islamic fundamentalists active in Belgium.

In late February 1986, the municipal council of Uccle (a municipality of Brussels--Capital) suspended the teaching license of three teachers of Islamic religion pending an inquiry to determine whether or not they belonged to any of the Islamic extremist currents. The municipal council of Jette (another municipality of Brussels-Capital) adopted a motion which condemned the "actions of Islamic fundamentalism", demanding that the government take action to put an end to such actions.

In early March 1986, the municipal council of Saint-Gilles (another municipality of Brussels-Capital) demanded of the government that action be taken by the immigration study commission.

PRL mayors from the municipalities of Brussels-capital (Ixelles, Koekelberg, Schaerbeek, Uccle, and Woluwe St. Pierre) and the heads of the PRL groups from other municipalities in the Brussels urban area spoke of their "concern in view of the diffusion of a teaching and slogans inspired by Islamic fundamentalism and hostile to the traditions of democracy and tolerance in Belgium", and demanded increased vigilance by the Belgian authorities in the organization of Islamic religious instruction.

From early March, a councillor from the FDF (French-speaking Front of Brussels) presented a resolution asking the government to take steps to stem the "rise of Islamic fundamentalism".

In mid-March, the municipal council of Koekelberg voted a motion by a PS councillor condemning Islamic fundamentalism. They furthermore demanded that the Ministry of National Education reorganize the courses of Islamic religion as soon as possible.

At the end of March, the PS group from the municipal council of Ixelles proposed to create supervisory committees made up of teachers, municipal representatives, and teachers of Islamic religion, in order to establish criteria for the content of religious instruction.

At the beginning of April 1986, the municipal council of Molenbeek appointed the teachers of religion. On 13 February, the municipal council had refused, by a large majority, to approve the list of religious teachers (Le Soir, 17 February 1986), due to incidents between Iranian students commemorating the anniversary of the revolution and counter-demonstrators.

On 24 April 1986, the municipal council of Etterbeek adopted a motion condemning Islamic fundamentalism, although not present in the municipality. For PRL councillor J.D. Defeld, "the Third World War has already started". "Etterbeek Adopts Motion to Combat Fundamentalism Possible but Absent" (Le Soir, 28 April 1986, p. 6). Leon Defosset, mayor of Etterbeek, did not believe in the legality of this motion, which, in his view, ran counter to religious freedom.

At the end of April 1986, the municipal council of Brussels-City also condemned Islamic fundamentalism.

6 Response of M. Jean Gol, Minister of Justice, to the parliamentary question of deputy José Desmaret (PSC, that is, French-speaking Social Christian Democrats).

7 On 19 April 1989, the deputy of the Vlaams Blok (neo-fascist type Flemish political party), F. De Winter introduced a draft law in the Chamber, the particular object of which was to amend article 19b of the law of 4 March 1870 in such a manner as to abolish the provisions relating to the Islamic religion, and to withdraw the recognition which it had enjoyed since 1974.

Certain municipalities of Brussels-Capital -- Schaerbeek and St. Gilles -- refused to organize courses of Islamic religious instruction in their schools. To the mayors of these municipalities, the ICC was not authorized to appoint religious teachers, even if the State had conceded these prerogatives to it. The mayor of St. Gilles did not wish to have fundamentalist teachers subservient to the authorities of Islamic countries.

The Minister of Education of the French Community, Jean-Pierre Graffe (PSC), questioned on this subject by the Ecolo deputy Henri Simons, in April 1989, admitted that these municipalities were entitled to reject Islamic religious instruction in their schools. In his opinion, pending a decree of execution of the law of 1978, the organizational authorities were entitled to declare that they were "not party to the arrangement" which existed between the Ministry of National Education and the ICC.

On the Islamic side, the murder of Mr. Al Ahdal remained unsolved; this was disturbing.

On 1 October 1989, parents of students at the municipal schools in Saint Gilles and Schaerbeek which had refused to organize courses of Islamic religious instruction, supported by the "Belgian Association for Unity and Mutual Assistance among Islamic Parents" brought suit against the above mentioned municipalities on the grounds that the schools had failed to offer Islamic religious instruction in their program.

On 1 December, both municipalities were ordered by the court to organize courses of Islamic religious instruction. Both municipalities appealed.

On 12 December, St. Gilles initiated a procedure to appoint three teachers who were not proposed by the ICC.

On 19 December, the municipality of Schaerbeek announced that Islamic religious instruction would be organized for children whose parents had brought suit.

8 E.g. Vic Anciaux (VU, Flemish democratic nationalist party), Secretary of State of the Region Brussels-Capital for immigration affairs, declared that the creation of the school would jeopardize integration but that legally it could not be prevented.

9 This minister was M. Wathelet.

10

Muslim Organizations and Islam-State Relations:
The Italian Case

Stefano Allievi

The Islamic presence in Italy is quite new and, in some ways, different; particularly if we compare it with that of northern European countries. Being a new phenomenon, it is also what we could call a statu nascendi: more a movement than an institution.

It is nevertheless possible, even at this moment, to draw its image roughly: the resultant picture, like photographs taken in motion, will be slightly blurred, because the situation itself is in fast evolution. But it is nevertheless clear enough to be able to identify some significant social facts and social processes, and try to understand their present state and future direction.

To let the reader actually visualize the phenomenon, this paper has been divided into two sections: the first is mainly descriptive, and the second contains some interpretations and considerations on the topic of the title.

Introduction: the return of Islam

From the historical point of view, the presence of Islam in Italy is not exactly a novelty: we should speak more precisely of its return. In fact Italy has been acquainted with an occasional Arab presence in Sicily since the 7th century, that is, since the very beginning of the history of Islam. A real Islamic domination of the island occurred from the 9th until the 11th century (and not only of the island, if we consider, for instance, the Emirate of Bari, but also different experiences like the Muslim colony of Lucera, etc). But the Islamic heritage is visible also elsewhere, in different areas, from the South to the North, throughout the country: through

Puglia, Tuscany, Liguria, Sardinia, etc, up to Aosta Valley. There were even mosques, for a very special group of Muslims (slaves, captured in different Islamic countries, from Maghreb to Bosnia, and often sold to the French navy), in towns such as Genova, Livorno and Napoli during the 18th century.

The Vanvitelli's Royal Palace of Caserta, in the 18th century, was also built by utilizing hundreds of Muslim slaves. On the other end of the Peninsula, Algerian soldiers fought with the French army in some of the battles of the Risorgimento, against the Austrians, and entered first into Milan, liberated in 1859. The monument to Napoleon III still reveals the Arab names of the soldiers who lost their lives in Solferino, Magenta and Montebello. These are but some of the moments in a long history, generally unknown even inside Italy.

In more recent times the presence of Islam vanished, particularly if we compare the Italian situation with the French or the British (or the German, the Belgian and the Dutch), for one simple and good reason: Italy does not have an important past as a colonial country in Muslim lands. Commercial contacts, obviously, have always gone on: for commerce and trade, the Mediterranean has often been more an advantage than an obstacle, more a bridge than a wall - a 'liquid continent', as Fernand Braudel used to call it. But the only political contacts of a certain importance took place between the two World Wars: the most important was the special statute given in 1919 to the Muslims of Tripolitania and Cirenaica, a part of the so-called 'Impero' in Lybia (that in any case was not entirely applied, suspended in 1922 and totally abrogated in 1928).

During the Fascist period more active initiatives were taken, particularly when Mussolini tried to play the role of 'protector' of Islam. He liked to be represented - the iconography on the subject is of some interest - holding the 'sword of Islam', given more or less spontaneously to him in Tripoli, in 1937, by a group of native chiefs. Mussolini took this gift with some rhetorical and at the same time committing words: "Fascist Italy intends to guarantee the Muslim populations of Lybia and Ethiopia peace, justice, welfare, the respect of the laws of the Prophet, and wishes to show its sympathy to Islam and to the Muslims of the entire world" (Mussolini 1938). Already ten years before, in 1928, Mussolini defined Italy, not only as a "friend of the Islamic world", but also as a country "conscious of its functions as a great Muslim Power" (Mussolini 1934).[1] Indeed, in the Fascist period, and particularly in the thirties, there was a real attempt at 'Muslim politics' on the part of Italy. Other examples could be the programs in Arabic of Radio Bari, founded in 1934, the empowerment of the Institutes for Oriental Studies in Rome and in Naples, and the frequent visits to Rome of the Great Mufti of Jerusalem. However, for the most part the Muslim politics of Italy remained more a hope or a dream than a reality: Italy did not become a "Western school" (De Felice 1988) for the young Islamic nations facing the Mediterranean.

Fascist politics did not have any major effect on Italian culture, for which Islam remained an unknown reality and, if anything, an old enemy. Popular memory has been influenced more by the history of frequent incursions on the Italian coast of the Saracen pirates, whose traces remain clearly visible in traditions ('giostre del Moro' *et similia*) and architecture (the 'Saracen towers' that can still be seen along the coasts), much more than by the Crusades - which, despite the presence of the Popes on the Italian peninsula, were primarily a French affair.

Together with this historical memory, the current wave of the so-called Islamic resurgence (and, in the minds of some: Islamic threat, Islamic danger, or Islamic challenge), generates, in the Italian case, what we could call a double return of Islam: from the depth of the past as well as from the topical subjects of the present - from history and geopolitics.

On the contrary, from the sociological point of view, no doubt, the Islamic presence is clearly a new phenomenon: linked to the arrival and presence of immigrants. For more than one century, and up to no more than twenty years ago, Italy had its own emigrants going to different receiving countries. It was the biggest European supplier of labour for the other Western economies. 1973 was the symbolic turning point, the year in which the number of Italians returning to the country was, for the first time, higher than the number of those leaving it. The real 'boom' of immigration into Italy has been even more recent: the eighties and the nineties. It started with the arrival of different groups of immigrants, mainly from the Philippines and other Catholic countries (El Salvador, etc.), particularly as maids. There were also immigrants from Egypt and other Muslim countries, coming in different waves. The last groups of workers, both legal and illegal, have come from the countries of the

Maghreb, Subsaharian Africa, and also Albania, etc.[2]

In general these immigrants were Muslims, who, so to speak, immediately brought Islam with them, differently from the first waves of immigrants from Muslim countries to France, Germany, etc., in the first decades after the Second World War up to the seventies.

Islam, then, has just arrived in Italy: it is the last of the newcomers. It arrived with the first few mosques (in reality, simple halls of prayer) organized in university towns by the Union of Muslim Students in Italy (*Usmi*), in the beginning of the seventies. It was a very small presence, with unique characteristics in Europe. Before the activity of the *Usmi*, Italy had only a single mosque in Rome.

What is singular about the Italian situation is precisely that the first mosques were created not by and for communities of foreign workers, but by and for an elite of students, mainly coming from the Middle East (primarily Syria and Jordan, many of them Palestinians). Only later did the number of workers exceed that of the students. At that point the mosques changed their role, and frequently their legal statute, although not often their leadership (or, at least, not yet).

What is clearly evident is that, in Italy, Islam is establishing itself very quickly, compared with the rest of what we could call the European part of the Umma. The whole typology that characterizes the Islamic institutionalized presence is already visible: mosques, associations, Sufi orders (*turuq*), political movements, intellectual production, transnational powers (particularly in Rome), intervention of states of origin, converts, free lancers, etc. But all that exists is still in a very fragile state of organization. The leadership at the national level, for example, is not clear so far: the struggle is still in course. Therefore, it might be useful for the reader to give here a sort of morphology of Islam in Italy,[3] starting from the numbers - usually an easy task, but not so in Italy.

Some statistical data. The Muslim presence in Italy is difficult to evaluate for the simple reason that even the number of immigrants is far from being under control. Italy is one of the countries in Western Europe with the smallest percentage of immigrants; but it has one of the highest percentages of non-EEC foreigners, and, probably with the possible exception of Greece, the highest number of irregulars, both in percentage and in numbers.

Approximately 900,000 foreigners were legally resident in Italy in 1992.[4] Among them some 760,000 were non-EEC members, of which more or less 280,000 (31%) came from Muslim countries, or from countries with a Muslim presence in their population. Currently the numbers are not much higher, at least with regard to legal residents (surprisingly enough they are even a little bit smaller: some 3,000 foreigners less in 1994 than in 1992). But things have probably changed more for the illegals. If we add an estimated number (in current literature, the numbers change depending on the source and on the thesis to be proved...) of irregulars, converts and those who have obtained Italian citizenship, we can obtain a probable number of 500,000 persons of Muslim origin that are not mere 'birds of passage', continually moving up and down or in and out of the Italian peninsula. This number consists of those who are established enough to activate a religious demand. The number, obviously, does not say anything about their effective and practical 'islamicity'. Any higher numbers, reported here and there, are due to the thirst for grandeur of some Muslim leader, or to the 'scoopmania' of some journalist, and should be rejected.

More or less one third of the Muslims come from Morocco, but the rest (differently from the absolute preeminence of the Turks in Germany, the Algerians in France or the Indopakistanis in Great Britain) are divided among several countries of origin: from Tunisia to former Yugoslavia (many of the recent refugees, as well as some groups of gypsies, are Muslims), from Senegal to Albania, from Egypt to Iran, from Somalia to Pakistan, from Algeria to ...Italy, etc. Among the illegals, most come from the Maghreb (mainly Morocco and Tunisia), but increasingly they comprise also Bosnians, Albanians, Senegalese, etc. We can see here one of the peculiarities of the Islamic presence in Italy: a multi-pole presence, with practically a complete absence of Turks (except for some unrecognized refugees), a modest presence of Muslim Asians, and no more than a symbolical presence of immigrants coming from former colonies (Somalia in particular).

Islam, however, cannot be described by numbers. Let us give some more indicative social data.

First of all, the mosques. From the point of view of religious organization, Italian Islam is proceeding along the same path as in other countries of Europe, but at what seems a remarkably higher speed. Until 1970, as we have already seen, there was only one mosque in Italy. In the seventies few new mosques were created. Between 1981 and 1990 we witnessed a first diffusion of mosques in different regions of the country. But real growth is more recent, and strictly linked to the laws of regularization, whose effect was evident and measurable. Immediately after the regularization of workers we saw a rapid 'regularization of Islam'. Evidently the demand was already 'there': only the supply was lacking. Now we can count more than 60 mosques, and globally at least 100-120 halls of prayer and possibly more: their expansion rate escapes every census, even that of the Muslim organizations. Only three of these are 'real' mosques, from an architectural point of view; among these is the recently officially inaugurated great Islamic centre of Rome; the others are in Milan and Catania.

The ethnic community more frequently at the origin of the mosques, when it is possible to single it out, is the Moroccan, but there are also Tunisian, Algerian, Iranian, Egyptian, Somalian, Pakistanian, Lybian, Turkish and Italian mosques. More frequently the origin of the mosque is not ethnical but associative, particularly in the past, as a result of the activities of the Usmi network. All mosques are what we could call 'first generation (or, better, first wave) mosques'. In fact, differently from what has happened in most of the European countries (for reasons linked to the economical cycle, and also to the legislative processes), the Muslims in Italy started to build their mosques practically immediately after their immigration. They did not wait for the birth of a second generation to be islamically educated, like in the case of several Muslim communities in different European countries, particularly in the seventies. The reason for this speed in growth is probably that, from the very moment of the arrival of Muslim immigrants, mosques have played an important social, and not only a religious role. (This social role is probably linked to (1) the different economic cycle in which the immigration process took place, in central and northern Europe countries on one side, and in Italy on the other. This cycle was characterized by mass industrial production yesterday, and by disseminated jobs now. (2) The different types of jobs on the labour market: small service more than industry. (3) A different kind of socialization in the countries of origin, in which Islam plays a different and bigger role today than ten or twenty years ago. (4) The absence of significative other networks of socialization, such as ethnic associations, amicales, etc. The result of the whole process is that the mosque network and Islamic organized presence is one of the very few moments and places of socialization and of collective visibilization among immigrants from Muslim countries in Italy.

Sufi orders and religious movements. The organization of the turuq, the sufi orders, is not one of the easiest subjects to study. Even if they are not secret societies, they are always, at least, discrete societies. Those who belong to one or another of them do not declare their membership at the first moment, and sometimes deny it. And that is the case also for some religious and political Islamically based movements.

Probably the membership in the turuq is, percentage-wise, more a characteristic of converts than of those who are Muslims of origin. But there are some exceptions. The most evident of them is the Senegalese tariqa of the *Mourides*, with which the majority of the Senegalese living in Italy associate, even if they are not explicitly members, or were disinterested therein before leaving their country. In fact the tariqa plays a role that is not only religious, but social (protection and insertion) and economical as well (Schmidt di Friedberg 1994).

In Italy one can find the traces of others Sufi orders. Two branches of the *Tijaniyya* are active: one is Senegalese (still probably the most important tariqa in Senegal from the standpoint of numbers). The other one is mainly composed of converts. The *Burhaniyya*, an Egyptian tariqa that is active also in Europe, and has its European centre in Germany, is also present among certain groups of converts. Mainly (and sometimes exclusively) composed of converts are the groups which refer to the *Naqshbandiyya*, the *Darqawiyya*, the *Alawiyya* and others, all with a few dozen members at most.

Another reality of a certain importance is represented by the political and religious movements that are starting to be present and influential in the Italian Muslim world. Some of them are more established than others: for example, the *Jama'at at-Tabligh*, that began its activity in a couple of mosques in central Italy, and is now rapidly increasing; and the *Muslim Brothers*, who are much more important as an ideological reference than as an organized structure, and whose ideological imprinting is evident among the leadership of the Usmi and of Islamic centres of a certain importance. Concerning this last group, if we try to find a Western parallel, we could make a comparison between the high diffusion of the writings of Qutb and Mawdudi and those of Marx and the Marxists some years ago: although reference to them was practically indispensable in a wide cultural area, one did not have to belong to a communist organization to read them. As in the case of Marxism, we should be able to maintain the distinction between the two levels, which, in any case, are both present.

Obviously we find a wide range of references to the Islamic movements of the country of origin of the different groups of immigrants: from the *Nahda* to *Hamas*, from the *Fis* to the *Jama'at-i-Islami*. None of them, however, seem to play more than a symbolic role, and only inside the group directly concerned, we find a more militant attitude and activity. There are, of course, banners of identification for the Muslims as a whole, for the entire Umma: Bosnia, Palestine (for some), or Afghanistan in the past.

Finally, there are the groups which are neither Sufi orders, nor religious or political movements. We generally call them religious families: particularly the Shi'ites, but also the Ismailis and others, which have their own organizational structures. The Shi'ites have their own network of organizations, mosques, reviews and even converts, obviously with a clear link with the European Islamic cultural centre based in Rome, i.e. the Iranian embassy to the Holy See.

Unlike other European countries, in Italy the national organizations that the French call Amicales, as well as other kinds of ethnic and national associations, play a modest role locally, and are virtually inexistant at the national level. Probably this is due to the fact that the presence of immigrants is less concentrated in this or that nationality, but also because the 'Muslim network' was built first. Some recent developments indicate that the situation may be changing.

Main social actors. Various groups and organizations are trying to represent Islam in Italy, and the contest is far from being concluded. At the moment, however, no one monopolizes the leadership of Italian Islam.

The most important actors are, at this moment, the following:

The Islamic Cultural Centre of Italy (*Centro islamico culturale d'Italia*). It is the group which is at the origin of the Great Mosque of Rome. It is probably possible to define it as a "diplomatic-state Islam": the board of the centre is officially composed of the ambassadors of the different Islamic countries, even if the leading role is played by Saudi Arabia through the *Rabita*, the *League of the Muslim World*. Morocco plays an important role, too, and for the moment the leadership of the centre has been appointed by this country.

The *Union of Communities and Islamic Organizations in Italy (Ucoii)* was founded in 1990 as the representative of the 'real' Islam, in opposition to the 'official' Islam of the Centre of Rome. It has in its promoting committee the Islamic Centre of Milan, historically one of the most powerful and best organized Islamic institutions in Italy (Allievi 1994), and the Union of Muslim Students (*Usmi*), whose role has already been pointed out. The *Ucoii* is quite active both in internal organization and in external public relations, both with the media and Italian society at large. It publishes a Muslim bi-lingual monthly (in Italian and Arabic), *Il musulmano* (that has recently 'suspended' publication for lack of funds) and its main purpose is to obtain an *Intesa* (agreement) with the Italian state in order to obtain recognition of the Islamic religion as one of the "non-Catholic" religions of the country (like other denominations that have obtained similar recognition: some Protestant denominations, the Union of Hebraic communities, etc.).

On Italian territory other Islamic social actors are playing a role, as well. In some areas of the country some regional networks (usually with the older or the better organized mosque at their centre) are quite active and relatively independent from the federation and the others subjects quoted above. The transnational powers, like the *Rabita* and the Lybian *Da'wah*, have some influence. Certain states too, particularly Morocco, Tunisia, Egypt and Iran, have been trying to establish control over their citizens, to a greater or lesser extent. The converts (both the Sunnis and the Shi'ites) have recently started to build their own networks, at a national and even European level. Finally we have what we call the free lancers, a typology not rare in Europe: normally 'sociological' Muslims, quite often intellectuals, that play a role of interface between the Muslim world and the non-Muslim society. These are often more recognized as Muslim representatives by the non-Muslim majority than by the Muslims themselves.

The intellectual production. The intellectual production of Italian Islam is, from a certain point of view, a little surprising. We can already count a dozen attempts to create Islamic reviews in Italian, even if they frequently do not survive. There are also various publishers, whose main interests include Islam. By these, we do not mean those who publish books on Islam, but rather militant publishers, often right-wing or massonic.

Easily visible, also in this case, is the role played, in this phase of the establishment of Islam, by the converts. They know the Italian language better, have the necessary know-how, and also seem to be more able to find the necessary financial resources (two or three of them were publishers even before their conversion...). The converts, therefore, with their special way of thinking and of living Islam, have become, at least partly, mediators with the media and, more generally, with the society as a whole. It is probably a temporary phase, but capable of significantly influencing the image of Islam conveyed to the external society. This image may seem more mystical, in some groups, and more radical and militant in others, than the daily reality lived by the Muslim immigrants.

Islam, society and the State: seeking legitimation

When speaking of this topic, we always need to keep in mind the novelty of the phenomenon. We may, nevertheless, point out some aspects of the open process going on between Islam and the State, or, better, some elements of analysis of the visibilization of Islam in the public sphere.

In Italy we may observe, from several points of view, a relatively acceptable level of social integration of the Muslim communities. More exactly (and this may be one of the reasons of the relatively good level of acceptance), Muslims are not being perceived, for the moment, as Muslim communities, but much more as immigrant communities; and not even as ethnic communities, but, more generally, as non-members of the community, as *extracomunitari* (not EEC members), as they are commonly defined (statistically, in the press, in the socio-political jargon, but also, very often, in scientific and pseudo-scientific research).

What has been perceived in other countries as the 'Muslim question', a hot point in the debates concerning the presence of immigrant communities, has not arisen in Italy, so far. Recently, however, the press[5] has started to touch on the subject.

At the national, institutional level the situation is partially different: there is a Muslim question. But it is rather brought up by the Muslims themselves. The Islamic community, particularly through the action of the *Ucoii*, is in fact trying to establish an *Intesa* (agreement) with the Italian government, in order to obtain a status compared with that of other religious minorities.[6] One should remember that in Italy the State has had a central agreement with the Catholic church (called the *Concordato*), since 1929, when the so-called Lateran Pact was signed by the Italian State, represented by Mussolini, and the Vatican. The text was up-dated in 1984.

Others religions, once "tolerated" and then "admitted" cults, are now simply called, in the republican Constitution, religious confessions "different from the Catholic". These religions can apply for an *Intesa* with the State. This status, already obtained by some Protestant denominations and by Judaism, has been applied for by several others (the Jehowah Witnesses, Buddhists, etc.). Among them is also the *Ucoii*, whose text (no more than a simple project so far) is based more or less literally on that of the *Union of the Jewish Communities*, converted into law in 1989, obviously with some minor differences. But the longwinding burocratical process, and even the discussions, have not yet officially started, for several reasons. One of them, on the Muslim side, but not necessarily the most important (that may actually depend primarily on the State), is a problem that other European countries know very well: the question of which Islamic body should be the official representative of the Muslim communities. This is not only a question of legal representation but also, and even more so, a question of grassroots leadership.

The first text of a possible *Intesa* has been proposed by the Ucoii, which is by far the most representative umbrella organization among the Muslim communities, but which is only a de facto association, not recognized by the State. The Italian State has, on the contrary, recognized the Islamic Cultural Centre of Rome as a non-profit organization (*ente morale*):[7] that is, not a 'church' and even less a 'religion', but something more similar to a private association. The centre of Rome, which obviously does not want to be excluded from this process and even claims the exclusive representation of the Muslims in Italy, can count on the support of the Islamic countries.

The position of the Islamic Cultural Centre of Rome was recently firmly repeated on the occasion of the official inauguration of the mosque, on 21 June 1995, in the presence of the President of the Italian Republic and civil and religious authorities: it is a request for an exclusive representation of Islam.[8] But a problem arises concerning its real connections and activities with the immigrants (the grassroots leadership quoted above). Theoretically, there is an even more serious juridical contradiction: the fact that the centre represents Muslim foreign countries, whereas the *Intesa* (and the concept that lies behind it) has always concerned, at least in the past, citizens of a different religion, and not foreign nationals[9] - nor, as in this case, (even) foreign countries. The problem also concerns the *Ucoii* which, less exclusively, for simple numerical reasons represents more Muslim immigrants than Muslim Italian citizens in any case.

The way the process for the *Intesa* is going on is instructive in itself. A first text had been elaborated by some Muslim intellectuals, most of them converts, which included partial recognition of (some principles of) the shari'a, particularly on family law. This text was circulated in very restricted circles, but was amended in the end. Now a new more 'moderate' text, practically based on the *Intesa* regarding Protestants and Jews, has been elaborated and proposed, first inside the Muslim communities, then in the Muslim press, and later towards the public opinion (mediated by those who are interested in these problems: researchers, journalists, members of the Catholic church). The last step has been to submit the text directly to the government: to the Prime Minister, who shall decide whether the right moment or need exists to start the procedures for the *Intesa*, and to the Ministry of Internal Affairs, which is officially in charge of the project. Some meetings have taken place, officially, with representatives of the Minister.[10] The whole process has been taken up by the *Ucoii*, created just a few months before the elaboration of the text, with this aim clearly in mind.[11]

At the same time, the Islamic Cultural Centre of Rome has been trying, weakly, to take part in this process. We should not forget some elements of the history of the Centre of Rome: the decision to give permission to build the mosque in Rome and the donation (literally: for free) of the land (30,000 square meters in a valuable area near the residential quarter of Parioli) in 1974, after the visit of King Faysal of Saudi Arabia to Rome in 1973. As most can remember, 1973 was the year of the first oil shock, a turning point in the history of the Western economies. Is it by chance that this decision was taken exactly in that period? Let us return to the facts. The Islamic Cultural Centre of Rome was officially created in 1966; not until 1974, only three months after its request, with a procedure unusually quick for Italian bureaucratic habits, was it recognized as a non-profit organization. Like in an old style detective story, we could say: do we need more evidence?

The Great Mosque, whose construction started in 1984, has been officially inaugurated now, but its internal organization and leadership is still not established and not strong enough. In any case, it tried to score some points on the question of the *Intesa*: in 1991 (not incidentally, just one year after the birth of the *Ucoii*, and when a text of a possible *Intesa* had already been circulating for several months), the Centre asked the Ministry of Internal Affairs to start procedures for an agreement between the Muslim community and the State. But a letter sent by the Ministry asking for more information (a necessary bureaucratic step) went without any answer: no text of any kind was ever elaborated or proposed. Clearly the request was just a step to mark the presence of the Centre, and its will to demonstrate its role (heavily discussed, in any case, among the Muslim community) as representatives of the Muslims of Italy.

In a way, we could speak at this stage of a sort of institutional bricolage, a do-it-yourself strategy that also shows the very primitive stage of the matter. On the other hand, it is quite evident that the different interlocutors know each other poorly. This holds true both on the part of the Muslims as well as on that of the State, not to mention society as a whole. Even the State does not have, for the moment, the instruments to improve its knowledge of the whole matter. For example, the commission in charge of drafting an *Intesa* is composed of a few officials appointed by the different ministries only, with no special knowledge and/or experience of Islam. The problem is that the whole organization of the Muslim communities, as well as the problems that they are facing, are not comparable to that of other religious minorities, normally composed of citizens and, very often, with an existent internal structure such as that of clergy-structured religions, like the Catholic church. From this point of view, Islam is a totally different world, at least for the moment.

In my opinion, the general public and a fortiori the state institutions still do not perceive the role that Islam plays - in Italy probably more than in other European countries for the reasons mentioned above - as a sort of substitutive instrument of socialization, in view of the practically complete absence of other agencies of socialization among immigrants of Muslim origin.

Institutional relations with public institutions: the quest for recognition

Relations with the public institutions can be defined as relatively good, but with one important characteristic: these relations exist and work much more on the local (municipal, and occasionally regional) level than on the national one. At the local level the phenomenon is clear, and symbolized by the fact that quite a few halls of prayer are placed in centres for immigrants, dormitories, or even, more importantly, in places offered by the municipalities, often for free or for a symbolic rent.[12] An extreme case is that of Palermo, where a former church was restored by the regional government of Sicily and given, practically as a present, to the Tunisian community (or better, the Tunisian government), the most important Muslim community in the region. But in this particular case, a decisive role was played by the political liaison between internal and international interests, and above all the linkage between the ex-Socialist Party in Italy (whose former leader, Craxi, is a personal friend of prominent members of the Tunisian leadership - including President Ben Ali - and used to spend his holidays in his properties in Hammamet, where he is currently living to escape from the Italian justice) and the Tunisian government. This 'politico-religious' intervention on the part of local governments can be seen not only in Palermo, but also in Rome, partly in Milan, and in other cities.

A similar and higher level of relations, again at a local level, takes place with religious and church organizations, particularly on immigrant problems. Public opinion in general has so far shown very little rejection motivated by Islamic 'arguments';[13] probably curiosity and exotism still play a bigger role than explicit discrimination and racism. Or better, discrimination and racism, when they are present (and they are present, here and there, in several towns with a significant number of migrants), are less motivated by cultural-religious considerations, but rather by ethno-racial categories. There are, as always, some exceptions; and this may be only a period of transition.

The political representation of Islam

In Italy we still do not have Islamic parties nor significant numbers of citizens of Muslim religion who participate in political elections, both on the local and the national level. But we do have a debate among Muslims (and particularly, but not only, converts) about their political role. Some small Muslim organizations (or, better, some leaders) have their special linkage with certain political parties or MPs. This linkage seems due much more to the pre-conversion political tendencies of some converts than to a real organized strategy of the Muslims as a whole.

More importantly, as mentioned before, we have a national umbrella organization of Muslims which has launched the project of the *Intesa* with the State in order to recognize the Islamic presence in Italy; this also implies the necessary political activity of lobbying. Some meetings have taken place at an official political level, and here and there discussions have begun about which Islamic body should be considered as representative. But the problem is far from being considered a 'key question', that is, something important on the political agenda. We cannot even say that the problem is truly under discussion.

Other questions could be asked about the perception of Islam in Italian society, even as a political problem. It is important to mention here that the awareness of a Muslim community (or, better, different Muslim communities) living on Italian territory is very recent, practically discovered during the Gulf War, more as an imitation of how other countries were reacting than as a real desire for knowledge.[14] Only some small responsive and attentive circles are starting to analyze the phenomenon, even though, sometimes, for their own purposes, in a sort of reciprocal manipulation. An example is the use of the problem of the Intesa in order to attack the privileged statute of the Catholic Church.

Tendencies of Islam in Italy: a probable scenario

A country that believes itself to be monolithically Catholic is starting to discover that this image is no more than an ideal construction: Islam is the second religion in the country. And even though Islam has not yet reached a very high level of organization, and is still not that evident, and will not be so for years to come, it is nevertheless clear that for Italy this is a historical turning point. After being identified with the enemy for centuries, Islam is now starting to become part of the social and cultural landscape of the country: mosques and minarets, like cathedrals and town halls (and skyscrapers and commercial centres...), are part of the skyline of our cities: a domestic matter, not only an international one.

For Italy, which did not even live the rupture with Protestantism, nor the pluralistic situation that in many countries is the result thereof, this is really a dramatic change, a sort of revolution in its self-perception. It might, however, be an easier change than in other European countries, not because of its Catholic culture, but possibly because of its Catholic church. We have already said something on the role of the church structures in the help given to immigrants in general, but also on the attention paid to the Muslim immigrants in particular. More than this, we cannot forget that the Church based in Rome is not only Italian, but also universal - the centre of the most intricate religious institution in the world. This means something - at different levels.

An universal body has universal needs. One could be that of insistently reminding Muslims of the need for reciprocity, the rights of minorities (Christian minorities in Muslim countries), the need for a minimum of equality and justice (and freedom of religion) in treating them. On the other hand, the Vatican interpretation of the question seems to be that the Catholic Church must also give an example: so, in the countries in which Christians are the majority (and in a Catholic country, Italy par excellence), Muslims should live their religious life freely. There is a desire for mutual understanding (an example could be the meeting of the religious leaders in Assisi), and a need for diplomacy among religions. These and other reasons can be used to explain the mainly positive attitude of the Catholic hierarchy towards Muslims, even if some pre-conciliar reactions and some resistance still exist, even in the hierarchy. These reasons also explain why the attitude of the Vatican (and particularly of the Pontifical Council for Interreligious Dialogue) seems to be more open than that of many dioceses. In the absence of a State strategy, this seems to be the only long-term policy activated toward Muslims. A policy that makes the role of Rome crucial.

But Rome is crucial also for another reason: this time from the Muslim's viewpoint. This reason is contained in a hadit,[15] in which Muhammad, answering the question of a disciple asking which of the two conquered cities, Constantinople or Rome, would be conquered first, says: "The city of Heracles will be conquered first, that is Constantinople". For Muslims living in Italy (and elsewhere) this text simply means: Rome will also become a Muslim city. When this will happen is not known, the Prophet has not said that; but after Constantinople also Rome will be conquered by Islam - according to the Prophet's word. Is it then so surprising that this topic is increasingly gaining importance in the ideological (and not only in the eschatological) reference of Muslims in Italy? This topic gives in fact an undoubtable centrality to the city of Rome for the whole *Umma*, and this seems to be (or, at least, seems to be considered) also a central argument for the role of the Muslim associations based in Italy. The whole process is at its very beginning. It will be of great interest to follow the next stages. In and outside Rome.

Notes

[1]   The speech cited was pronounced at the Senate on 5 June 1928.

[2]   For a historical analysis and a panorama of the actual situation of migrations in Italy, see Allievi (1991).

[3]   Taken from Allievi & Dassetto (1993). Prof. Dassetto and I, in our research, have tried to describe the 'social morphology', as Durkheim calls it, of Islam in Italy, in its different forms, during long and extended field work (the field is... Italy).
Because of the lack of sources of information (there were practically no studies, very little local research, and not even a sufficient quantity of empirical evidence of the

Islamic presence, not to mention theorization and interpretations - hic sunt leones, that was all), our study took on, out of unexpected necessity, the characteristics of an exploration, a travelling investigation. In one year and an half we travelled (sometimes together, sometimes alone) all over Italy, region after region, town after town, in a sort of investigative process, in the etymological meaning of the word: to search, to look for, to inquire into, in order to discover something. Nearly four months 'on tour', more than 13,000 km. covered by car and as many by others means of transport, hundreds of witnesses and social actors interviewed, a higher number of contacts on various items, a non-definable quantity of hours of conversation involved, are the physical evaluation of this effort. The result was a first provisional map of the mosques, the places of meeting, the organization of the Muslim communities living in Italy, a quantitative evaluation of their weight (in every region of the country), and a first attempt of interpretation of the social and religious role they are playing, and of some reactions of the non-Muslim society.

[4] The period of our research.

[5] The best (and the worst) example has probably been the (articles related to the) police operation made at and around an Islamic centre in Milan, the so called 'Viale Jenner mosque', at the end of June 1995 (the 27 and sqq.), and the following opening of a debate over the risk of an Islamic danger. But some previous examples of a certain interest can be cited. For instance, an inquiry into the Islamic presence in Milan in the Corriere della Sera, the best selling newspaper in Italy together with Repubblica, on 3-4 and 5 february 1995, clearly 'building' the Islamic enemy, and others. Some few examples also in Belluati, Grossi & Viglongo (1995: 69-78), a research on media and racism with some (few) pages dedicated to Islam; but the period of observation is not recent (June-August 1991), and the themes monitored concerned some Islamic items abroad, not Islam in Italy. A couple of examples, instead, in Allievi & Dassetto (1993: 262-275).
Regarding television, the only research available is in Marletti (1995). The period of observation is October 1992 - May 1993, and again the analysis does not concern Italian Islam (Islam settled in Italy), but the image of Islam (in general) perceived through the italian TV.

[6] On the juridical problems of non-Catholic confessions, see Long (1991). On Islam in particular, see Castro (1993: 65-75). For the text of the *Intesa* proposed by the Muslims see *Il musulmano*, n.7-8, 1993, and several articles in the previous numbers; see also Paolucci (1993: 175-193). More detailed and comparative analysis are in S. Ferrari (1996), acts of a recent international conference held in Como in June 1995, to be published also in English edition (particularly the texts of S. Ferrari, F. Castro, G. Conetti and C. Mirabelli).

[7] Recognition was granted with d.p.r. n.712, 21 december 1974; what a 'Christmas present', given only three months after the demand of the Islamic Cultural Centre, that is a quite unusual speed.

[8] See the (unpublished official speech of the President of the Council of Administration of the Islamic Cultural Centre of Rome, the ambassador of Morocco M. Zine El Abidine Sebti, on the occasion of the inauguration of the mosque, which I attended, and some articles in the newspapers the day after, 22 of June.

[9] Even if, juridically, the Intesa concerns the members of a religious group. But de facto the majority of them was, in the other cases concerned, composed by citizens. For some considerations about this problem S. Allievi, L'islam in Italia. Profili storici e sociologici, in Ferrari (1996).

[10] We will try here to reconstruct, for the first time, the different steps of the project of *Intesa*. The text of the *Bozza di Intesa tra la Repubblica Italiana e l'Unione delle Comunità ed Organizzazioni islamiche in Italia*, as it is called by the Muslims who proposed it, was sent for the first time to Prime Minister G.Andreotti in the summer of 1990, but no answer was received. In the meantime, in spring 1991, a meeting was organized with the Minister of Internal Affairs, Scotti; and another one, informal, with some members of parliament in the summer of the same year, on the occasion of the 'Islamic summer camp', in Fabriano. A second time it was sent to the new Prime Minister, G.Amato, on 5 November 1992. In the same period a delegation of the *Ucoii* met some high functionaries of the Ministry of Internal Affairs and with the Minister of Social Affairs, not specifically on the questions related with the Intesa. Astonishingly rapidly, on 11 November 1992, the undersecretary to the President of the Council of Ministers, Fabbri, answered that a commission for the *Intesa* (an internal one, not yet a bilateral one) had been charged with the necessary procedures. Again on 11 January 1993 another letter was sent by the Ministry of Internal Affairs, direction for the cults affairs, communicating the nomination of the commission and asking for some more information, concerning the Muslim community, its organization, structure, mosques, finances, etc. For lack of organization (and of information 'in the proper manner' on some subjects, such as finances for instance), the Ucoii has not yet answered to this letter. In the meantime the Ucoii has met several political representatives, such as members of parliament of different parties and the President of the Parliamentary Commission on Constitutional Affairs (A.Ciaffi, on 26 February 1993). The only real official meeting at the government level, with the undersecretary in charge also of the Intesa, took place on the occasion of the XXV Islamic Conference, in Rome, on 24 December 1994, with a visit and a discourse by the undersecretary M.Borghezio of the former government (Prime Minister S. Berlusconi) and a meeting with the staff of the Ucoii (which I also attended, unofficially, as an observer). But no concrete planning and agenda of meetings have been established, and no decisions have been delivered: just an exchange of ideas and projects.

[11] Interestingly enough, "obtaining an Intesa with the Italian State" is mentioned as one of the first points in the internal statute of the Ucoii, in the article on goals and objectives (n.3). It is then one of the reasons for belonging to the Ucoii; and in fact the elaboration of the text is the first significant act of the Ucoii. And, looking at the limited time passed between the foundation of the Ucoii and the elaboration of the text of the Intesa, it is clear that the two things had been planned together, one in function of the other.
At the moment the Ucoii, with a decision taken in June 1995, has appointed an internal 'commission of three sages' in order to develop the project of the Intesa and the necessary official and political steps: the three are N. Dachan, one of the founders of the Ucoii, A. Abu Shwaima, amir of the Islamic Centre of Milan, and H. Piccardo, a convert who is in charge of the external and press relations of the Ucoii, and director of the review Il musulmano.

[12] Several examples in different regions are referred to in Allievi & Dassetto (1993).

[13] We remember just a couple of cases: the burning of a small mosque in Sestri Levante, in Liguria, the day after its inauguration, the only 'clear' case of rejection, and the 'punishment' of the Imam of the mosque of Latina, in Lazio, by a group of naziskins - but in this second case he was probably just perceived as an immigrant, and not as a Muslim, and much less as a Muslim leader.

[14] For a discussion of the question see Allievi, Battegay, Bastenier & Boubeker (1992). See also Allievi, S: Muslim minorities in Italy and their image in the Italian media (in Vertovec & Peach, 1995).

[15] For the complete text and some considerations on its meaning see Allievi & Dassetto (1993: 289-291).

11

Islam in the Discourse of Public Authorities and Institutions in Denmark[1]

Lars Pedersen

The presence of Islam in Denmark is mainly as a result of labour migration which began in the late 1960's. It was however, only during the 1970's that the number of immigrants reached a substantial volume. Labour intensive industries in Denmark produced a demand for unskilled manpower which drew a reservoir of workers who came largely from a number of Muslim countries including Turkey, Pakistan and Morocco.

Today this group of immigrants have either been badly hit by marginalization in the labour market or else occupy the lowest levels of the market, with poor working conditions and low wages etc. The development of Islamic institutions in Denmark relates directly to this wave of immigration and to these social conditions.

While the Muslim minority tends to organize itself around the local mosques, one of the dominating trends has been towards the creation of larger associations. The development and growth of these social-religious institutions is still continuing under persistently difficult conditions. The development of such institutions takes place in a period which could be defined as a *state-political phase*. The existing mosque associations have been formalised under circumstances which are actively defined by the state system. Priority is in fact given to initiatives administrated under the hegemony of Muslim states (Pedersen 1991 & 1993).

The number of Muslims living in Denmark today is estimated at around 95,000.[2] The largest group within this (35,000) are of Turkish origin. It is estimated that 75,000 Muslims hold foreign citizenship while 20,000 are Danish. Sociologically speaking therefore, Muslims form the second largest religious community in Denmark, followed by Catholics (40,000), Jehovas Witnesses (26,000) and Jews (9,000).

Immigrants create institutional frames within which their religious life can evolve. Organizational efforts are not of course limited to the religious domain but are also applied to other areas. To a large extent immigrants find that Danish associations and political organizations do not provide adequate representation of their interests and are therefore obliged to structure themselves according to their own demands and aims. A desire for political and cultural self-help organizations has evolved. These organizations are not only centres for the formulation of wishes and demands, but are also centres for the re-defining of new collective identities. With the emergence of these self-help organizations the administration of the cultural heritage has entered a new phase in the collective history of the new ethnic minorities in Denmark as it has in Europe on the whole.

As Werner Schiffauer noted (1988) in connection with Turkish immigrants in Germany, the structural totality for immigrants is broken through migration. Religious and other social relations are no longer identical. Religious relations have become explicitly religious, representing one possible relation among many others. Religion has in principle become a private matter. Religious practice, which previously - at least in rural areas - was an integrated part of society, is transformed in character through migration; it is individualised and changes in its symbolic value.

In a radical sense the *system world*, to refer to Habermas (1981), destroys and restructures the *life world*. Primordial loyalties such as kinship are replaced by market economic systems as leading principles for the organization of social relations.

Despite the systematic rationality of the *system world* the changes are not represented as a smooth process without contradictions. On the contrary, the social conditions of the immigrants are extremely constrained, both socially and culturally and this leads to the development of cultural references that are unique. The changes which take place against this background provoke the need for a radical reconsideration of cultural roots and identification.

It seems helpful to assume that it is precisely in the dislocation between the *system world* and the *life world* that social and cultural relations are disturbed. In a climate formed by these disturbances, the importance of the nature of the inclusion of the Islamic institutions is clearly underlined and thus provides significance to the construction of an *Islamic way of life* (Pedersen 1993).

In this essay however, I will concentrate on critical aspects related to the discourse of the public authorities and institutions in relation to islamic (religious) life, both directly and also in a broader sense, which obviously has wider social implications and significance. The question of religious freedom has in this perspective, due to the specific social processes involved, risen to become a question about democracy.

The concept of religious community and religious freedom in Denmark

Protestantism is the official religion in Denmark. Legally speaking it is organised as a State church. Aside from the Danish National Church, the Folkekirke, we can distinguish between 1) religious communities that are legally defined as *recognised* by royal decree,[3] and 2) religious communities that are legally defined as *unrecognised*, but whose ministers are nevertheless empowered to perform marriages which are valid under civil law, and 3) religious communities which are not seen as religious communities at all (e.g, Scientology, Moonies). Each of these categories carries certain rights, or a lack of them. Islamic communities fall into the second category.

The official view expressed by the Ministry of Ecclesiastical Affairs is that the question of general recognitions through royal decree is irrelevant and will no longer be given. It is assumed by the Ministry that the only occasion in which the question of distinction according to formal status has had any social relevance was in connection with marriage procedures. Marriages performed within the Danish national Church and within the *recognised* religious communities have a civil legal validity. In 1969 priests of *unrecognised* religious communities gained the possibility to obtain the right to perform marriages which were legally valid. The Ministry assumed that this thereby achieved a *de facto* equality between different religious communities. The *unrecognised* religions now maintain the same actual rights as the so called recognised religions. They maintain that they are in fact to be seen as such (Communication with the Ministry).

My interviews with leaders and imams from Islamic organizations in Denmark suggest however that the problem is much more complex than the Ministry of Ecclesiastical Affairs would have it and that it cannot be reduced to the formalistic level. The religious leaders spoken to do not agree with the conclusions reached by the Ministry. On the contrary they talk about problems in being able to function on an equal footing; the suspicion they meet from local authorities; a lack of understanding regarding their special needs and a lack of help in establishing the physical and organizational framework needed to sustain a well functioning religious life. The problem carries a large symbolic significance and it also influences the real possibilities of the development of independent Islamic institutions.

There are in fact a number of practical consequences affecting different areas vital to the development of religious life:
- Conditions for mosque associations to obtain immigration permits for new imams are difficult as well as the permits with regard to duration of work and residence are unsatisfactory.
- Economic conditions, especially in relation to the tax system.
- Differences in ascribed authority concerning the registration of births and deaths.
- Difficulties concerning the establishment of suitable burial conditions.

On this symbolically important issue Muslims who have been in Denmark for 25 years, whether still holding foreign citizenship, or having acquired Danish citizenship, still do not have the same opportunities or access to a well functioning religious infrastructure which the majority of the Danish population have. This paradox is not decreasing, despite the growth in the number of Muslims holding Danish citizenship.

In the interviews which I conducted with Islamic leaders and imams in Denmark I asked how they would characterise the concept of *religious freedom* in Denmark. The answers which I received ought to be seen as alarming and can be briefly summarised into three types:
1) The Danish constitution guarantees *religious freedom.*

Islam is not included in the Danish understanding of democratic rights, human rights or religious freedom. The Danish claim of religious freedom is contradicted by the practical difficulties which Muslims encounter in trying to live according to Islam.

2) Islam and the Muslim countries are far more tolerant towards their respective Christian populations and towards Christianity in general than the European countries are towards Islam. We want the same rights here as the *Dhimmis* have in our countries.

3) The situation is worse in our own countries where we cannot live freely as Muslims. The main task for any Muslim is to strive towards creating a true Islamic state, where both the political and legal system are aligned in accordance with the aims and principles of Islam. We do not expect the West to defend Islamic interests. Due to democracy and to the principle of protecting the interests of minorities in the West everything is provided for: We can practise Islam in the family; we can educate our children in our homes or in a school. We can establish an organization, a mosque in whose constitution we can write as its aim that; 'We are Muslims, we serve Muslim interests and we want to protect the Muslim community'. We can register such an organization for 200 Dkk and the whole thing will be accepted. The problems which we suffer in the West are due to Muslims themselves; due to our own disabilities and lack of capacity.

All of these answers are of course open to debate. But the point here is not whether the imams and leaders are right, the fact of the matter is that they actually evaluate the social position of Islam in this perspective. The idea of equal *rights*, despite differences in legal status as the Ministry sees it, is in any case clearly not being translated into equal opportunities; therefore as the Islamic leaders see it, there are no equal rights.

Islamic interests and public institutions in Denmark

An evaluation of the social situation of Islam cannot be restricted to the formal level of establishing Islamic institutions. If we are to talk of *religious rights* within a secular society such as the Danish one with any kind of real bearing, then we must also include the public institutions which connect more immediately to the perspective of the *life world*.

In the following I shall focus on the discourse of those institutions where social integration is confronted on a larger scale, and where the problems of religious interests and rights can be defined as a matter of principle.

I will go into some detail concerning education since this is obviously an area where the conflict is being increasingly articulated.

The law and legal Acts defining the organization of education in the *Folkeskole* (the Danish public primary school) presume that the education is to be based on the life conditions of the individual pupil. Values such as participation, responsibility, freedom of spirit and thought, and democracy are stressed. The degree to which this is interpreted can vary to some extent from school to school.[4] Such a thing as a national curriculum is an unknown phenomenon in the Danish school system.

Conflicts in the *Folkeskole* vis a vis Muslims who wish to adhere to Islamic principles are primarily articulated with respect to specific aspects of education, i.e Physical education; Sex education; Religious education; Music; School outings; Days off for Muslim feastdays, ...and the wearing of the hijab. The schools handle conflicts within these separate issues differently, but they certainly constitute a grey area in the social life of the schools.

Physical Education, including swimming lessons is an obligatory *subject*. Dispensation can be obtained for health reasons, but not for religious ones. This matter has been underlined in a ministerial circular on the participation of immigrant children in physical education. The ministry urge schools to show respect and flexibility (Cirkulæreskr 1986-01-13).

Sex Education is an obligatory *theme*. On the whole it is not generally given as separate course, but as an integrated part of other relevant subjects. Dispensation from attendance is not possible (Bekendtgørelse 1972-06-15, nr 313).

This particular theme has provoked strong emotional response right from its inception. In 1972 a complaint was lodged at the European Council for Human Rights against the Danish state by three Danish Christian parents who wanted their children to be dispensated from the education. The Danish State was not convicted, but the acquittal was based on a reference to the liberal Danish law on private schools which gives parents the right to move their child to such a school (Eilschou

Holm 1980).[5] This case is still a leading one in the question of the right to dispensation from certain themes in the education system in Denmark.

In connection with this it should be noted that the *relative* number of private, publicly funded, so called Islamic schools,[6] in Denmark is the highest in Europe with respect to the sociological number of Muslims; by January 1995 there were 14 such schools.[7] In certain specific geographic areas up to 30% of pupils of a certain grade and nationality attend an Islamic private school. The majority of these schools are based in the Arab and Pakistani communities, and in recent years there has been a move from within the Turkish community to establish private Islamic schools.

Voices are being raised against the establishment of these Islamic schools including some from among high ranking administrators within the Ministry of Education.[8] The Islamic schools are thus regarded as an abuse of the 'liberal' Danish free school system and the tradition of 'tolerance' upon which it is based. This form of (ab)use is seen as serving 'totalitarian' aims.

Critics argue that the underlying motive of the Islamic schools is to 'avoid integration' into Danish society and that the teaching in these schools does not give the child an open, tolerant or democratic mind.

The main source drawn upon in *Christian education* is the Evangelical-Lutheran Christianity of the Danish National Church. Christian education occupies the very centre of religious education in the public primary school and is seen as a basis for understanding Danish culture and other religions. This notion of Christian education has been stressed and reinforced in the latest revised school law (Bekendtgørelse 1991-06-20, nr 484).[9] Dispensation from participation can be obtained on condition that parents declare that they will undertake the necessary education of their children themselves (Lov om Folkeskolen 1993: pgf. 6). The school authorities have no legal right to ascertain whether or not parents do actually carry out this undertaking in practice. Around 2% of pupils in the Folkeskole are exempted from participating in Christian education. This figure varies widely on a local basis. There is no central record of how many *Muslim* pupils are exempted. A consultant in the Ministry puts the estimate at around 50% of *Muslim* pupils being exempted.[10] My investigations show large variations. There are schools and classes where almost all Muslim pupils participate and at others the rule seems to be that none do. Much appears to depend on the way in which the schools present the subject to the parents.

A number of strategies are employed by school leaders in dealing with Muslim pupils and their parents in matters relating to conflicts arising from the curriculum. The following three strategies can be identified from my data:[11]

(1) The public primary school is qualified as being not only a *Folkeskole* (literally. *Peoples school*) but a *Danish* Folkeskole. When I began interviewing, I naively interpreted *Danish* as being a reference to a pedagogical norm. That is to say in the way the law concerning educational practice has usually been defined; explicitly stressing the child and taking this as its point of departure. This interpretation soon showed itself not to be the case when dealing with Muslim pupils. Stressing the *Danish* aspect was by contrast a means of constructing a pedagogical continuity which defined *Danish-ness* as the central value of the cultural norm, leaving *Muslim-ness* to its marginality.[12] This discourse is of a passive, mildly repressive, tolerant character. Practical solutions are attempted in matters such as; concerning nudity in connection with physical education; days off for Muslim celebrations which are accepted on the basis of mutual agreements; the lack of questioning Islamic dress, etc. If the parents persist in the long run in wanting their child's education to adhere more closely to Islamic principles they are advised to transfer it to a private Islamic school.

(2) *Islam* is seen as a patriarchal form of repression. The schools define Islam as constituting a pedagogical threat whose social consequences should be repressed. The schools take a positive attitude to this in the sense that they see themselves as defending the pupil. On the other hand the schools take a tactical, partly intimidating and repressive strategy towards the parents, in particular towards the father who is regarded as the demonised villain. A take it or leave it attitude, without flexibility and with no concern about finding solutions. Taking the day off on religious feast days is considered as unauthorised absence. Parents are reminded that they have the choice of taking their child to an Islamic private school if they are not willing to accept the rules of the school and the school

system. Rather than seeing the establishment of Islamic free schools as a result of a deficiency in the public school system the law is used as a threat against parents. At the same time these private schools are seen as an exploitation of the same law.

(3) A small number of the school leaders interviewed defined Islam as constituting a positive universe for the pupil. The law of the *Folkeskole* is understood as not respecting the guarantee of religious freedom contained in the Danish constitution. These school leaders are applying a very loose interpretation of the law of the *Folkeskole*. One school leader admitted that he would have serious problems if Denmark had visiting inspectors who checked on the educational activities of Muslim pupils.

In summing it all up one can say that the Danish *Folkeskole* has great difficulty in acting as a *folkeskole* (a school of the people) towards its Muslim pupils and their parents, and prefers to act as a *Danish* school (towards the Muslims).

Interviews conducted within the Danish *Health-system* and questionnaires distributed to the directors of hospitals indicate a willingness to meet the needs of Muslim patients in the matter of religion. Islam's existence is manifestly a *silent* one and is dealt with only *incidentally*. Despite the good will, experience in this area does not show a trend, at a common strategic level, towards professional interaction between the various departments of a hospital. Out of 19 participating hospitals, only at one was it for example possible to obtain meat that would be acceptable by Islamic ritual standards. It is quite common for hospitals not to receive demands from Muslim patients concerning *halal* food, although they are aware that Muslims will usually choose vegetarian meals. In this connection it should be noted that while the system providing *kosher* catering for patients has broken down, a service was for many years available for Jewish patients. At no hospital is there an established Islamic infrastructure, nor do they include access for imams or provide rooms for prayer. This does not however mean that the hospitals take a negative attitude towards meeting such needs. The interviews which I conducted would suggest the opposite. The demand however is simply not being expressed! This could be taken to indicate that no problem exists in this area but could equally be taken as a sign of the immense scale of the problem: The Muslim patients do not expect - perhaps wrongly - the hospital system to meet their religious needs at all, as they know that Islam is generally understood to be a foreign religion.

The option of having boys circumcised has gradually disappeared from the hospital services in recent years. Generally this is attributed to cuts in expenses combined with the opinion that this kind of religious demand should not be regarded as an illness as such.[13]

Islam also lives a silent existence within the *prison system*. Muslim prisoners have the same formal religious rights as prisoners of other faiths (Communication with the directors of 18 prisons).[14] Only one prison in Denmark has a prayer room (an annex to the prison church converted in 1994), and one prison has a telephone line to an imam. At none of the prisons is halal-food available. Alimentary matters are nowadays to a large degree left to the initiative of the prisoners themselves. If a prisoner wishes to have halal-meat the prisons are for the most part ready (at least in theory) to help in obtaining it through the supply shops within the walls of the prison itself. In open prisons the prisoners can buy food freely at shops of their own choice and can therefore of course purchase halal-meat if it is available (i.e if the prison is in the vicinity of Copenhagen). Halal certified frozen chicken is widely available throughout the country.

In the *labour market* it is interesting to note the way in which the central public institutions and active organizations view a matter such as Islam. As Moustapha Diop has put it, the work place cannot be isolated simply as a place of production; 'il est aussi lieu de vie où des aspirations des acteurs sociaux concernés s'éxpriment au travers d'une système de représentations, au travers de l'imaginaire' (Diop 1988: 82). Since the work place is in this sense also *life-world*, the discourse and practise of the parties in the labour market are potentially challenged.

A commission was formed in 1992 by the Ministry of Labour whose purpose was to contribute to the formulation of a coherent policy to 'strengthen the integration of immigrants and their rights as being Danish by birth'. The contribution from the commission was to be formed in 'respect to the differing cultural, linguistic and religious backgrounds of immigrants' (Arbejdsmarkedsstyrelsen 1993: 1 /Author's translation). There was however, 'no wish from the Confederation of Danish Employers or the main Danish Confederation of Trade Unions to see the issue of religious rights raised in connection with the work of the Commission. They view the issue as being a local one and one that is outside Labour Law' (Interview with the secretary of the Commission).[15]

Moving to the relevant main labour exchanges at the local level we can note an awareness of Islam being perceived as a social issue. In certain geographical areas labour exchanges act in a flexible manner while in others Danish cultural values are stressed as the code for entry into the labour market.

From the point of view of Muslim workers involved, this flexibility is arbitrary however and does not form a real alternative to a system of guaranteed right.

Among the trade unions, labour market conflicts involving religious issues are also rare, and the matters are not met and dealt with at the central union level but only on an extremely local level. In the cases reported to me concerning loss of employment due to circumstances related to religious affiliation - dress code being a typical issue - the strategy of the trade unions has always been to avoid conflict with the employer. Trade union actions have been to limit damage in support of the employee so that he or she should avoid losing the right to claim unemployment benefits.

Issues concerning Islam are not handled openly at the level of the *system world*; the strategy is to limit it to an invisible and marginalised issue. Local conflicts concerning days off work for the most important religious celebrations, access to rooms for prayer, and dress codes for women remain isolated, invisible and silent. No considerations are taken for the relevance of religious rights. With the extremely high rate of unemployment among the Muslim minorities the argument is that demands of a religious nature are not of significant relevance.

At the present time four Muslim *graveyards* have been established in Denmark. Or rather separate Muslim sections have been formed within existing graveyards. They have been established through the initiative of local graveyard administrations. In all of these cases the graveyards are owned by city councils. While these initiatives have been the result of good intentions, they have resulted only in partial solutions. Respect for the Muslim burial traditions and the conditions articulated by the Islamic religious leaders in the country have been met only to a varying degree.[16]

There is a widespread call from among the Islamic leaders for separate graveyards, in line with the Mosaic community and the Roman Catholic Church.

In Denmark the *slaughtering* of livestock without prior stunning is permitted 'when the slaughtering is done according to Jewish and Muhammedan rites' (Bekendtgørelse 1986: pgf. 1, part 2). Certain conditions are to be respected. The slaughter of animals other than poultry is required to be done in an export abattoir. If the animal exceeds 70 kg a machine is to be used to hold the animal and turn it upside down.

Ritual slaughter has been debated from time to time in the Danish media. Various official commissions have contributed to the debate and certain reservations towards the idea of ritual slaughter have been upheld.

The arguments articulated by these commissions in favour of ritual slaughter without prior stunning have two main angles: (1) 'Religious communities exist in Denmark for whom it is of essential importance to be able to obtain meat from animals slaughtered according to the religious practices of these communities' (Det Etiske Råd Vedr. Husdyr 1988); (2) Existing scientific evidence of excessive pain on the part of the animal is insufficient.

In addition to these two main arguments, a third has been forwarded: the export of meat from animals slaughtered without prior stunning will increase with the development of the inner market in the E.E.C. (Betænkning 1154: 50).

The argument against slaughter without prior stunning is related to the suggestion by some investigations that the animal suffers excessive pain and that this aspect should take precedence over the wishes of the religious communities involved (op.cit.: 49).

Among the Muslim leadership we find that the discussion of prior stunning ranges in a continuum from acceptance to complete denial. The Islamic Cultural Centre in Copenhagen and the Muslim World League have approved stunning in an agreement with the Danish Livestock and Meat Board.[17] The rest of the imams whom I interviewed expressed harsh opposition to this approval.[18] The commissions mentioned are aware of these conflicting standpoints and also note that from the point of view of the *Jewish* community meat from these animals is not regarded as *kosher*.

Islamic interests and the multi-cultural society imagined

As discourses and domains of action connected to Islamic religious interests show, Danish society is in the process of a complex, often contradictory discussion involving new social initiatives in the inclusion of a growing Muslim minority. The borderline of an arena which has generally been seen as belonging to the private sphere, has been crossed.

It is important to recognise that many Danish public institutions are based on decentral ruling and this emphasizes the importance of dialogue between institution and user/client. This has a number of consequences including the fact that religious interests can be more easily met on a positive footing within some institutions rather than others. The degree of readiness can vary therefore from institution to institution. Despite the heralding of the value of dialogue we find a relatively uniform (negative) attitude towards Islamic values articulated. The *symbolic violence* (Bourdieu 1977) is based on a blindness towards seeing the institutional strategies as being cultural. Danish values are so to speak, seen as universal. The conflicts arising in the relationship between public institution and Muslim client are accordingly seen as conflicts between modernity and traditionalism.

From my presentation of the discourse it can be seen that while Islam might be met with tolerance, it is also simultaneously met with unease. Islam is treated as a foreign religion, not as yet integrated into, or rooted in the social and cultural life of the nation.

The relationship between the State and Islam is being re-formed. At the same time, Islamic religious communities are being given more social space. These things happen simultaneously with the continuous changes in the distinction and shape of the relationship between the *system world* and the life world.

The historically based social conditions which have placed the Muslim minority on the cultural periphery and left them without hegemonic or symbolic power provide a special dynamic to *life world* processes and gives substance to an *Islamic social structure*.

From the point of view of a large proportion of the Muslim minority the Islamic institutions are regarded as a defense of their cultural autonomy; a counter pole to the fragmentation of social life which emanates from the *system world*. It is possible to suggest that the *system world*, through the State authorities and public institutions represents a hegemonic discourse and that this constitutes a form of symbolic violence vis a vis the Muslim minorities. But if this is so then they in turn respond in the form of a *community of interpretation* (Said 1981), or an *imagined community* (Andersen 1991) created through the Islamic institutions.

A Muslim identity, or Muslim cultural identification in Western European modernity can be understood as being created in an asymmetrical communicative relation involving changes in the relationship between the *system world* and *life world*. As Benedict Andersen (op.cit.) and others have stated, identity is not something inherited, but remembered; something remembered from the present time and not from the past - it has a narrative character with a reversed genealogy.

The question here is not whether Muslims should behave in one way and only in one way, the important issue is that it is possible for individuals to understand their lives within a given narrative unity and use this as the basis for a collective perceived identity. We can also go further and say that in this process, since identity is formed from a particular social position, people may accentuate or enhance certain characteristics which they possess.

I would like to paraphrase Appiah (1994: 161): If to be a Turk, an Arab, or a Pakistani is registered as being a Muslim, which in turn implies a refusal to assimilate according to European norms, it therefore follows that to be a Muslim in such a culturist or racist based society you have to deal constantly with assaults on your dignity. It would not be sufficient for you to insist on being treated with equal dignity *in spite* of being a Muslim, because to demand that would imply acquiescence; that being a Muslim was to some extent undignified. The strategy therefore must be the demand to be respected *as a Muslim*.

I have sketched out the way in which religious rights for Muslims are articulated within Danish society. I have shown the ways in which national authorities and institutions have responded to the symbolism and expression of religious affiliation. But it is also of equal importance to examine how the situation is articulated by the Muslim minority. It is in this light that the relationship between the State and Islam holds an important symbolic meaning which transgresses the narrow formal boundaries as defined by the State administration. The democratic problem is inscribed in the differences whose principle character lies in the gap between the Islamic discourse and the discourse expressed by the institutional public.

There is no reason to believe that Danish society cannot also meet and integrate the religious interests of Muslims as part of a democratic reform of the religious system. How these isolated issues are tackled will be of central importance as it might well play a role in how social and economic marginalization is represented in the political language of the Muslim minorities. Social and economic marginalization today are to a large extent interpreted by the Islamic leaders as confirmation of the marginalization of Islam. Knowing that 'cultural relativism' is only possible in theory and not in practise the task is therefore to develop models for negotiating the possible.

Notes

[1]   This paper is based on data from my research project *Muslim minorities and democracy in Western Europe (EU). Limits of Religious Freedom - The relationship between State and Islam.* The project is being carried out at Third World Information, Aarhus, and is being financed by the Danish Research Council for Humanities.

[2]   This number does not include the 18.000 refugees from Bosnia-Hercegovina. Within the first half of this year the first 2000 of these have at last been granted political asylum.

[3]   We have 9 such *recognized* religious communities of which the Jewish community is the only non-Christian one.

[4]   The *Folkeskole* is the responsibility of the local city council which are free to delegate certain tasks to the school councils. The majority of the members of these school councils are parents elected by the parents at the school in question. The school leader is the administrative and pedagogical leader of the school and is responsible before the city council and the school council (Lov om Folkeskolen 1993).

[5]   In many areas private schooling is in fact a real alternative to public schools. According to the Ministry of Education some 15% of Danish pupils today attend private schools which in turn receive 85% of their expenses from state funding.

[6]   The term *Islamic* can of course be debated. In this connection it is used to distinguish the schools established by different new ethnic minorities from the Muslim (sic!) Middle East. These schools are in any case distinct from other private school in that they all include Islamic education in their curriculum, in one way or another.

[7]   If we look at the absolute number of Islamic schools, Denmark comes in as number 2 behind the Netherlands which by 1995 has 29 publicly supported Islamic schools (according to an editorial comment by P.S. van Koningsveld & W.A.R. Shadid).

[8] These administrators are not expressing any official position of the Ministry and there has as yet been no action taken against these schools.

[9] Theoretically, it is actually possible not to learn about Islam in school. Much criticism and research (e.g J.Bæk Simonsen et.al 1994) has been levelled at the type of material employed by teachers in dealing with Islam. The widespread use of newspaper articles for example which directs attention towards political events rather than towards the ethics, religious experiences and dimensions involved. Since however, there is no state authorized material for such lessons, the choice has been left up to the teacher

[10] My contact with this consultant was in the spring of 1995.

[11] The data referred to is based on interviews with school leaders from 15 schools where over 50% of the pupils were understood to be of Muslim origin.

[12] This view is confirmed in an analysis of minorities and "the national idea" in the Danish primary school. Jette Kofoed (1994) concludes that minority children are met on the one hand with a continuing demand to behave "Danish", while on the other are constantly reminded that they will never really be Danes. This means that they are not given a both-and choice with regard to simultaneous identification with their parents and an imagined Danish background, or even an either-or choice concerning the construction of social identity but on the contrary are placed in a neither-nor situation.

[13] These decisions are not taken by the Directors of the hospitals but by the local and regional councils responsible for the health-system.

[14] Denmark has signed the European Council's standard minimum rules for the treatmentof prisoners that guarantee these rights to be universally understood (Europarådet 1987: pgf. 46-27).

[15] Mutual relations in the labour market are regulated by the independent conclusions of collective agreements between the representatives of the two parties in the labour market and *not* by law.

[16] The problems are primarily; the wish for a *total* physical and enclosed separation; the geographical orientation of the body towards the *qibla*; the understanding of eternal grave peace; ensuring that no one steps on the grave; the Danish demand for a coffin to be used; the widespread wish among Muslims to be able to take an active part in closing the grave in order to obtain religious credit.

[17] The agreement reads: "In order to comply with the Danish legislations of slaughtering the Islamic Cultural Center and the Muslim World League accept that stunning of the animals to be slaughtered can take place by the so-called 'Cash Knocker'".

[18] This also holds true for the Turkish imams interviewed. My interviews with these imams were held prior to a fatwa issued by Diyanet Isleri Baskanligi. This fatwa, which to my knowledge was issued at the occasion of Kurban Bayram in 1995, states that "stunning the animal using electric shock during slaughtering in order that the animal should not suffer does not invalidate the sacrifice... unless the animal dies from the electric shock", assuming that the general (Islamic) procedure is followed (Letter from Diyanet to the author, september 1995). It seems obvious that this fatwa was issued as a result of inquiries from the Turkish diaspora as it would have no significance in the Turkish national context. It seems also to be obvious that the imams in general have not been informed of this position; e.g the social councillor at the Turkish embassy in Copenhagen responsible for the Turkish State imams was not aware of it, but advised me to direct my inquiry to Diyanet.

12

The Establishment of
Islamic Schools

A Controversial Phenomenon in Three European Countries

Claire Dwyer & Astrid Meyer

During the 1980s a new phenomenon emerged in various European countries: the call for state-funded Islamic schools. The demand to institutionalise Islamic schools can be seen as a continuation of the process by which a variety of Islamic institutions have been established in the last decades including mosques, circumcision, Islamic religious education, cemeteries and *halal* butchers. If in some cases such institutionalization has passed almost unmarked, in many cases initiatives have depended on the acceptance of the receiving society. This has been particularly the case when initiatives need the financial support of the authorities, or represent a challenge to existing legal precedents. Thus it can be argued that the form the process of institutionalization of Islam in each European country takes, depends not only on the initiatives of the Muslims involved, but also on the response of the receiving society. This point is stressed in a recent comparison of the process of 'recognition' of Islam in three European countries (see Rath, Groenendijk & Penninx 1991). Rath *et al.* stress that two interdependent factors play a decisive role in the process of institutionalization: first political decision-making, culminating in specific legislation and regulations, and secondly ideological assumptions about the place of Muslims in society. They recognise that the institutionalization of Islam in Europe is taking place in different ways in each country in response to the existing legislation which evolved as a result of the political decision-making process in an earlier historical phase. In practical terms legal systems provide a structure for political and ideological processes since "people, including both indigenous population and migrants, tend to create a pattern of demands and desires within the possibilities (and impossibilities) allowed by the law" (Rath *et al.* 1991: 103). On the other hand they argue that legislation and regulation are not unequivocal, and allow scope for different interpretations. Thus ideological assumptions exert a major influence on the political decision-making process and consequently on the way in which social resources are distributed within the nation-state. This is particularly the case when the existing legislation is less explicit.

In this paper we apply these assertions to the institutionalization of state-funded Islamic schools in the UK, the Netherlands and Belgium. The situation concerning state-funded Islamic schools in these countries is rather different: in the UK none of the attempts to gain state-funding have so far been successful; in the Netherlands 29 state-funded Islamic schools are functioning, while in Belgium only one such school is recognised and receives state-funding. A comparison of the institutionalization process is made by focusing on the political decision-making process at both the national and the local level in each country, and by examining the ideological assumptions about Muslims embedded in the debates surrounding this decision-making. Our approach does not imply that the role which Muslims play in the process of institutionalization is not important or does not influence this process, on the contrary. However, this is not the issue we want to address here. We limit the scope of this paper to the responses of the receiving society to the process of institutionalization and in particular to the responses of the authorities involved.

The position of Islam: a comparison between the UK, the Netherlands and Belgium

Unlike some other European countries there is no legal framework for recognition of religious communities in the UK. Thus many of the older religious communities operate under legal provisions which are particular to each church, there is no general religious framework. The Church of England has established status with the monarch as the head of the Church and representation for Anglican Church leaders in the House of Lords. Other Churches are governed by their own legislation passed by the House of Commons. Thus while some religious leaders, including Catholic Bishops and the Chief Rabbi are accorded seats in the House of Lords this is on an individual basis and such rights are not accorded automatically. As Nielsen (1992: 43) suggests "the traditional religious communities, including the main churches and the Jewish community, have historical privileges" although these are largely to do with status rather than actual material advantages. Most Muslim organizations and mosques within the UK operate under the law which regulates charitable organizations. Since there is no formal recognition of the position of Islam within the UK the recognition of Muslim rights has tended to be established on a piecemeal basis within particular areas. Although there has also been an increasing interest from the government in the establishment of a representative Muslim Council with whom they could negotiate, such a council is difficult to establish given the heterogeneity of the British Muslim population.[1] The attempt to gain state-funded Islamic schools is a particular issue over which British Muslims have attempted to gain equality with other religious groups, which has involved negotiation both at the local and the national level.

In the Netherlands and Belgium there is no established church. The relation between state and religion in both countries is based largely on similar principles. In both countries the freedom of religion and the separation of Church from State are embedded in the Constitution. However, there is an important difference in the juridical recognition of religious denominations. Belgian legislation is characterised by a formal recognition of religious denominations. This recognition has a number of (mainly financial) advantages for the denominations involved (Leman, Renaerts & Van den Bulck 1992a: 47). In 1974 Islam was formally recognised and thus in theory equated with the Catholic, Protestant and Jewish denominations. In practice the position of Islam in Belgium is far from equal with other recognised denominations. Due to the absence of a representative council of the Muslim community in Belgium,[2] facilities which have been realised for other denominations such as the payment of salaries of religious functionaries and partial grants for the purchase or building of places of worship, have not yet been realised for Muslims (Janssen 1993: 35). The recognition of Islam however, has had a great impact on the development of Islamic religious education in schools established by the government, which will be discussed later.

In the Netherlands there is no such thing as the formal recognition of churches or religious communities and thus also not of Islam. There can however be a *de facto* recognition in the form of piecemeal decisions on specific areas, as in the UK. Here the principle of equality (article 1 of the Dutch Constitution) plays an important role, since it implies that facilities which are offered to Christian denominations cannot be denied to other religious groups. This also implies equal treatment in the sphere of education.

Although there are differences in the juridical position of Islam in general, the legislation in both the UK, the Netherlands and in Belgium offers possibilities, in theory at least, for the establishment of state-funded Islamic schools. We will now give a brief account of the existing legislation concerning the establishment of denominational schools and of the process of institutionalization of Islam in the sphere of education in the three countries involved.

Islam and education in the UK

The 1944 Education Act established the present educational system within the UK. This act recognised a division between state-funded schools and private or independent schools. The latter schools, which account for the education of 8% of children in England and Wales are run by religious or private foundations which have charitable status. These schools are registered and subject to government inspection. Within the state-funded sector of education there are two categories of schools: non-denominational schools and religious schools. These religious schools, known as voluntary-aided schools, are funded primarily by the state although they must find some additional funding for capital costs. These religious schools, which are predominantly Christian but include a small number of Jewish schools represented a compromise in the 1944 Education Act to accommodate the religious authorities (and other private foundations) who had previously been the main providers of education (Nielsen 1992: 53).

The majority of Muslim children in the UK are educated within state-funded schools, either denominational or non-denominational. Within these schools Muslim parents have sought to ensure that their concerns are met by campaigning to provide places for religious observance, provision of *halal* meat, availability of single-sex physical education and permission for girls to wear appropriate dress, including the headscarf. Despite some well-publicised cases[3] these issues have been largely resolved at the local level (for example see Joly 1995). However, perhaps two of the most significant concerns that parents have raised are the provision of single-sex education of girls and the nature of religious education and worship within schools.

The existence of single-sex education within the UK is a significant difference between the UK and the Netherlands and some Muslim parents have been concerned to ensure that single-sex schools are available for their children.[4] This has been one concern that has prompted some parents to support Islamic schools, particularly for girls of secondary school age. Religious education and worship has emerged as a key issue for parents with the passing of a second Education Act in 1988. This Act reiterated that both religious education and "a daily act of collective worship" should be compulsory in all schools. This legislation has led to some concern among Muslim leaders and parents since the Education Act stated that the content of religious education and the nature of religious worship should be "predominantly Christian" in nature. A number of Muslim organizations have been concerned to inform parents of their right to organise alternative religious worship for their children (Sarwar 1994) as well as seeking to clarify the requirements for religious education when the majority of children within a school are not Christian.[5]

Nevertheless, the passing of the 1988 Education Act was to cause concern among many Muslims that their needs were not recognised within the existing legislation and to encourage support for Islamic schools which would provide a basis in Islamic religious education. Thus for some Muslim parents the provision of single sex education has been a motive for seeking an Islamic education for their children, for others it has been a desire for a school which provides Islamic religious education. There has also been concern about the quality of education and the alleged "under-a-chievement" of Muslim children within existing schools.[6] One response has been to suggest that Muslim children will have higher levels of achievement if they are educated in schools which reflect their cultural and religious backgrounds.

There are two options for Muslim parents who require an Islamic education for their children. They can choose a private Islamic school, which is not state-funded, and pay for their children to be privately educated. There are approximately 30 private Islamic schools in the UK which have been established by a variety of different Muslim organizations and they provide for the educational needs of perhaps 1% of the 500,000 Muslim pupils in the UK. Although there are a few well-funded private schools, such as the prestigious King Fahd Academy in Regents Park (London), the majority of the remainder are small schools which are not well financed. The second possibility is to establish state-funded Islamic schools following the same models as Christian and Jewish voluntary-aided denominational schools. This is the possibility which has been explored by several schools recently which have sought to obtain state--funding for existing private Islamic schools. Although there is no theoretical impediment within the law to such schools being established the attempts by Islamic schools to gain such recognition and obtain state-funding have been unsuccessful.

In the section which follows we outline briefly two recent attempts to obtain state-funding by the Islamia Primary School in Brent, London and by Feversham College, Bradford.

Attempts to gain state-funded Islamic schools within the UK
Islamia School, Brent

The Islamia School in Brent, north-west London, is a primary school which was founded in 1982 by a private foundation, the Islamia Schools Trust. The school first applied for state-funding in 1986 but its application was turned down on the grounds that the school, housed in a two-storey Victorian mansion, was too small to be viable. Attempts to expand the school, via extension and the purchase of adjacent vacant school buildings, were blocked by the Brent Planning Subcommittee, who were reluctant to support the school.

A further appeal to the Department of Education and Science in 1988 was rejected on the grounds that there were surplus places in neighbouring schools. Significant in this second rejection was the lack of backing from Brent Council (previously a coalition, now Labour controlled) which argued that an Islamic school was contrary to their policy of 'multicultural education'. The application for state-funding for the school was formally rejected by the Secretary of State for Education in May 1990. The school appealed for a judicial review and in May 1992 the High Court ruled that there was 'manifest unfairness' in the decision to reject the school. The decision was thus referred back once again to the Secretary of State for Education and in August 1993 the application was again refused on the grounds that surplus school places existed in other schools in the borough. This refusal was controversial for a number of reasons. First, the school was supported - at least, in principle - by the now Conservative controlled Local Education Authority. Secondly, the government had reprieved from closure another primary school in the borough despite it needing major capital expenditure. This school therefore contributed to the surplus places. Finally, the question of existing surplus places seemed spurious in the case of the Islamia school which was oversubscribed and had a long waiting list. This was particularly true since the question of surplus places had not previously been considered in the case of other voluntary-aided schools. The decision also appeared to contradict the government's policy, evident in the 1988 Education Act, of widening parental choice in education. The conclusion of the Islamia school's founder, Yusuf Islam, reflects the frustration of the campaigners: "It's an outrage. We have come to expect a great deal of injustice. We get the impression that the Government just does not want to see a Muslim school and is pursuing a policy of starving us of funds" (*The Times Educational Supplement* 27/8/93: 1).

The Secretary of State for Education denied that they had discriminated against the school and reiterated that government policy was not opposed to any denominational schools if they met the requirements and that the Islamia Schools Trust should apply to establish a state-funded school within an area where there were no surplus places available.

Islamia was seen as a test case for state-funded Islamic schools within the UK. It was recognised as a school which had excellent grounds for its application for state-funding although it had had difficulties in gaining local authority support. Certainly Brent was a particularly sensitive location for the establishment of the first Islamic school in the UK because of its high profile within the contested politics of multicultural education in the 1980s.[7] Brent Council had a publicly stated commitment to progressive multicultural education and thus the establishment of an Islamic school in Brent could have been regarded as an admission of failure. The Islamia Schools Trust is now exploring the possibility of either reapplying or establishing another school on a different site.

Feversham College, Bradford

In contrast, the second Islamic school which recently attempted to get state-funding enjoyed full support from the local authority. Feversham College is a Muslim girls' secondary school in Bradford which provides education for 280 girls and is run by the Muslim Association. The school has been well supported by the city council which offered the school new premises in September 1994 at a nominal rent. The school applied for state-funding in June 1994 with the full support of the Local Education Authority. In February 1995 this application was rejected. The reasons given for the rejection were: the accommodation of the school did not meet health and safety standards; the school did not meet the needs of the national curriculum in the teaching of technology and the management of the school was insufficiently developed to deliver the national curriculum. The Secretary of State for Education, Gillian Shepherd, stated that: "I am very much aware of the strong local demand for single-sex places for Muslim girls and the wide support for the school among the Bradford Community....Whilst I have had to reject this present application, I do not want to be seen as closing the door on this or any other Muslim school joining the state sector" (*The Independent* 17/2/95).

Supporters of the school were disappointed at the rejection and saw it as further evidence that Islamic schools were treated more harshly than other applicants for state-funding. They were concerned that no indication of concerns about safety standards were given on previous visits to the school, and that the application was rejected outright rather than offering the possibility for the school to work towards achieving the recommendations. The school intends to lodge another application as soon as possible after the points raised in the rejection have been remedied.

Both these cases illustrate the struggles of Muslim groups within the UK to establish state-funded Islamic schools on the same grounds as other denominational groups. Although these cases have proved unsuccessful there are likely to be continuing efforts from Muslim organizations to establish such schools and effectively to challenge the discrepancies within the existing legislation. It is likely that new applications for voluntary-aided status will be lodged in the future and those schools which have been rejected may reapply.

In addition several Muslim organizations are exploring the possibilities of alternative routes to gain state-funded Islamic schools. The 1988 Education Act created a new category of Grant-Maintained (GM) schools. Such schools are independent of Local Authority Management and are funded directly by state government. GM status could be obtained either by state schools choosing to 'opt out' of Local Authority Management or by existing independent schools choosing to 'opt in' to the state system. Thus it is possible that grant-maintained status could be an alternative route to state funding for Islamic schools. Initially routes which were explored were the possibility of existing state-schools 'opting out' to become Islamic schools. Cumper (1990: 386) discusses this option for a school in Birmingham. However, despite being a GM school which has a predominantly Muslim intake this school remains a non-denominational state school. More recently, several independent Islamic schools, including The al-Furqan school, (Birmingham) and the Islamic Academy (Leicester), are reported to be exploring the possibility of 'opting in' to become a GM School (*The Muslim News* 24/3/95). Yet this route remains to be tested as a means of gaining a state-funded Islamic school.

Muslim educationalists remain divided over the issue of grant-maintained schools (Knight & Hedegus 1994). Grant-maintained schools would exist outside the support of a Local Education Authority which have often been highly responsive to Muslim concerns. Thus, as Knight & Hegedus (1994: 7) argue an Islamic grant-maintained school might be more vulnerable than an Islamic voluntary aided school. Another concern is the political future of grant-maintained schools in the light of a change of government. Hence a number of Muslim educational groups are involved in discussions with the Labour Party (the party in Opposition) to gauge their potential support for public funding of Islamic schools.[8] It is clear that despite the current lack of success British Muslims remain committed to seeking ways in which the existing legislation can be challenged to create the possibilities for state-funded Islamic schools.

Islamic schools in the Netherlands

In the Netherlands parents have the constitutional right to arrange the education of their children on the basis of their own religion. Article 23 of the Dutch Constitution guarantees freedom of education and offers the possibility to establish denominational, including also Islamic, schools. Moreover the Constitution guarantees financial parity for denominational and non-confessional state schools. Every school is entitled to 100% state-funding when a number of conditions are met. These include a minimum number of pupils, qualified teachers, a prognosis that the school is viable and that it is following the Dutch curriculum.[9] If all conditions are met an application for a new school cannot in theory be rejected and state-funding should be granted.

As in the UK, various motives seem to have led Muslims to establish their own schools. Firstly the failure to have Islamic religious education realised in non-confessional state schools. In addition to a general religious education (*Kennis van Geestelijke Stromingen*), parents have the right to demand education in their own religion for a maximum of three hours per week as part of the school curriculum. The school is obliged to provide facilities and teachers are provided by the local religious community. Local authorities can choose to pay for the teaching but there is no legal obligation to do so. Regulation of religious education is not explicit and this has allowed local authorities a fair amount of leeway in terms of ideological and political manoeuvring (Rath & Meyer 1994). Additional demands can be posed by local authorities such as the condition that the lessons should be given in Dutch which is not stipulated in the legislation. This condition has served to obstruct the provision of Islamic religious education in various cities (Roovers & Van Esch 1987: 40-4; Shadid & Van Koningsveld 1990: 111). In the school year 1993-1994 Islamic religious education was only given in public schools in four Dutch cities: Apeldoorn, Rotterdam, Tiel and Ede (Karagül 1994: 110).

Other reasons given by campaigners for Islamic schools are the disappointing academic achievement of Muslim children in existing schools (i.e. the non-confessional state schools and Christian schools) and the fact that Muslim parents are rarely involved with their childrens school. Campaigners expect that Islamic schools will increase the participation of parents. Moreover they argue that such schools enable Muslim children to develop a positive sense of their own identity. As a boardmember of the Dutch Islamic Foundation for Education states: "For those children (=Muslim children authors) it is better to develop an identity of their own in their "own nest". Who they are, where they come from and why they are here. When they are 12, 13 they can enter into Dutch society more firmly and make a greater contribution than they do now" (Koolen 1989: 11).

Since the early 1980s Muslims have tried to establish state-funded Islamic schools (Landman 1992: 260-1). The first schools were established in Rotterdam and Eindhoven in 1988. From that year on the number of Islamic schools increased: in 1989 four new Islamic schools were opened, in 1991 20 Islamic schools were established, in 1993 the total number was 29. Since then no new Islamic schools have been realised. This is mainly due to new legislation, stipulating more stringent requirements for the establishment of new schools, which is intended to reduce the total number of schools in the future.[10] All Islamic schools in the Netherlands are primary schools. Although there have been some applications for secondary schools, no such schools have yet been established (Onderwijsraad 1994: 30).

Three of the Islamic schools in the Netherlands were the initiative of a national foundation, the Dutch Islamic Foundation for Education (ISNO), which promoted a 'liberal' type of Islam (Shadid & Van Koningsveld 1992: 165). The foundation was attached by statute to the Dutch Islamic Foundation (ISN), which controls a large number of Turkish-Islamic mosques and cooperates with the Turkish Directorate of Religious Affairs. In November 1993 the ISNO was disbanded. The three existing schools that were established by the ISNO are now administered by three independent foundations. The other 26 schools were established by several local Islamic organizations with various backgrounds.

The increase in the number of Islamic schools does not mean that the establishment of Islamic schools in the Netherlands is without controversy. Although the national government has stressed on various occasions that freedom of education also applies to Muslims,[11] a broad public and political debate took place about Islamic schools. Opinions about the desirability of such schools were strongly divided. Moreover in several cities where applications have been made for the establishment of Islamic schools the local authorities have reacted in a negative way. Often the arrival of these schools has been considered as an expression of distrust in existing schools (Sikkes 1989; Teunissen 1990). According to Shadid & Van Koningsveld (1989), who explored the attitude of several city councils, Islamic schools would probably never have come into existence without the constitutional freedom of education. Only by appealing to the existing legislation could campaigners overcome the paternalism shown by many city councils. We will now discuss in greater detail the situation in one Dutch city, Utrecht.

Islamic schools in Utrecht
A first attempt

The first attempt to establish an Islamic school in Utrecht was an initiative of the abovementioned Dutch Islamic Foundation for Education (ISNO). Their application, made in 1988, encountered considerable opposition from the city council. Particularly the Alderman for Education, in that period C. Pot, appeared to be a strong opponent of the establishment of the school in question. The school was not, in his opinion, an Islamic school, but a so-called 'nationality school', which would only cater for children of Turkish origin. Only members of D'66 (left-wing liberals) and CDA (Christian Democrats) voted for the application, the others followed the advice of the Alderman. Thus the application was rejected by a majority of the city council on two official grounds: firstly, the application did not meet the legal requirements since the foundation had not marked explicitly the area from which the school would receive its pupils; and secondly the school was perceived as a 'nationality school'. The existing legislation stipulates that such schools are not to be considered for state-funding.

Several legal procedures followed after the decision of the city council. First the ISNO appealed against the decision via the Provincial Executives of Utrecht who in 1989 rejected both arguments of the city council. The latter in turn appealed against this decision to the Council of State and the Crown. In 1992 the Crown decided in favour of the ISNO: the school in question was an Islamic school according to the Dutch legislation and not a 'nationality school' as the city council of Utrecht had argued. A year later, in 1993, the case was heard by the Council of State. They judged in April 1994 that the decision of the city council was not valid. In the meantime the ISNO decided to withdraw the application on the grounds that they did not want to hamper the initiative taken by the SIOU which had applied for the establishment of two Islamic schools in 1992 (see below). According to a spokesman of the former ISNO the continuation of the application for an ISNO-school in Utrecht could lead the local authorities to play the ISNO off against the SIOU. Nevertheless the ISNO is an important example because it demonstrates how campaigners have successfully appealed to the existing legislation.

The Aboe Da'oed school

In 1992 a local organization, the Utrecht Foundation for Islamic Education (SIOU),[12] made a new attempt to establish two Islamic primary schools. Long before the application was made boardmembers of the SIOU contacted the Department of Education of Utrecht and with the cooperation of several civil servants the application was formulated. In contrast to the ISNO-application, that of the SIOU was approved by the entire city council. This decision might have been influenced by the results of the various procedures concerning the ISNO-application, which made clear that it was not feasible to directly oppose the establishment of Islamic schools. Despite this it is evident from the minutes of the meeting of the Committee of Education of the city council that similar arguments against the establishment of Islamic schools were made as in 1988. The Alderman for Education, J. Van Lidth de Jeude who succeeded C. Pot, pointed out that nevertheless the application met all the requirements and thus should be granted. In theory the SIOU could open the two schools in August 1993 but a new law was enacted in July 1992 which demands, among other things, approval of the Ministry of Education and Science for the establishment of all new schools. Thus preparations for the schools were delayed for several months. On 16 April 1993 the board of the SIOU was invited to the Ministry. In a meeting they were told that approval would be given for the establishment of one school on the condition that the foundation withdraw the application for a second school. If not, the Ministry would refuse the establishment of both schools on the grounds that the required prognosis did not prove the viability of the schools, however figures for this argument were not supplied. The SIOU, fearing protracted juridical procedures, agreed with the condition of the Ministry and on 16 May 1993 approval was received for the establishment of one Islamic primary school. With the approval of the Ministry the SIOU expected no further problems. However now the Department of Education of Utrecht which initially had been very cooperative delayed the actual establishment of the school. They preferred to postpone the opening of the school for another year, which was not the wish of the SIOU. The allocation of accommodation for the school took several weeks. Thus it was only two weeks before opening that the SIOU could start preparations and in August 1993 the first and only state-funded Islamic school in Utrecht was established: the Aboe Da'oed school.

Islam and education in Belgium

As in the Netherlands freedom of education in Belgium is a constitutional right and offers the possibility to establish denominational schools. In order to be recognised and gain state-funding such schools have to meet a number of conditions, which are also very similar to those in the Netherlands.[13] In Belgium however denominational schools are not fully state-funded: accommodation for the school is not financed by the State.

The call for Islamic schools seems to be less strong in Belgium than in the UK and the Netherlands. According to Wagtendonk (1991: 160) this is due to the fact that Islamic religious education in Belgian state schools is provided on a large scale. In contrast to the Netherlands, in Belgian municipal and state schools religious education or ethics is obligatory and paid for by the government. Only recognised religions have the right to claim religious education in their religion. Islamic religious education became possible after the formal recognition of Islam in 1974. From 1975[14] the number of schools that offer Islamic religious education has increased immensely, although many matters, such as the education of teachers, inspection and a fixed curriculum, are not or only partly arranged.[15] Unlike in the UK and the Netherlands, in Belgium the right to have religious education, including Islamic religious education seems to be a generally accepted matter. Even some Catholic schools offer the possibility for Muslim pupils to follow this education.

However, the wish to establish Islamic schools seems to be based not only on the need for Islamic religious education. As in the UK and the Netherlands, Muslims in Belgium give various reasons to promote the establishment of an Islamic school. Firstly there is the wish to have their children educated in an "Islamic tradition" (Leman et al. 1992b: 63). Moreover the existing education in so called 'black schools' is seen as problematic. Parents hope an Islamic school will serve two goals: a stronger self identity and better educational standards.

So far only one recognised and state-funded Islamic school has been established: the Al Ghazalischool in Brussels. The founder of this (French) primary school is the Islamic and Cultural Centre (ICC) in Brussels, which is governed by diplomats from Muslim countries represented in Belgium and has a director who works in the name of the Muslim World League (Dassetto 1990: 15; Foblets 1991: 93). Since the 1960s the ICC has played an important role in the process of recognition of Islam in Belgium (Dassetto & Bastenier 1985; Tamarant & Omar 1990). Moreover in 1975 the Centre was appointed by the Ministers of Education to organise Islamic religious education in Belgium schools (Foblets 1991: 93). The privileged position of the ICC was soon to be criticised[16] and in 1990 the ICC has ceased to be in charge of the organization of Islamic religious education.[17] According to an ICC spokesman the establishment of the school in Brussels was one of the reasons why the Belgian government decided to withdraw the authority of the ICC to organise Islamic religious education.

Initially the ICC also had plans to start a Dutch Islamic school in Anvers, however, because of practical financial problems and the fear of "hostile reactions" this plan was abandoned. A spokesman of the ICC explained: "I think that it (=an Islamic school authors) will only increase the problems in Anvers, where the situation is already critical enough with the Flemish Block (..) It creates a sort of red cloth for the bull of racism. We also have to consider that, because increasing racism is, of course, also negative for us."

The arrival of the Al Ghazalischool in Brussels

An application for recognition and state-funding for the Al Ghazalischool was submitted in August 1989. This initiative of the ICC caused considerable political commotion. The application was submitted during a period of discussion about an eventual reduction of the total number of schools and a better distribution of immigrant children within existing Belgian schools. Moreover the initiative coincided with the efforts of the Royal Commissioner on Immigrant Policy to establish a representative body of Islam in Belgium. The ICC blocked the plans of the Royal Commissioner "since it would make a peaceful discussion about the place of Islam impossible" (Leman 1992: 12).

The arrival of an Islamic school in Brussels was made public in a short article in *Le Soir* on 24 August 1989. Although the Minister of (French) Education, Jean-Pierre Grafé, had from the beginning made it clear that the application of an Islamic school was to be treated the same way as any other application,[18] a fierce debate broke out after the announcement in *Le Soir*.[19] The discussion soon appeared to take on the character of a so called 'moral panic'.

A first political reaction came from the Secretary of State of Brussels and coordinator of immigrant policies, Vic Anciaux. Anciaux recognised the right to establish Islamic schools but argued such schools would be an obstacle for the "pursued integration". In a letter Anciaux tried to persuade the director of the ICC to abandon the establishment of an Islamic school.[20] The Royal Commissioner on Immigration Policy, Paula D'Hondt, stated in a radio programme that she shared the view of Anciaux. She wondered if it was reasonable for a religious leader, who had only been in Belgium a few months, who did not speak Dutch or French and was barely familiar with the Belgian situation, to take such an initiative.[21]

In the beginning of September the director of the ICC stated that the establishment of the school would not be postponed. On 3 September 1989 the matter was discussed in the government of Brussels. It was decided not to interfere in the establishment of the Islamic school, but to follow the matter closely.[22] However, the same evening Charles Picqué, president of the regional government of Brussels and mayor of Sint-Gillis, stated in a radio programme that he would resist the establishment of the school "by all means".[23]

While the school started in the buildings of the ICC in the Jubelpark in Brussels, other politicians intervened in the discussion. The (Flemish) Socialist Party supported the arrival of the Al Ghazalischool, but also pleaded for a discussion between Belgian and Islamic representatives.[24] The chairman of the *Christelijke Volkspartij* (Christian people's party) on the contrary strongly opposed the arrival of the school. He stated that his party was preparing a juridical report aimed at preventing the establishment of Islamic schools.[25] The extreme right-wing Flemish party, Vlaams Blok, argued that the recognition of Islam had to be withdrawn.[26]

By the end of October the attention of the press for the Islamic school in the Jubelpark had declined. Meanwhile after several visits of the education inspector the Al Ghazalischool was recognised and gained state-funding.

Political debates: a comparison

In the UK, the Netherlands and in Belgium the establishment of state-funded Islamic schools, or attempts to gain such schools have led to considerable political debate. Here we trace the variety of arguments that have been used in these debates in the three countries involved.

Arguments which have been expressed when the right to establish Islamic schools is at stake are the freedom of education and the principle of equality. The latter implies that all religious groups, including Muslims, should be treated equally and have the same rights. In the Netherlands these arguments were stated by the Secretary of State for Education, N.J. Ginjaar-Maas, in a note which followed the debate about the first Dutch Islamic schools. The principle of equality has also been used in Utrecht. For D'66 (left-wing liberals) this principle was a decisive factor in their decision about the ISNO-application. They found themselves compelled to support the ISNO-schools on the grounds of legal equality but were opposed to Islamic schools in principle. Similarly in the UK the Education Secretary, Gillian Shepherd, has been careful in her rejection of the most recent application to acknowledge the potential for Muslim schools. Likewise the opposition party, the Labour Party, although divided on the question of voluntary-aided Islamic schools, acknowledged that: "The right to such status (=voluntary-aided status authors) already exists in law and it has been exercised and enjoyed in practice by Anglicans, and Roman Catholics. In equity, that right can not be denied to others" (*Labour Party Education Policy Review* 1990: 49). This principle of equality was also consistently used by the campaigners for Islamic schools themselves. Yusuf Islam, the leader of the Islamia Schools Trust in Brent argues: "We want our children to be brought up with a basic knowledge of Islam while at the same time receiving a standard education and enjoying a facility which has been enjoyed by Christians and Jews for forty years" (*The Times Educational Supplement* 30/8/85: 5).

In Belgium however, the arrival of the Al Ghazalischool was for some politicians reason to question the freedom of education. Jaak Gabriëls, chairman of the *Volksunie* for example wanted to prevent the establishment of the school "at any price", because: "Islamic schools could lead to a disintegration which belongs to a fundamentalistic tenor of Islam. That can not be the intention of our tolerance, even if the constitution guarantees the free choice of education, because that article was not written with such an intention. If it (=revision of the constitution) is possible, I would indeed promote it" (*HUMO* 13/9/89). According to Gabriëls Islamic schools can not be compared to schools of other denominations and therefore the principle of equality would not apply to Muslims. The chairman of the *Christelijke Volkspartij* (Christian people's party) in Belgium holds a similar opinion. He thinks that the comparison with Christian or Jewish schools can not be made since those schools do not question "the fundamental rights and liberties of the Belgium society" (*Het Laatste Nieuws* 12/9/89). Nevertheless in general the right to establish Islamic schools is also acknowledged in Belgium. The majority of the debate about Islamic schools however is not about the right to establish such schools but about their desirability.

Central to the debates in the three countries is the complex question of integration, a term which is contested and has different meanings in different contexts.[27] Debate about this term has also been central to earlier discussions about multicultural education in all three countries. Thus the debate about Islamic schools fed into already contested discussions about the most appropriate ways in which the perceived under-achievement of so called 'ethnic minority' children could be alleviated.

Opponents have argued that Islamic schools will not aid integration. They expect that Islamic schools will be predominantly, if not exclusively, attended by immigrant children. For them the primary way in which integration can be achieved is the 'integrated' school. For example, Thea de Wit, city councillor for D'66 (left-wing liberals) in Utrecht argued: "Strictly speaking we are not really supporters of sending children to school separately. And especially with the question of immigrant children and their links with Dutch society it is to be recommended to place all children in one school (=non-confessional public school), in this way they will get to know each other and learn to respect each other's culture." A similar argument was expressed in Belgium by Secretary of State of Brussels, Vic Anciaux: "It is impossible to integrate children, who are educated in a totally isolated environment, in a harmonic society. I opt for an education of immigrant children within our schools" (*Het Laatste Nieuws* 18/9/89). In both statements 'Muslims' are constructed as 'immigrants' who should integrate in the Dutch and Belgian society via existing schools and not via Islamic schools. Likewise the leader of the ruling Labour Group of Brent Council, Nitin Parshotam argued: "The Council sees itself as the enabling mechanism through which all the aspirations of the different groups of the local community can be met ... at present we have a commitment to "multifaith" schools" (*The Times Educational Supplement* 17/6/88: 9). In statements such as these 'integration' is seen as only possible if children of different cultural and religious backgrounds are able to mix together at school. This understanding of 'integration' can be seen as consistent with the principle of multicultural education where the multicultural school becomes the site of the creation of a multicultural society.[28]

Supporters of Islamic schools however offer a different understanding of the ways in which 'integration' might occur by stressing the role of the Islamic school in providing a strong sense of identity. Thus J.F. Huibers, Member of Parliament for the CDA (Christian Democrats) in the Netherlands, thinks Islamic schools will promote integration, because: "There children have the space to hold on to and to develop their own identity. That is crucial for their development. The culture at home corresponds with the one at school and that is good for the motivation to learn" -

(*Nieuwsblad Migranten* 19/6/92: 8). Often parallels are drawn with the experiences of other minority religious groups who have used religious schools as a means to integration. For example in the UK, the Catholic bishop of Leeds, David Konstant, expressed support for Islamic schools at a conference on education: "The experience of my own community (which has been a persecuted minority) is that having our own school within the state system helped us to move out of our initial isolation so as to become more confident and self-assured. The effect of the separate schools has been integration not divisiveness" (*The Times Educational Supplement* 4/1/91: 3).

Likewise in the Netherlands the Christian Democrats have expressed support for Islamic schools. In Belgium such a statement is only heard from MP Mieke Vogels from Agalev (left wing) who thinks that individuals might integrate better in Belgian society if "they first collectively sought and found their identity". In Belgium the dominant idea is that the wish to develop the own identity is sufficiently met by the Islamic religious education on state schools.

The ideological construction of 'Muslims' can have different expressions. While it is sometimes based primarily on the assumption that Muslims are newcomers to a society it can also be part of a wider discourse which suggests a particular ideological construction of Islam. This construction of Islam suggests that Islam is antithetical to 'Western' values. The views cited above by Gabriëls provide an example of such a position and similar statements about Islam were also evident within debates about Islamic schools in the UK and the Netherlands which expressed concern about the standard of teaching, the position of women and the threat of 'fundamentalism' (see Roosblad 1992, Parekh 1990). The following statement from the former Alderman of Education in Utrecht, C. Pot, who was a key opponent of the establishment of the ISNO-school in Utrecht in 1988, comes in response to the question as to whether he fears the creation of "ghettos of foreigners" which could become the source of Islamic fundamentalism: "I wouldn't know, but I certainly won't exclude it. At the moment this thinking does not play an important role, but if those Muslims are pushed into isolation by giving them their own schools and organizations then it is quite possible" (Güler & Van der Heijden 1990: 72). Such expressions of the dangers of fundamentalism were also evident in the popular British press which often considered the question of Islamic state-funded schools in the context of other issues like the Rushdie Affair.[29] Within the UK the negative ideological construction of Islam was particularly centred on the alleged position of women within Islam, reflecting the fact that many Islamic schools which might potentially apply for state-funding were girls schools. Thus a member of the Blackburn Labour Party, Pat Guinan, opposed the Party's Education Policy which gave cautious support for state-funded Islamic schools arguing that Islamic education: "is an education whose basic purpose is to produce women prepared for docile and devout acceptance of a reactionary family and social structure where women are possessions" (*The Guardian* 19/7/89: 4).

From the above illustration of the arguments used in the debates it is clear that there are several ways in which 'Muslims' are ideologically represented. Sometimes they are perceived as equivalent to other religious groups, on other occasions however Muslims are constructed as 'immigrants', 'ethnic minorities' or 'fundamentalists'. It is our contention that these constructions play a part in the way in which the legislation is operated to accommodate Muslim needs. What is also evident from this account is that although the process of institutionalization of Islamic schools in the three countries discussed has had different outcomes there are also many similarities in terms of the types of arguments that were used in the debates.

Conclusion

Attempts to establish Islamic state-funded schools have been made in the UK, in the Netherlands and in Belgium during the last decade. Although the existing legislation in each country makes the establishment of such schools possible, at least in principle, the results of these attempts have been quite different.

In the UK so far none of the attempts to gain state-funded Islamic schools have been successful; in the Netherlands 29 schools have opened in a relatively short period; in Belgium only one Islamic school has been recognised and receives state-funding. In the account that we have given above we have outlined the processes and debates surrounding the attempts to establish some of these schools. We have illustrated that, despite differences in the existence of state-funded Islamic schools in each country, debates about such schools have been very similar. In this final section we offer some tentative suggestions as to how the differences between the three countries in terms of the establishment of Islamic schools might be explained.

In the Netherlands the principle of equality is enshrined in the first principle of the Constitution and enables Muslims to demand the same rights as other religious groups, including the right to establish Islamic schools. The principle of equality and the freedom of education seems to have favoured the establishment of Islamic schools. Moreover the specific legislation concerning the establishment of new schools is quite explicit and seems to leave little space to local authorities for political manoeuvring.

The same arguments could be made about the legislation in Belgium. In Belgium however the recognition of Islam in 1974 seems to influence - although not directly - the establishment of Islamic schools. Recognition of Islam made Islamic religious education in state schools possible. The fact that this education has been realised on a large scale seems not only to make the call for Islamic schools less strong than in the UK and the Netherlands, it also influences the political climate. The dominant political view in Belgium is that the religious needs of Muslims are sufficiently met by the Islamic religious education organised in state schools and so the establishment of Islamic schools is 'unnecessary'. In contrast to Islamic religious education this form of institutionalization evokes strong resistance, stronger than in the Dutch case. Although the Belgian Constitution also stipulates the principle of equality, this principle seems to have less impact in Belgium than in the Netherlands. The establishment of the Al Ghazalischool in Brussels was for some even reason to question the constitution.

The British case is more controversial. Since there is no constitutional recognition of Islam or of the right to freedom of education, British Muslims find that their case for equality is less strong legally then might be the case in Belgium or the Netherlands. However, it has been determined in principle that denominational schools can be established for other religious groups as well as Christians and Jews and the Secretary of State for Education has been at pains to emphasise this possibility. It might be considered that the principal barrier to the establishment of Islamic state-funded schools in the UK remains the established Church, particularly when the UK is compared to Belgium or the Netherlands. It has been argued that the ideological role of the established Church has been strengthened, particularly in relation to education, with the incorporation of legislation about religious education and religious worship in the 1988 Education Act (Sahgal & Yuval-Davis 1992: 11). However, at the same time, individual members of the established Church, and other religious groups, have been prominent in supporting the rights of Muslims to enjoy comparable rights, as we illustrate in this article, and thus the established Church may, in practice, have a supportive role in the recognition of Muslims in the UK (Modood 1994). Nevertheless, the existence of an established Church remains an important ideological force which can be evoked in debates about the recognition of minority religious groups within the UK. Since Muslims do not have recognised rights within the British state as a religious group they can only gain institutional rights through a piecemeal challenging of existing legislation.

There are also additional differences within the British educational system which may have militated against Islamic schools being established more easily in the UK than in other European countries such as the Netherlands or Belgium. The existence of independent schools means that there has always existed an alternative to state-schools for Muslim parents to choose an Islamic education for their children, provided that they can afford it. The situation has also been complicated in the UK by radical changes in the education legislation since 1988 which has prompted a range of different opportunities for state-funded Islamic schools. The contradiction inherent within this changing policy has been the government's avowed commitment to increasing parental choice in education and yet their lack of support for Islamic schools which are community run and funded and clearly have strong parental support.

While concluding that there are differences in terms of the legislative possibilities which allow the establishment of state-funded Islamic schools in the three countries we have considered, we also contend that there are many similarities. In all three countries there has been considerable opposition to the establishment of Islamic state-funded schools and attempts to establish them have given rise to political debate. From our account of these debates it is clear that 'Muslims' are not only represented as a religious group which should be treated on the same footing as other denominations. On the contrary other representations, militating against the establishment of Islamic schools, seem to dominate the debate. Thus while the establishment of state-funded Islamic schools seems to depend upon the existing legislation, it is also strongly influenced by the ideological representations of 'Muslims' which are embedded within the political decision-making process.

Notes

[1] This issue was first mooted during the 'Rushdie Affair' but is a continuing component of the government's relationship with British Muslim representatives.

[2] For a fuller discussion of the problems concerning the establishment of a representative council see Blaise & De Coorebyter 1990, Foblets 1991; see also the contributions of Leman & Renaerts and Michot in this volume.

[3] For example, girls in Altricham Grammar School for Girls were refused the right to wear a headscarf to school (*The Times* 24/1/90: 1).

[4] However, a number of studies have also emphasized that this is not a concern for all Muslim parents (see Shaw 1988: 141; Joly 1986).

[5] A Muslim working party is involved in the preparation for an agreed syllabus for religious education (*Q-News* 28 January 1994).

[6] This issue was debated at the Conference of the National Muslim Educational Council [July 1993] and at the Conference of the Association of Muslim Schools [February 1994]. See also *Countering Under-Achievement among Muslim Children in the state-sector*, Discussion paper of the British Muslim Parliament, January 1993.

[7] See Dwyer 1993.

[8] See *The Muslim News* 24/3/95.

[9] Wet van 2 juli 1981, houdende Wet op het Basisonderwijs, *Stb.* 1981, 468; Wet van 1 juli 1992, houdende een tijdelijke regeling voor de bekostiging van nieuwe basisscholen voorafgaand aan een algehele wijziging van het stelsel van stichtings- en opheffingsnormen in het basisonderwijs (Tijdelijke wet bekostiging nieuwe basisscholen), *Stb.* 1992, 365; Wet van 15 december 1993, houdende wijziging van het stelsel van stichtingsnormen en opheffingsnormen in de Wet op het Basisonderwijs, *Stb.* 1993, 716.

[10] See note 9.

[11] See TK 1988-1989, 21 110, nr. 1; Memorie van Toelichting bij Wet op het Basisonderwijs, TK 1976-1977, 14 428, nrs. 1-4.

[12] The board of the SIOU consists of members of Moroccan, Turkish and Surinamese backgrounds.

[13] Schoolpactwet van 29 mei 1959 tot wijziging van sommige bepalingen in de onderwijswetgeving, *Belgisch Staatsblad* 19 juni 1959.

[14] In that year the Ministers of Education, Humblet (French) and De Croo (Dutch) sent a letter to all heads of schools in which they requested them to offer Islamic religious education to Muslim children if their parents wished such education (Blaise & De Coorebyter 1990: 39-40). A new law which made Islamic religious education formal

was enacted three years later (Wet van 20 februari 1978 houdende wijziging van artikel 8 van de Wet van 29 mei 1959 met betrekking tot het Schoolpact, *Belgisch Staatsblad* 11 maart 1978).

[15] Leman et al. 1992b: 60; *Limburgs Mozaiek*, 1995 4(33): 2-4.

[16] Opposition came from parts of the Muslim community (see Dassetto & Bastenier 1985: 15-17; Shadid & Van Koningsveld 1995: 52) and some local authorities. In 1986 two municipalities in Brussels, Schaarbeek and St. Gillis, refused to organize Islamic religious education in their schools. They questioned the legitimacy and the unofficial recognition of the ICC by the Belgium government (Blaise & De Coorebyter 1990: 15).

[17] In 1990 the Belgium government installed a Provisional Council of Wise Men to advise the government on the establishment of a representative organ for Islam. On the advice of the Provisional Council a Technical Committee was recognized for the organization of Islamic religious education in state schools (KCM 1993: 171-2).

[18] *Het Volk De Nieuwe Gids* 25/08/1989.

[19] For a general outline of the political discussion on the Al Ghazalischool see Blaise & De Coorebyter 1990.

[20] *Het Belang van Limburg & Het Volk* 29/08/1989.

[21] Het Nieuwsblad 30/08/1989.

[22] Het Laatste Nieuws 05/09/1989.

[23] *De Standaard* 08/09/1989.

[24] *Het Volk De Nieuwe Gids* 12/09/1989.

[25] Het Laatste Nieuws 12/09/1989.

[26] *Het Belang van Limburg* 21/09/1989.

[27] For a fuller discussion of the contesting definitions of 'integration' in the context of debates about the UK as a multicultural society see Parekh 1990.

[28] See Halstead (1988: 203) for a discussion of the contested definitions of multicultural education and their implications for Islamic schools in the UK.

[29] See for example the column in *The Sun* (19/7/89) entitled 'What the Angry Muslims Want'.

13

Making a Place for Islam in Politics
Local Authorities Dealing with Islamic Associations

Jeroen Feirabend & Jan Rath[1]

Islam is slowly but surely gaining a firm foothold in Europe. Until a few years ago adherents of this global religion were fairly uncommon in this part of the world. During the past decades, however, their numbers have gradually increased and they now constitute living religious communities. A wide range of institutions and organizations has been established for their own benefit, such as praying rooms, schools, businesses, broadcasting associations, libraries and political organizations. Some of these institutions have been established without any direct intervention from the society at large. They have come into being within the Muslim community relatively unnoticed and neither the Muslims themselves nor others have felt it incumbent to demand or arrange formal recognition or regulation by the state. The establishment of other institutions, however, has been accompanied by intervention. At times the state or (semi-)private organizations have taken the initiative to apply or adapt the prevailing laws and regulations. At other times Muslims, striving for treatment on an equal footing with established religions, have taken the first step. On a number of occasions these initiatives have been aimed at receiving material support.

In this paper we focus on this latter form of institutionalization, in other words that which extends to the public domain. We focus, moreover, on the attitudes and actions of the surrounding society. The way in which the institutionalization of Islam takes place depends not only on the attitudes of Muslims themselves, but also on the space granted to Muslims. After all, whether or not the established society enthusiastically supports the demands of Muslims or even goes on ahead of them, or remains uncommitted, or frustrates their materialization makes a world of difference.

Curiously enough the process of making space for Islam has not been systematically examined. Elsewhere a programme of research was presented aiming at filling the gap of sociological knowledge (Rath, Groenendijk & Penninx 1992; see also Rath, Groenendijk & Penninx 1991). This suggested a number of theoretical considerations that should help to structure future research. Here we restrict ourselves to touching on a few points.

To begin with, the authors identified a number of different factors that are assumed theoretically speaking to play a role in decisions about making space for Islam. The *laws and regulations* are one set of factors. They constitute the legal framework within which demands for facilities or (legal) provisions are judged. At the same time they influence, if not shape, the way in which and the extent to which Muslims formulate their demands. A central position within the processes of making space is taken by the *state*. It is obvious that the state is bound by rules, laws and regulations, which basically - but simplistically - mean that the state has to meet the demands of Muslims, provided that they comply with the legal requirements concerned. Also there is the judiciary, a relatively independent institution providing legal security to all citizens. Finally there are numerous *private individuals and organizations* that for a diversity of reasons set themselves up as interested parties and for that reason intervene in the establishment of Islamic institutions. One can think of political parties, trade unions, church organizations, residents' associations, the media, the business community, academia and so on. Hereby a distinction is possible between organizations based on religious principles and other organizations. Together they exert influence on the state and its decisions about the eventual maintenance or amendment of the laws and regulations.

The authors also formulated a number of assumptions about the interrelationship of these factors, especially about the interrelationship of the state on the one hand and the laws and regulations on the other. Although the state - just like any other participant in the political decision-making process - has to conform to the prevailing laws and regulations, thereby applying the principle of equality, the (national) legal framework does not necessarily determine the outcome. This has to do with the fact that the national government sometimes delegates its power to local authorities as part of a policy of decentralization. The latter are assumed to have a better insight of the situation at the local level and can be entitled to decide at its own discretion. The space for Islamic institutions can vary accordingly. Apart from the political organization of the executive, there are ideological factors involved. The room to act within the law is not inherently strict and clear: legal rules can be abstract, broad or ambiguous, while the purpose behind such rules may not be sufficiently evident. Civil servants or politicians who concern themselves with practical politics can in such circumstances use their discretionary powers to make certain decisions. In the sociology of law it is assumed that such cases occur within 'semi-autonomous social fields', i.e. social systems existing between the legislator and individual citizens and producing its own rules (Moore 1973).

All this means that the attitude of the state is not in the least a pure legalistic matter, but one affected by the judgement of actors involved. We have to keep in mind that all these actors for their part are exposed to the influence of other semi-autonomous social fields. External political pressure or struggles between or within departments of the local or national state, for one, can influence the room to act.

Decisions with regard to Islamic institutions are thus not only affected by the legal framework and political circumstances but also by the ideological climate. Here we are talking about opinions, representations and evaluations of society and its members, about the distribution of social resources, about the relationship between the state and citizens, about the permissibility or desirability of cultural diversity, about the social meaning of religion, about Islam and its adherents, as well as the practical conclusions that could be drawn from these. To be sure: these opinions and representations do not need by any means be grounded in the *truth*, whatever that may be. After all, their social significance is merely based on the *idea* that they are true. In practice they help people make sense of the world in which they live, and serve as legitimation for specific actions, in this case decisions about the assignation of space for Islamic institutions. At the same time they also serve as guiding principles for social actions, in other words they suggest ways in which politicians, civil servants and others may use their discretionary powers. These processes take place continuously and are historically specific. Laws and regulations have not always existed in the same form. On the contrary, the present laws and regulations with regard to religion and religious activities are the product of ideological debates that took place in an earlier historical period. As far as the laws and regulations can be regarded as a more or less 'fixed' factor - because their development takes place extremely slowly - contemporary ideological opinions and representations play a role according to the room for manoeuvring within the laws and regulations.

In summary, it may be stated that a profound understanding of the dynamics of the process of institutionalization of Islam, in particular the attitudes and actions of the society at large, can be accomplished by describing and analyzing the laws and regulations and the political decision-making in more 'technical' terms, but also by gaining a clear insight into the ideological positions of the actors concerned, as well as the interrelationship of both phenomena.

Let us now work out these notions in a concrete case, namely how local authorities in the Netherlands deal with Islamic associations. In particular we will examine to what extent, in what form and under what conditions local authorities have allowed Islamic associations to participate in the local decision-making process. This sort of participation can be important for Muslims - in addition to other, more individualized forms of political participation such as the exercising of voting rights (Rath 1988) - since local authorities are in a position to make space for Islamic institutions such as mosques and religious education at primary schools. In the Netherlands there is no legal provision stating that *religious* c.q. *Islamic* associations are natural participants in the local decision-making process. As the law stands Islamic associations cannot demand participation, and nor indeed can any other religious organizations, but they do have a moral right. In Dutch 'pillarized' society it was quite common for the state to deal with religious organizations. Indeed this was part of the politics of accommodation of religious groupings. Today, however, with the pillarized system in decline, the local authorities have rather more freedom to decide whether or not religious c.q. Islamic associations should be co-opted to have a say in local politics.

We have examined this process in two cases, namely in the cities of Rotterdam and Utrecht.[2] These cities were chosen because it was expected that they occupied opposite positions in regard to Islam and Islamic associations, the city of Rotterdam being more supportive of Muslims' demands (Cf. Rath & Meyer 1994). Studying these opposite cases may deepen our insight into the issues concerned.

Rotterdam[3]

Until the early 1980s the local authorities of Rotterdam held a strictly reserved attitude towards Islamic associations, an attitude which contrasted sharply with the one towards secular and often left-wing associations of Mediterranean immigrant workers. The latter were heavily subsidised to cover the costs of accommodation and of social-cultural and educational projects, and were furthermore strongly supported to found an umbrella organization. Through this Platform for Foreigners in Rijnmond (*Platform Buitenlanders Rijnmond* - PBR) immigrant workers were able to channel their demands into the local political arena. Islamic associations, although rooted in the same immigrant communities, were *not* allowed to participate in this PBR. They were looked upon by the Platform-members as strongholds of 'undemocratic' extreme nationalist, if not fascist movements such as the Turkish *Grey Wolves* or the Moroccan *Amicales* (de Graaf 1985: 37). Significantly, the exclusion of Islamic associations was fully in line with the position of the local authorities who had stressed in a memorandum that the establishment of relations with Islamic organizations could endanger the separation of church and state, and that the Grey Wolves and Amicales employed the mosques as a "means of control and even oppression".[4] The result was that secular, left-wing associations were able to monopolise the relations between immigrant communities and the local authorities, leaving Islamic associations outside the local political arena.

In the beginning of the 1980s the municipal civil service - particularly the Migrants Bureau - the bureaucratic department responsible for the development and implementation of the local ethnic minorities policy - started a profound discussion about whether the exclusion of Islamic associations should be tenable any longer. In an internal memorandum on this topic it was argued that many places of worship did not comply with building and fire safety regulations and that the local authorities had to take action. A strict application of the rules, however, would probably have resulted in the closure of many mosques. According to the memorandum, this option was out of the question considering their importance as a meeting place. Instead it was recommended that Islamic associations should be provided with extra "services", for: "(...) mosques are by far the

most important self-organizations. It is important to take mosques seriously and to respect this expression of identity for the sake of the accessibil-
ity of these groupings" (Gemeente Rotterdam 1981).

This resulted in a series of informal exploratory talks between the
alderman (Labour Party, PvdA) of ethnic minorities affairs and a number
of leaders of Islamic associations.

Two years later, in 1983, the Migrants Bureau produced a new memorandum which again, but now with greater emphasis, called for a more
active attitude of the local authorities towards Islamic associations. While
referring to the visits of the alderman to Islamic associations, at which the
latter expressed a strong wish for recognition and support, the memorandum contained a plea for: "(...) co-operation with the groupings that are
nearest to migrants' hearts. For Turks and Moroccans, these are the
mosques."

The memorandum concluded by remarking that: "(...) support, in the
form of service and (limited) subsidy, and recognition of mosques -
implicitly but, if possible, also explicitly - provides us with social partners
in the policy on migrants. This policy is unthinkable without the association or, better, collaboration with the people involved" (Gemeente
Rotterdam 1983).

For the first time the participation of Muslims in the local decision-
making process was explicitly articulated. On September 16, 1983, this
line of policy was unanimously endorsed by the municipal executive
- being the mayor and aldermen, not the entire municipal council.

The civil servants of the Migrants Bureau did not want to simply pay
lip-service to the recognition of Islamic associations, and as a token of
their seriousness, representatives of these associations were invited in 1983
to join the Working Party on Self-Organizations of Immigrants. This
working party was to advise the authorities on the new policy on
subsidising ethnic minority associations. For the first time, Islamic and
secular, if not anti-Islamic, associations of migrant workers had to sit side-
by-side and co-operate. The working party advised - with secular associations against it - to open up the possibility of subsidising social-cultural
activities of Islamic associations.

In April 1984 the Alderman for Special Groups presented the details of
the new line of policy to the municipal executive. He again emphasised

the social importance of Islamic associations, the "extreme isolation" of Muslims and their possible lack of "willingness to integrate". The "extreme isolation" should be reduced and further prevented by the establishment of political relations with Islamic associations in the form of a so-called "critical dialogue". The alderman also proposed granting limited subsidies for costs of accommodation and socio-cultural activities of Islamic associations, provided that these complied with the local ethnic minorities policy : in other words, were aimed at the social integration of ethnic minorities in Dutch society. In so doing Islamic associations would be put on the same footing politically as secular autonomous organizations. The municipal executive initially hesitated to support these proposals on a number of grounds, one being a reluctance to support *religious* organizations, but eventually gave its support to the policy outlined.

With the process of recognition becoming evident, the endorsement of the revised policy by the entire municipal council could no longer be put off. The fact that in the meantime various Islamic associations had submitted applications for concrete projects increased the pressure on the council to make a political stand at last. In March 1985 a majority of the municipal council endorsed the proposed policy, albeit after lengthy discussions. Extreme left-wing parties, such as the then communist and pacifist-socialist parties (CPN resp. PSP), opposed any equation of Islamic associations with secular organizations of immigrants. In the view of the communists, Islamic associations were strongholds of people who sought to protect their own identity and were thus unwilling to merge with the Dutch. The pacifist-socialist and a number of liberal (VVD) councillors argued that the separation of church and state did not allow any subsidising of religious organizations. Both maintained good relations with the left-wing and secular member-organizations of the Platform for Foreigners in Rijnmond. During the debate it appeared that councillors of one and the same party took opposite positions. At the end of the series of debates it was decided that limited block grants would be assigned for socio-cultural activities of Islamic associations, provided that these were not at odds with the municipal policy and contributed to the integration of ethnic minorities.[5]

In the meantime the "critical dialogue" of the local authorities with the leadership of Islamic associations continued. Soon the alderman and his civil servants expressed their need for a representative body of Islamic associations in Rotterdam. In their view the dialogue was complicated by the large number of Islamic associations, their variety and the turnover of participants. It was felt that a more permanent body of consultation would help to overcome these bureaucratic problems. Muslims in Rotterdam (and elsewhere) had taken various initiatives to create an umbrella organization, but so far these attempts had failed. In spring 1988, however, the Cooperating Turkish Mosques Rotterdam (*Samenwerkende Turkse Moskeeën Rotterdam*) presented themselves and invited other, non-Turkish Islamic associations to join their umbrella organization. In June 1988, the multi-ethnic and multi-national Platform for Islamic Associations in Rotterdam (*Stichting Platform Islamitische Organisaties Rotterdam* - SPIOR) was established. The vast majority of Islamic association in Rotterdam eventually joined the SPIOR.[6] Interestingly, the civil servants involved in the "critical dialogue" had been involved in the foundation of the SPIOR, by writing the articles of association and by promoting the funding of SPIOR. Partly due to their commitment, the SPIOR was officially recognized relatively quickly and financially supported by the local authorities.

Nowadays the SPIOR participates in the (informal) Network of Cooperating Organizations from and for Immigrants in Rotterdam, and is consulted by the local authorities in various matters concerning immigrants in general, and mosques and Islamic religious education at public elementary schools in particular. In relation to the eventual establishment of the so-called city-province of Rotterdam, there are plans to formalise this network into an advisory council for immigrants, which would imply the first formalised structure for political participation of immigrants, including Islamic associations, in Rotterdam.

Utrecht[7]

The city of Utrecht has a relatively long-standing tradition of political participation of immigrant workers. As far back as 1973 the local authorities established a separate advisory council through which immigrant workers could voice their interests: the Migrants Council (*Migrantenraad*), the first of its kind in the Netherlands. The political marginality of immigrants was put on the political agenda by the Working Party on International Policy (*Werkgroep Internationaal Beleid*), a working party in which both left-wing immigrants and native Dutch participated. They first and foremost criticized the poor functioning of the welfare foundations - then the Regional Foundation for the Assistance of Foreign Workers, now the Regional Centre for Foreigners - that had been set up in the 1960s to take care of immigrant workers during their time in the Netherlands. They argued that as long as non-Dutch immigrants were disenfranchised an alternative channel for political participation should be available. The Migrants Council would advise the local authorities on various matters concerning immigrants. The proposal to found a council was especially promoted by one member of the Working Party on International Policy who was also a member of the municipal council. The municipal council endorsed the proposal with only the communist party (CPN) opposing it.[8]

Representatives of the various immigrant communities were elected onto the Migrants Council.[9] Some of them were board members of local Islamic associations. Amongst other things, the Migrants Council mediated between the local authorities and Islamic associations in an (unsuccessful) attempt to establish a communal mosque for the Muslims in Utrecht. In October 1978, the Migrants Council was abolished, because the Ministry of Culture, Recreation and Social Affairs had decided to cease funding the council. It is also assumed that links between some members of the council and right-wing extremist organizations as the Grey Wolves and Amicales played a role in the decision to abolish the council.

In 1981 the local authorities established two new advisory councils: the Surinamese-Antilleans Working Party (*Werkgroep Surinamers-Antillianen*) and the Foreign Workers Working Party (*Werkgroep Buitenlandse Werknemers*) in which Mediterranean groupings were represented. The latter consisted of one representative from each national community, and one or two representatives of the regional welfare foundation and civil servants.[10] At the beginning of 1990 both working parties merged into the Ethnic Groups Advisory Council (*Adviesraad Etnische Groepen*). These political bodies did not have a formal position in the policy-making process.

In contrast to the Migrants Council, only subsidized immigrant associations were entitled to membership. In practice, however, only secular, left-wing associations were granted subsidies. Islamic associations were *de facto* denied any subsidy and thus representation in this new advisory council. In 1991, for example, the Turkish Cultural Centre (TCC) tried to gain access to the advisory council. The statutes of this organization did not contain any explicit reference to an Islamic foundation, although this was more or less the case.[11] The application was never formally discussed, officially because the TCC did not meet the condition of structural financial subsidy, but unofficially because the TCC was accused of being a cover organization of the extremist Grey Wolves. The accusation came from a member association of the advisory council, the left-wing *Turkish Democratic Workers Movement* (TDID).

All this meant that non-Islamic left-wing associations were able to monopolize the relations of immigrants with the local authorities, a situation approved of and secured by the local authorities. Oddly enough, the same authorities were sometimes in need of some form of consultation with Muslims. In 1989 for example the *ezan*, the call for prayer, had to be regulated.[12] This required the local authorities to enter into deliberations with Islamic associations. In a number of meetings between the municipal executive and civil servants and the Islamic associations about the *ezan*, Islamic associations expressed the wish to establish a more structural contact with the local authorities. This led in fact to the establishment of the *Islamic Associations Platform (PIO)* and for a while Islamic associations believed that they would finally gain political recognition. However, the platform did not exist for long. On the first and only meeting of the municipal executive and Islamic associations the possibility of financial support for Islamic associations was discussed. The Alderman of Welfare (**Labour Party, PvdA) - the first responsible for the local ethnic minorities policy - just repeated the statement that subsidies for Islamic associations including the Islamic Associations Platform were out of the question, which basically implied that the Islamic Associations Platform would not be viable.

Recently, with the inauguration of the new municipal executive in April 1994 and especially with the inauguration of a new Alderman for Welfare (also Labour Party) slight changes in the attitude towards Islamic associations can be observed. The new alderman seems to have a more open stance towards Islamic associations than her predecessor. This is suggested by her visits to local mosques, but also by the fact that the local authorities have started subsidizing a project located in a mosque and organised by an Islamic association. Now there are even talks about the possible participation of Muslims in a new advisory body for ethnic minorities in Utrecht. Whether Islamic associations will gain the same recognition as they did in Rotterdam, remains to be seen.

Ideological representations of Islam and Muslims in the Netherlands

Above we observed a remarkable difference in the processes of making space for Islam in local politics: the city of Rotterdam has welcomed the participation of Islamic associations in the political decision-making process and even promoted the establishment of a separate political organ through which Muslims can voice their political interests, whereas the city of Utrecht has *de facto* excluded their participation. This has happened within one and the same general legal framework, with regard to Muslims coming from the same regions of origin (predominantly Turkey and Morocco), and under the primary political responsibility of aldermen belonging to the same political party (Labour Party, PvdA). Their attitudes and actions show nevertheless a strong divergence. An explanation for this divergence can possibly be found in the ideological domain - especially in the normative evaluation of real and alleged characteristics ascribed to the people concerned - together with changes in the policy process with regard to immigrant ethnic minorities.

The local authorities of both Rotterdam and Utrecht have acknowledged in general terms the rights of Muslims to participate in local politics. Often, however, this right is conceived primarily as an individual right, Muslims are expected to participate as individuals in the existing political structures, for example as supporters or members of existing political parties. But when it comes to forms of collective participation the 'liberal' attitude changes. An independent Muslim political party for instance is suddenly considered problematic, although no politician would formally question the legitimacy of such a party. The reactions to the possible establishment of such a party in Utrecht in 1993 illustrate this. A councillor for the Christian-democratic party (CDA) in Utrecht sighed: "You cannot forbid anyone to establish a political party, but whether it is a positive development... that I would like to reconsider or discuss. But at some stage you can not withhold it, just as everyone has the right to become a member of a political party, so everyone has the right to establish a political party."

When the political empowerment of Islamic *associations* is at stake a wide variety of opinions about Islam and its adherents are expressed. It is taken for granted that Islamic associations are undemocratic and function as covers for extreme nationalist, if not fascist, political tendencies. Likewise it is assumed that foreign powers interfere in local politics through Islamic associations, and that Muslims, compared to native Dutch, are traditional in the sense that they allow and even expect religious leaders to play a prominent role in politics. It is assumed that political leaders are not elected on the basis of their political capacities, but (self) appointed on the basis of religious capacities. This is judged negatively and considered to be an anachronistic, rather backward way of establishing leadership. This view is expressed by a Christian-democratic councillor in Utrecht: "There are also other ways. There exists something in addition to your imam. I am also a member of a church-community, that community also has a minister. But what I mean is that I will not address myself to him if I have a housing problem. Then I go to the housing department, I do not go to my minister. That is the way things went in the past. I mean those days are gone."

In Rotterdam the local authorities were pleasantly surprised when they could finally deal with "modern" Muslims who, as a high-ranking civil servant put it, "were getting the picture right". These leaders were obviously seen as exceptions. Similarly, in both Rotterdam and Utrecht it was taken for granted that Islamic associations were working under the influence of foreign powers. Oddly enough, in Utrecht this constituted another reason for the political exclusion of Islamic organizations, whereas in Rotterdam this encouraged the authorities to include them in the political process. A civil servant pleaded for financial support for the SPIOR as a means to avoid the interference of foreign powers: "A negative consideration of not providing financial support is - and I mean that without intending to cast doubt upon the integrity of the SPIOR - the eventuality that foreign funds, thus influence from outside, will be playing a role."

By the same token Muslims were regarded as caring little about the highly esteemed separation of church and state in Dutch society. A councillor for the liberal party D'66 in Utrecht argued: "The laws of the Morocco-men are interwoven with their religion, well that is a problem. I do believe that it has to be clear to anyone how Dutch society functions. We keep church and state separated and I consider that an acquired right that should not be changed. And that has to be made very clear towards mosque organizations. Once that is clear, well I think we can live together very well."

By dealing with Islamic organizations the authorities would automatically get caught in the same trap. In Rotterdam and particularly in Utrecht the principle of separating state from church has long been used not to subsidise the activities of Islamic associations. In Rotterdam, however, when dealing with the decision as to whether to subsidise the umbrella-organization SPIOR, the authorities claimed that "the social interests of its followers should not force the state to full non-intervention". The point is that by claiming this the spokesman simply sanctioned the idea that Muslims would have a different attitude in this matter and that dealing with them did bring the principle into jeopardy.

In democratic societies such as the Netherlands it seems logical that local authorities dealing with any organization should apply the constitutional principle of equality. All religious c.q. Islamic organizations should then be treated on equal terms. And since it is assumed that Christian organizations have no direct relations to the policy process - they are neither subsidized nor co-opted[13] - Islamic organizations are likewise excluded. This, however, seems inconsistent with the empirical evidence presented above. Paradoxically this inconsistency does not undermine the political significance of the abstract principle of equality. Contrary to what many people assume, the categories equated do not necessarily need to be religious categories. As a matter of fact, this happened in Rotterdam. In the official discourse Muslims were no longer primarily equated with other religious categories, but with the category of immigrant ethnic minorities. This ideological transformation paved the way for a more supportive attitude towards Islamic associations. During the process of recognition the religious identity of the organizations concerned appeared to be less significant, whereas their compatibility with secular organizations of immigrant ethnic minorities was given greater emphasis. Once Islamic associations became equated with non-Islamic c.q. secular organizations, they became eligible for specific subsidies and participation in the political decision making.

A pragmatic consideration for this change is that Islamic associations reach large numbers of immigrants, who are not reached by secular organizations. Furthermore, there is the fact that the implementation of the local ethnic minorities policy is expected to be better served by collaboration with Islamic associations. In a letter to his colleagues in the municipal executive the Rotterdam Alderman of Special Groups explained that: "In policy-making with regard to migrants, greater and greater interest is attached to the so-called self-organizations as representatives of ethnic minorities. They can become as it were social partners in the process of integration. (...) The predominant form of self-organization is the mosque organization."[14]

So, while the leadership of the Rotterdam Islamic associations considered the recognition by the local authorities an important move in the direction of improvement of the position of Islam in the Netherlands, the local authorities themselves considered it an important move in the direction of integration of ethnic minorities.

Conclusions

During the past decades Muslims in Europe have constituted a number of religious communities. A wide range of institutions has been established on their behalf, prompting intervention by the state and others to regulate the space for such institutions. The process of making space for Islam, however, is not self-evident. Although the state has to conform to the prevailing laws and regulations, thereby applying the constitutional principle of equality, the legal framework does not necessarily determine the outcome: the law is not always strict and clear, but can be abstract, broad or ambiguous, while the purpose behind such rules may not be sufficiently clear. Furthermore, due to the national policy of decentralization, local authorities can have a greater say in the implementation of general rules. This leaves room for political and ideological struggle. Civil servants and politicians involved in practical politics can then use their discretionary powers to 'colour' their decisions.

This explains why the processes of making space for Islam in local politics in the cities of Rotterdam and Utrecht in the Netherlands have such different outcomes. The local authorities of Rotterdam have encouraged and supported the inclusion of Islamic associations in politics, while the authorities of Utrecht have adopted a more exclusionary attitude.

This divergence seems more surprising since advisory bodies are generally considered a legitimate means of political participation and form a commonplace phenomenon in everyday politics in the Netherlands. Yet, the (material and immaterial) support by the local authorities is only optional. Within this relatively 'liberal' legal framework political and ideological factors sometimes play a decisive role. The local authorities of Rotterdam and Utrecht do share a similar ideological representation of Islam and its adherents. This representation revolves around negatively evaluated notions of Islamic collectivism and traditional leadership, and around fears regarding the interference of foreign powers, the absence of democracy, the influence of political extremism, and the undermining of the separation of church and state. The provision of space for Islamic associations in Rotterdam was a political action coupled with changes in the ideological domain in the sense that characteristics associated with Islam were gradually put aside, and that socio- or ethno-cultural characteristics of immigrants came to the fore. The principle of equality was now applied to immigrant ethnic minority groups rather than to religious groups, and was placed within the political framework of the local ethnic minorities policy which aimed at the integration and upward social mobility of immigrant ethnic minorities. Ever since, Islamic associations have been given the opportunity to participate in local politics, if only as ethnic minority associations which means that Islamic associations have not been granted a 'natural' position outside the field of the ethnic minority policy. Furthermore, they have been put in a position in which they have to compete with secular (and often left-wing) organizations of immigrant ethnic minorities for (financial) provisions and political influence. The secular organizations that thus previously monopolised the relations between immigrant communities and the (local) state have been tempted to oppose the participation of Islamic associations amongst others by emphasising the (alleged) Islamic character of these associations, i.e.

their traditionalism, extremism etcetera. Within the present legal, political and ideological framework, this opposition has only had limited effect.

Notes

1   The authors wish to thank Claire Dwyer for her assistance with completing this chapter.
2   An analysis of the national situation is given by Yar 1993.
3   For a more detailed description see also Rath 1993 and Rath & Meyer 1994.
4   In the memorandum *Migrants in Rotterdam* the local authorities emphasized that the Dutch state did not accept "the slightest responsibility, including financial ones, for the church" and that it could never be its intention to give "the Muslim community" preference over other "religious communities". Gemeente Rotterdam 1978: 71-72.
5   *Report on the (public) meeting of the Commission on Co-ordinated Welfare-policy, Welfare-planning, and Special Groups.* Gemeente Rotterdam, March 26, 1985.
6   Only Sunni organizations that support the objectives of SPIOR are entitled to membership. Reijnierse 1992: 13.
7   For a more detailed description see Feirabend 1993.
8   The Ministry of Culture, Recreation and Social Work (CRM) supported the Migrants Council with a 95% grant for the running costs of the secretariat. The additional 5% was sponsored by the local authorities.
9   Jaarverslag Migrantenraad 1974-1975: 15.
10 *Notitie inzake het instellen van een categorale werkgroep 'Buitenlandse Werknemers',* Gemeente Utrecht, Afdeling voor Bedrijfsvoering, Februari 4, 1981.
11 An Islamic Associated is registered at the same address. The treasure of this organization is also the treasurer of the TCC.
12 On March 1, 1988, the Law on public manifestations came into force. This law put the *ezan* on a par with the Christian public calling for prayer. See Groenendijk 1994.
13 This is not entirely true, but that does not matter in the discussion. See for instance Gemeente Utrecht, *Verslag commissie voor welzijn,* d.d. 19 maart 1992.
14 Letter attached to the 1983 memorandum from the Migrants Bureau.

14

Muslim Minorities and Welfare Policy in Three Dutch Cities (1984-1994)

Herman Beck

In the early sixties labour migration to the Netherlands was initiated by Dutch private industry with government approval. Labour migrants were recruited from Mediterranean countries. Among those labour migrants were Muslims, most of whom originated from Turkey and Morocco. In the beginning no particular policy was outlined by the Dutch government with regard to these labour migrants.[1] According to the Dutch government there was no need for a particular policy because the residence of the labour migrants was only supposed to be temporary. It was only concerning matters of lodging and employment that some measures were considered necessary. The then Ministry of Cultural Affairs, Recreation and Welfare Work was put in charge of housing, while the arrangement of employment was considered to be the responsibility of the Ministry for Social Affairs.

During the seventies the residence of the labour migrants turned out to be of a less temporary nature than had been foreseen by the Dutch government. The beginning of the reunion of labour migrant families was one of the indications the labour migrants were planning to stay longer in the Netherlands rather than return to their country of origin. As a result of this unforeseen development the Dutch government was forced to draft a policy in which the notion of the temporary stay of labour migrants in the Netherlands was abandoned. The labour migrants were now counted among the immigrant minorities living in the Netherlands. The Ministry of Cultural Affairs, Recreation and Welfare Work expressed the basic principle of the policy which had to be pursued with regard to the immigrant minorities with the slogan: "integrating while retaining one's own identity".[2] According to the government, this two-track policy was considered to be a happy medium, because on the one hand it brought about the integration of individual members of minority groups into Dutch society, while on the other hand they were given the opportunity to continue to experience their identity within their own circles. The government expected the principle of retaining one's own identity to be helpful for a smooth reintegration of the labour migrant into his country of origin upon his return there.

However, in practice this policy of integration while retaining one's own identity turned out to be manageable only in the so-called 'soft' sector of welfare facilities. In the so-called 'hard' sectors of education, employment and housing, the two tracks of integration and retaining one's own identity were incompatible. The contradiction implied by the basic principle of the policy of "integrating while retaining one's own identity" and the fact that, in 1980, in reply to the *Etnische minderheden* (Ethnic minorities) report of 1979 the government acknowledged that the Netherlands had become an immigration country, resulted in the adjustment of the government policy with regard to ethnic minorities. The government's policy now focused on the emancipation of ethnic minorities, which was to be brought about by removing them from their underprivileged position and by realising a situation of cultural equality in an open multi-ethnic society.

Thus, according to the *Minderhedennota* (Minorities Memorandum) of 1983 this emancipation policy was intended to result in a society " ... in which the members of the minority groups in the Netherlands have an equal position and every opportunity to develop themselves on an individual level as well as on a group level".[3] One of the ways in which the government tried to encourage the emancipation of ethnic minorities was by stimulating the creation of selforganizations, through which ethnic minorities could have a say in government policy. Through this participation in government policy they could extend their social influence. At the same time local governments were credited with a more active and a more important role with regard to the minorities policy in the 1983 central government's *Minorities Memorandum*. In anticipation of this policy, the Minister of the Interior who had been in charge of the co-ordination of the minorities policy since 1979, had introduced a "temporary contribution for additional administrative costs caused by the minorities policy", on the basis of the ordinance of 1981, with the aim of stimulating local governments to develop activities in the framework of minorities policy.

Definition of the problem and method of working

This contribution focuses on the way the minorities welfare policy was developed in three Dutch cities and pursued during the decade after 1983, the year in which the *Minorities Memorandum* was published. After a brief introduction to the three selected Dutch cities, attention will be focused on the policy of the three local governments with regard to the religious needs of Moroccan and Turkish Muslim minorities in their municipalities.

Although the Dutch State is based on the principle of the *duplex ordo*, the division between Church and State and, therefore, its government, basically, does not deal with issues regarding religion, it is acknowledged that religion can be of fundamental significance with regard to the self-image of ethnic minorities both as a group and as individual members of that group. Therefore, religion can be considered to be a part of welfare policy. Apparently, this opinion was implicitly acknowledged by the Dutch government according to the fact that, in 1982, the Ministry of Cultural Affairs, Recreation and Welfare Work established a working group which was charged with the task of advising the government on " ... the need for accommodation where cultural minorities could give shape to their religious experiences, the desirability of government support here and the conditions under which this support could be granted".[4] In 1983 the so-called Waardenburg working group wound up their activities with a report and a policy recommendation. This report was called *Religieuze voorzieningen voor etnische minderheden in Nederland* (Religious Facilities for Ethnic Minorities in the Netherlands). It seems to have had some influence on government policy as is clear from the above mentioned *Minorities Memorandum*, which states that " ... activities of associations organized on a religious basis may be supported with government subsidies pursuant to subsidy rules with regard to facilities of a non-religious nature".[5]

It seems that the Dutch government were willing to grant a role to religion as far as it could contribute to the process of emancipation of minority groups and their individual members. This view created the possibility to subsidize the non-religious activities of associations organized on a religious basis. However, on the other hand, the Dutch government tried to limit the influence of religion as much as possible. By adopting this attitude the Dutch government neglected the fact that many individual members and groups from ethnic minorities considered religion to be of great importance in daily life. That is why the Dutch government was severely criticized, for example in Christian Democrat(ic Appeal) circles, where the remark was made that the fact that " ... religion was a power by which social life was impregnated was beyond the government's range of policy".[6]

This contribution focuses firstly on the way in which the three selected municipalities realized the right of ethnic minorities to have a say in local policy, which originated in the *Minorities Memorandum* of 1983. In which way were the immigrant Muslim minorities given the opportunity to participate in the local minorities welfare policy? Secondly, the minorities policy of the three selected municipalities will be examined on the particular aspect of the religious needs of ethnic minorities. This municipal policy will be compared with the policy recommendation of the Waardenburg working group and the 1983 *Minorities Memorandum*. Was the minorities policy of the three selected cities strictly according to the policy of the central government or can it be said that they developed a policy of their own, in which more attention was paid to the religious needs of the Muslim minority groups in their municipality? In view of the subsidy requests, did the local governments take into account the wishes of the Muslim minorities? Were Muslim minorities in a position to influence decisions because of their participation in the minorities policy?

These questions will be tackled on the basis of policy documents and interviews with officials who were entrusted with the municipal minorities policy, and on the basis of research in the municipal records. This research was focused on the requests for subsidies by Moroccan and Turkish Muslim minorities and on the decisions rejecting or granting the requests.

The three selected Dutch cities

The choice to study the minorities policy of the cities of Gorinchem, Breda and Tilburg was made due to personal circumstances. For the sake of comparison some national figures with regard to the Moroccan and Turkish minorities in the Netherlands will first be given. According to the Netherlands Central Bureau of Statistics (CBS), the Netherlands had approximately 14,394,600 inhabitants in 1984. Among theses 0.74% or 106,440 inhabitants were thought to be Moroccans and 1.08% or 155,300 were Turkish.[7] In 1992 the number of inhabitants in the Netherlands had increased to 15,129,150 including 195,536 Moroccans (1.29%) and approximately 240,810 Turks (1.59%).[8] As far as the three selected cities are concerned the following information can be given. This includes information on the political colour of the municipality and the most important political parties which were represented in the city council and from which the Burgomaster and Aldermen were chosen. After all, in daily municipal practice the Burgomaster and Aldermen are the people who take the initiative in outlining municipal policy.

By 1984, *Gorinchem* had 27,340 inhabitants, among whom were approximately 593 Moroccans (2.16%) and 914 Turks (3.34%). By 1994, the same city had 31,090 inhabitants, among whom were approximately 998 Moroccans (3.21%) and 1,119 Turks (3.59%). During the period under review the City Council had 21 to 23 seats, which were mainly divided among the following political parties: the Labour Party (PvdA), the Christian Democratic Appeal (CDA) and the People's Party for Freedom and Democracy (VVD). These political parties also provided the Aldermen, while the Burgomaster always came from the Labour Party.

By the end of 1984, *Breda* had 118,887 inhabitants, among whom were approximately 1,741 Moroccans (1.46%) and 930 Turks (0.78%). By the end of 1994, the city had 129,968 inhabitants, among whom were approximately 2,332 Moroccans (1.79%) and 1,119 Turks (0.98%).[9] During the period under review the City Council had 39 seats, which were mainly divided among the following political parties: the Christian Democratic Appeal (CDA), the Labour Party (PvdA), the People's Party for Freedom and Democracy (VVD) and the Democrats '66 (D'66). These political parties also provided the Aldermen, and the Burgomaster always came from the People's Party for Freedom and Democracy.

As far as *Tilburg* is concerned, figures are available from 1986 and 1992.[10] In 1986, the city had 151,799 inhabitants, among whom were approximately 1,745 Moroccans (1.14%) and 2,790 Turks (1.83%). By the year 1992, Tilburg had 160,644 inhabitants, among whom were approximately 2,626 Moroccans (1.63%) and 4,265 Turks (2.65%). During the period under review the City Council had 39 seats, which were mainly divided among the following political parties: the Christian Democratic Appeal (CDA), the Labour Party (PvdA), the People's Party for Freedom and Democracy (VVD) and the Democrats '66 (D'66). These political parties also provided the Aldermen, and the Burgomaster always came from the Christian Democratic Appeal.

	Total number of inhabitants	Turks	Moroccans	Burgo-master	Most important parties in the city council	Parties providing the Aldermen
the Netherlands 1984	14,394,600	155,300 = 1.08%	106,400 = 0.74%			
the Netherlands 1992	15,129,150	240,810 = 1.59%	195,536 = 1.29%			
Gorinchem 1984	27,340	914 = 3.34%	593 = 2.16%	PvdA	PvdA, CDA, VVD	PvdA, CDA, VVD
Gorinchem 1994	31,090	1,119 = 3.59%	998 = 3.21%	PvdA	PvdA, CDA, VVD	PvdA, CDA, VVD
Breda 1984	118,887	930 = 0.78%	1,741 = 1.46%	VVD	CDA, PvdA, VVD, D'66	CDA, PvdA, VVD, D'66
Breda 1994	129,968	1,274 = 0.98%	2,332 = 1.79%	VVD	CDA, PvdA, VVD, D'66	CDA, PvdA, VVD, D'66
Tilburg 1986	151,799	2,790 = 1.83%	1,745 = 1.14%	CDA	CDA, PvdA, VVD, D'66	CDA, PvdA, VVD, D'66
Tilburg 1992	160,644	4,265 = 2.65%	2,626 = 1.63%	CDA	CDA, PvdA, VVD, D'66	CDA, PvdA, VVD, D'66

PvdA=Labour Party; CDA=Christian Democratic Appeal; VVD=People's Party for Freedom and Democracy; D'66=Democrats'66

The figures make clear that during the period under research, the number of Moroccans and Turks increased both relatively and in absolute numbers not only in the Netherlands as a whole, but also in the three selected cities. Although it is often, wrongly assumed that *all* Moroccans and Turks in the Netherlands are practising Muslims, it is quite reasonable to suppose that with the increase of Moroccan and Turkish inhabitants in the Netherlands, the number of Muslims also increased. With this growth in the number of Muslims their needs for religious facilities in all probability also grew, which apparently caused them to appeal to a greater extent to the local governments to take measures in matters concerning religious facilities.

The municipal welfare policy with regard to the Muslim minorities

Since the autumn of 1983 the city of Gorinchem possessed a minorities policy document entitled *Beleidsnota "Minderheden in Gorinchem". Beleidsplan ter bevordering van een samenhangend minderhedenbeleid* (Policy Document "Minorities in Gorinchem". Policy plan for the promotion of a consistent minorities policy), which functioned as a guideline for the municipal minorities policy until November 1994. It is acknowledged in this policy document that the municipality of Gorinchem was stimulated to develop activities in the field of minorities policy by the 1981 ordinance of a "temporary contribution for additional administrative costs caused by the minorities policy". The municipality of Gorinchem subscribed to the main objective of the 1983 *Minorities Memorandum*, in which it was stated that " ... the minorities policy aimed at the realization of a society in which the members of immigrant minorities in the Netherlands will have an equal position and every opportunity to develop themselves both on an individual and a group level".[11] The municipality of Gorinchem wanted its ethnic minorities to be involved in its minorities policy so that it would be possible to take their wishes into consideration as well as possible. In order to guarantee the ethnic minorities a say in the realization of a consistent local minorities policy, it was decided in November 1981 to establish a minorities policy committee in which each association of ethnic minorities was represented by one member chosen or appointed from that particular group.

The composition of the minorities policy committee, its term and task were laid down by the 7 September 1982 bye-law of the municipality of Gorinchem.[12] Two main tasks of the Gorinchem minorities policy committee are: (1) to advise, whether requested or not, the city council and the Burgomaster and Aldermen on issues regarding the immigrant inhabitants of the city; and (2) to stimulate individuals and institutions working in the field of ethnic minorities to consult one another and to cooperate with each other.

Initially, under the 7 September 1982 bye-law the minorities policy committee was composed of fifteen voting members, whose number was increased to seventeen voting members under the 25 August 1988 bye-law. The alderman entrusted with the minorities policy was appointed chairman of the committee. Four of its members were chosen from the city council. The other voting members were representatives provided by the different minorities associations and foundations in the municipality of Gorinchem. The term of the voting members of the minorities committee was analogous with the term of the members of the city council. Besides the voting members, the representative of the Stichting Opvang en Begeleiding van Buitenlandse Werknemers (Foundation for the Receiving and Guidance of Foreign Workers) and the representatives of the unions had a voice but not a vote in the minorities policy committee. However, the 25 August 1988 bye-law no longer mentions the representative of the Foundation and the representatives of the unions. The official entrusted with the municipal minorities policy was added as a secretary to the minorities policy committee. For the sake of completeness, it must be mentioned that individual members of ethnic minorities were also able to participate in the regular central and local government bodies for public comment.

As for the 1982 minorities policy committee of the municipality of Gorinchem, both Moroccans and Turks were represented by three associations or foundations.[13] The other representative members of the committee were Greeks and Italians. From the very beginning, the municipality of Gorinchem tried to involve young people and female members of the ethnic minorities in the minorities policy committee. Notably, out of the three Moroccan associations or foundations one was established for young people, while out of the three Turkish associations or foundations one was aimed at young people and one at women. For our topic it is important that of the three Moroccan members of the minorities policy committee, one represented the Moroccan Mosque Foundation, and one represented the Moroccan Association Gorinchem and Environs, which according to its statutes is an Islamic-cultural association. The same was true of the Turkish members, one of whom represented the Turkish-Islamic Mosque Foundation. Apparently, the Gorinchem city council followed the fore-mentioned view of the 1983 *Minorities Memorandum* that activities of associations organized on a religious basis may be supported with government subsidies pursuant to subsidy rules with regard to facilities of a non-religious nature. In the annex to the decision concerning the 'Regulation on the granting of subsidies to organizations with activities in the field of welfare work for minorities' of 20 December 1984, however, it does explicitly state that religious activities are not eligible and that the intended activities must be proven to serve a social-cultural purpose.

The minorities policy committee, set up on the basis of the municipal bye-law on August 26, 1988, included four Turkish representatives, two of which representing Turkish youth organizations, one representing Turkish women and one representing an organization called the Turkish Islamic Foundation. Of the Moroccan community three organizations are still represented in the committee, all three of them Islamic-cultural societies according to their bye-laws, namely the Moroccan Association for Gorinchem and Environs, the Islamic Mosque Foundation for Gorinchem and Environs, and the Moroccan Islamic Association Annour.[14] In 1994 the Gorinchem city council decided to abolish the committee for minorities policy.

The committee for minorities policy did not meet the expectation that it could function as a participation body for ethnic minorities in Gorinchem. Nor did the committee succeed in adequately fulfilling its task of advising the Burgomaster and Aldermen and the city council about matters concerning the immigrant inhabitants of the city and of stimulating individuals and institutions working in the field of ethnic minorities to cooperate with and consult each other. The failure of the committee for minorities policy as an advisory, consultative and participative body can be explained in various ways:

(1) The difference between Moroccans and Turks and the internal discord within each nationality during the decade under review, led to a situation in which specific groups within each nationality preferred to set up an association or foundation of their own to promote their interests, rather than aiming at the common good of the entire minority. After all,

the city council accepted the possibility of appointing representatives for the committee, nominated by incorporated organizations or societies of immigrants that organize social-cultural and educational activities. By registering as an organization or association with the Chamber of Commerce, submitting notarized regulations, groups with different opinions and objectives within an ethnic minority group could try to obtain a seat on the committee for minorities policy. Once they were in, such representatives proved to be more interested in securing subsidies for specific (individual) activities than in serving the interests of the minority which they represented.

Such division was not conducive to procuring goodwill and funds for the benefit of religious needs. In the history of Islam in Gorinchem, one of the clearest instances of the adverse effects of division within an ethnic minority group is the attempt of the Moroccan minority to obtain from the city of Gorinchem a building that could serve as a mosque for the Islamic Moroccan community. The city was prepared to cooperate in finding an adequate building and in issuing the necessary permits. However, the discord between the two Moroccan associations caused the city to withdraw its support, since it did not wish to be involved in the quarrel. The city of Gorinchem then referred to the division between Church and State: religious activities and institutions were not to be subsidized.

(2) In 1986, the introduction of suffrage for members of ethnic minorities for the local elections, on the basis of the revised Constitution of 1983, entitling them to vote and be eligible for election, opened up the way for them to gain more influence and participate further on a municipal level. It was possible to get elected into the city council and thus gain influence and get involved in city politics. In Gorinchem, however, it was not until 1994 that a Moroccan was elected into the city council to represent the left-wing party of "GroenLinks". It is also possible to try and participate by voting for a party that promises, in the event of positive election results, to serve particular interests and undertakes to stand up, for example, for religious needs. The possibility, as a result of the revised suffrage, of gaining more, and more direct, influence on all areas of municipal policy may have diminished the interest in the minorities policy committee, which only covered welfare facilities.

(3) In 1989 the report of *Immigrant Policy* (*Allochtonenbeleid*) of the

Scientific Council for Government Policy was published in which an even stronger emphasis on integration was pleaded. The 'hard' sectors of the minorities policy, such as education, employment and housing, were to be given full priority.[15] Both the national and local governments seemed to share this view. A policy was drafted, centralizing the *ability to manage for oneself* of individual members of minorities, in particular young people and young adults. The policy as a whole is focused on guiding individual members of ethnic minorities towards participation in the labour market. The road towards a position in the labour market runs via training and education. On a local level, the money available for welfare facilities for minorities will therefore diminish. The animation to join the minorities policy committee, which is mainly occupied with welfare facilities for minorities, will therefore decline.

(4) The fact that an incorporated organization or association can directly apply to the local council for subsidies in the area of welfare facilities, makes being on a time and energy consuming participation body like the committee less appealing.

The actual welfare policy which the city council carried out to meet the religious needs of ethnic minorities is reflected by the decisions relating to subsidy requests by organizations and associations. I will come back to these decisions after discussing the municipal policy in the cities of Breda and Tilburg.

Between 1984 and 1994, the cities of Breda and Tilburg did not have any minorities policy committee or advisory board. Initially, at the beginning of the 1980s, the establishment of such a committee or advisory board had been contemplated. However, the idea was abandoned because it was feared that there would be too much emphasis on individual interests and too little attention for more general topics. The minorities policy pursued by both cities was referred to as an *ad hoc* policy. In practice this meant that the Burgomaster and Aldermen outlined the minorities policy to be followed annually and then submitted it to the city council for approval. In the preparation phase of the minorities policy, the councillors responsible for the minorities policy consulted with officials in charge of the minorities policy as well as spokesmen of the major minority groups in their cities. These spokesmen formed part of an informal network in which consultations took place with the major selforganizations of minority groups in Breda and Tilburg. Thus, both cities did set store by closely involving minorities in the preparation of the minorities policy; however, they only worked through an informal network that was to support the contact between local government and minority groups.

From the period under research, no memorandum of the city of Breda is available, detailing the general policy relating to minorities. The relevant municipal policy can be retraced by consulting a large number of separate memoranda, for example in the field of housing, work, education and training and welfare facilities. The city of Tilburg had its *Management Memorandum Minorities Policy Tilburg* (*Kadernota Minderhedenbeleid Tilburg*) of 1994, emphasizing the importance of selforganization of minorities. In this management memorandum, which clearly breathes the spirit of the 1989 report of *Immigrant Policy* (*Allochtonenbeleid*), the stimulation of the integration of minorities into the community of Tilburg is the central aim. Oral statements verified that the city of Breda shared this view. Integration then is understood as " ... the participation of minorities in social organizations/institutions in Tilburg (c.q. Breda) to a similar extent as the native population".[16] The intended participation is impeded by the gap between the autochthonous Dutch majority and the immigrant minorities. This gap is predominantly the result of disadvantages in education and skills, cultural differences and discrimination in various forms. It is thought that this gap may be bridged or at least reduced by stimulating the participation of immigrants in the labour market, aiming especially at teenagers and young adults.[17]

It is clear that, in their minorities policy, the cities of Breda and Tilburg focused on the hard sector of labour. As on the national level, a shift in policy has taken place on a local level, relocating the emphasis from welfare to education and labour in the hope that this might extend the emancipation and participation of minorities within and into Dutch society.

The actual policy that was carried out as appears from the handling of subsidy applications

The policy of the cities of Breda and Tilburg in the area of welfare facilities for minorities must be deduced from the decisions relating to requests for subsidies submitted by Islamic minorities. The minorities policy actually carried out by the city of Gorinchem must be approached in the same way. First it must be stated that all three cities endorse the principle of the division of Church and State. From this point of view, religious activities are not eligible for subsidy. Organizations on an Islamic basis that wish to be eligible for municipal subsidies for minorities, are required - as indeed are all other organizations and associations - to have notarized regulations, and to be registered as an organization, foundation or association with the Chamber of Commerce. Their subsidy requests are only considered if they involve non-religious activities, usually described as social-cultural activities.

The request to subsidize welfare activities was made to the municipality, which referred the request to the official entrusted with the municipal minorities policy. The official judged the request according to the municipal minorities policy and according to the subject involved. Things considered subsidizable were those regarding educational, recreational, social-cultural, organizational and information activities, especially if those activities aimed at stimulating the consciousness-raising of the position and social role of minority groups and promoted the contacts between the ethnic minorities and the autochthonous community. In other words: if the activities could be useful for the integration of ethnic minorities into Dutch society.

The official entrusted with the municipal minorities policy prepared a proposal for the city council (Gorinchem) or for the Director of welfare policy (Breda, Tilburg) with regard to a decision rejecting or granting a request of a minority for subsidy. In daily practice, the official in most cases consulted the minority organization before a decision was taken and asked for further information; or in the case of Gorinchem the minorities policy committee was consulted. However, at this point, the municipal records reveal that a minorities policy can be an exceedingly personal matter especially because there are no fixed standards of judgement.

For example, although basically all requests for subsidizing religious activities were rejected, there are several cases of Islamic women's organizations which made a request for subsidizing activities as part of the Ramadan and the *'Id al-Fitr*, the festival of the breaking of the fast, which is in fact a religious affair. These requests were always granted. Several reasons were given for the positive decision. Firstly, because it was considered a recreational and cultural activity, which was useful to all citizens. By the way, the same argument was used when a request by an Islamic youth organization was granted as part of the *Id al-Adha*, the sacrificial feast. A second reason for the positive decision was the priority given to women and young people of ethnic minority groups. Thirdly, Islamic women were considered to be doubly discriminated as members of ethnic minorities and as females. Finally, in one way or another, although never publicly stated, also the well-known prejudice of the subordination of women to men in Islam (through which they could be considered triply discriminated) also seemed to have some influence when the decision was taken.

Prejudices also seem to play a part in the case of the Foundation of Milli Görüş of Gorinchem. This foundation had notarized regulations and was registered with the Chamber of Commerce. When the foundation made a request to the municipality to subsidize some informational activities, the request was rejected, because the foundation was considered to be an undemocratic, almost fascist organization. After the same foundation had changed its name to Müslüman Gençlik Teşkilati, it made the same request, which was granted!

If its request is rejected, a minority organization has the possibility to call in the committee of objection and appeal. In this way a minority organization is able to a say in local welfare policy, just like all other citizens.

Islam, identity and integration

To Muslims in the Netherlands, Islam is not an unambiguous abstraction.[18] The meaning which Muslims in the Netherlands attribute to Islam depends on practical and social factors such as education, a satisfactory economic and social position, acceptance by Dutch society, the patronizing attitude of authorities in the countries of origin and the wish to stay or to return to their native country.[19] These factors are of great importance for the position awarded to Islam as an element that confirms and gives shape to a migrant's identity in the Dutch situation, which, religiously as well as socially and politically differs considerably from conditions in the countries of origin. Islam as an element that confirms and shapes a migrant's identity can function as a determinant of (1) the singularity identity, (2) the affiliation identity and (3) the consciousness identity.[20] For a Muslim in Dutch society, these different identities determine the choice to identify with a particular person, group or ideal.

The submitted requests for subsidies show that Muslims in the Netherlands award Islam an important role in finding ways in which they could give new shape to their separate identities within Dutch society. A new self-image was necessary to be able to survive as a Muslim in the social and political context of the Netherlands. This is indeed the very aspect which the three city councils might have anticipated in their subsidy policy regarding minorities. The different identities in the new self-image of Muslims in the Netherlands would have stimulated integration. Consciously or unconsciously - probably as a result of the presupposition that Islam would inhibit integration - the three cities in their welfare policy ignored the opportunities which the right to exercise a religion offered for the integration of Muslims in Dutch society. Granting subsidies for religious activities would in fact have been the very thing to have made a positive contribution to the identity and the self-image of Muslims in the Netherlands. Muslims would have felt accepted and received as Muslims into Dutch society. Thus they would have considered themselves full members of the Dutch community.

In the welfare policy as it was carried out by the three cities in the period under discussion, the meaning of Islam as a determinant for identity and, closely related to this, the importance of Islam for the emancipation and integration of immigrant Muslims in Dutch society were not taken into account, despite the possibilities offered by the *Minderhedennota* (Minorities Memorandum) of 1983. A possible cause may be the unsuccessful two-track policy of "integrating while retaining one's own identity", in which the preservation of the own identity was in fact aimed at keeping the immigrant Muslim attuned to his country of origin and not at all to possibilities of integration which offered identity and self-image. In the municipal welfare policy, the recommendation of the *Minderhedennota* (Minorities Memorandum) of 1983 that "In any case ... activities of organizations on a religious basis are eligible for subsidy on the strength of subsidy rules for facilities of a non-religious nature", has always been interpreted quite literally, namely that only applications for facilities of a non-religious nature were eligible for subsidy. However, the recommendation could have been interpreted in the spirit as a possibility of allowing *all* activities, including religious ones, of organizations on a religious basis to be eligible by subsidizing those activities using resources from subsidy schemes for facilities of a non-religious nature. Such an interpretation of the recommendation would rather have met the religious needs of Muslim minorities; in their subsidy request they have already indicated what meaning they attribute to Islam for their well-being in Dutch society. Granting subsidy requests would have been understood as acceptance by Dutch society of the migrant worker with his Muslim identity. The care and solicitude of the Dutch government for the well-being of Muslim members of ethnic minorities, represented by allocating subsidies in a religious field, would decidedly have had a positive effect on integration.

Concluding remarks

1. Depending on the municipality, minority groups can have a say in municipal minorities policy by several ways. Firstly, if available, through participation in a minorities policy committee. Secondly, through informal networks. Thirdly, because since 1986 they are entitled to vote, by participation in local politics. However, the municipal records make clear that, due to the lack of fixed standards of judgement, minorities policy - just like many other aspects of local politics - is based on the personal preference of the alderman who is responsible for the policy relating to minorities, and of the official entrusted with the municipal minorities policy rather than on the participation of minority organizations by having a say in this policy by the ways just mentioned. The Gorinchem minorities committee and informal networks in Breda and Tilburg never really gave an influential voice to Muslim minorities in these three cities in the municipal minorities policy.

2. There was never a minorities policy with clearly formulated and developed objectives. This lack of policy, however, is not typical of minorities policies only, but *mutatis mutandis* also applies to, for example, welfare policies relating to youth work. As far as one can speak of any minorities policy in the three cities, it closely followed the state policy and

no new initiatives or views were developed. Policy makers were not or wished not to be aware of the importance and function of Islam in the day-to-day life of a great number of Muslims in the Netherlands, nor of the role of religion in its emancipating effect on social and cultural aspects of identity and self-image. If, for example, more attention had been paid to the role of the mosque in meeting the religious needs of members of Islamic minorities, a more positive approach to subsidy requests in a religious field would have greatly contributed to the feelings of well-being of Islamic minorities in the Netherlands. Reinforcing these feelings of gratification would have stimulated emancipation and integration.

On the basis of the minorities policy of the three selected cities it is possible to state that local policy makers have failed by strictly adhering to the division between Church and State to use religion as a possibility to stimulate the emancipation and, as a result, the integration of ethnic minorities. The cities clung too scrupulously to the ideology of the division of Church and State, and as a result the meaning of religion in the field of functionality and effectiveness was ignored.

3. If some contribution in the nature of emancipation and integration did result from the welfare policy that was carried out in the three cities, it is to be found in the adaptation to Dutch requirements of subsidy requests by organizations on an Islamic basis. If religious needs may be satisfied and facilities can be obtained by calling them social-cultural, then the applicants are fully prepared to follow the ways of local authorities in formulating such requests.

4. Finally it must be observed that the division among the various Muslim minority organizations, associations and foundations was not conducive to the process of participation and influence of Muslim minorities on the local welfare policy.

Notes

[1] For an overview of the history of the government policy with regard to labour migrants see e.g.: Entzinger 1990, Tinnemans 1994.
[2] For this issue, see e.g.: ACOM 1979: 21ff, Penninx 1979: 148ff.
[3] *Minderhedennota 1983*: 10, as quoted in Smeets 1995: 14.
[4] *Religieuze voorzieningen* 1983: 1.
[5] *Minderhedennota 1983*: 110, quoted in Shadid and P.S. van Koningsveld 1995: 79.
[6] Klop 1982: 527.

[7] *Statistisch zakboek 1985*: 25, 35.

[8] Quoted in Martens and J. Veenman: 45.

[9] Information of De sociografische dienst van de Directie Beleid en Onderzoek van de Gemeente Breda.

[10] *Kadernota Minderhedenbeleid Tilburg* 1994: 4.

[11] *Beleidsnota "Minderheden in Gorinchem"* 1983: 3, 4.

[12] The municipality of Gorinchem followed the structure which also was supported by the Vereniging van Nederlandse Gemeenten (Association of Dutch Municipalities) in its memorandum *Gemeentelijk inspraakbeleid voor minderheden. Een inventariserend onderzoek* (Municipal policy regarding the participation of minorities. A Survey) of August 1982.

[13] Viz.: Moroccan: de Marokkaanse jongerenvereniging (Moroccan Youth Association); Marokkaanse vereniging Gorinchem e.o. (The Moroccan Association of Gorinchem and Environs); Stichting Marokkaanse moskee (the Moroccan Mosque Foundation). Turkish: Turkse jongerenvereniging (Turkish Youth Association); Turkse vrouwenvereniging (Turkish Women's Association); Stichting Turks-Islamitische moskee (the Turkish-Islamic Mosque Foundation).

[14] Viz. Moroccan: De Marokkaanse Vereniging Gorinchem en Omstreken (the Moroccan Association of Gorinchem and Environs); de Stichting Islamitische Moskee Gorinchem en Omstreken (the Islamic Mosque Foundation for Gorinchem and Environs); de Marokkaanse Islamitische Vereniging Annour (the Moroccan Islamic Association Annour).
Turkish: De Turkse Jeugd- en Arbeidersvereniging (the Turkish Youth and Workers Association); de Democratische Turkse Jeugdvereniging (the Democratic Turkish Youth Association); de Turkse Islamitische Stichting (the Turkish Islamic Foundation); de Turkse Vrouwenvereniging (the Turkish Women's Association).

[15] Entzinger 1990: 260-63.

[16] *Management Memorandum Minorities Policy Tilburg* (*Kadernota Minderhedenbeleid Tilburg*) 1994: 6.

[17] *Management Memorandum Minorities Policy Tilburg* (*Kadernota Minderhedenbeleid Tilburg*) 1994: 6.

[18] See e.g. Beck 1992.

[19] See e.g. Beck 1993.

[20] Kim 1994: 18-30.

Bibliography

Abumalham, M. (ed.): *Comunidades islámicas en Europa*. Madrid, ed. Trotta, 1995.

ACOM (Adviescommissie Onderzoek Culturele Minderheden): *Advies onderzoek minderheden*. 's-Gravenhage, Ministerie van Cultuur, Recreatie en Maatschappelijk Werk, 1979.

Agwani, M.S: *Islamic Fundamentalism in India*. New Delhi, 1986.

Ahmad, M: Islamic Fundamentalism in South Asia: The Jama'at-i-Islami and the Tablighi Jamaat. In: M. Marty and S. Appleby (eds.): *Fundamentalism Observed*. Chicago, 1991, pp. 457-530.

Akhtar, S: *Be Careful with Muhammad! The Salman Rushdie Affair*. London, Bellew Publishing, 1989.

Alexander, P: Notes on the "Imago Mundi" of the Book of Jubilees. *Journal of Jewish Studies* 33(1982), 197-213.

Ali, Y: Muslim Women and the Politics of Ethnicity in Northern England. In: Saghal, G. & N. Yuval-Davis (eds.): *Refusing Holy Orders. Women and Fundamentalism in Britain*. London, Virago, 1992.

Allemann, F. (ed.): *Muslime in der Schweiz*. CIBEDO-Dokumentation 27, Frankfurt am Main, CIBEDO, 1986.

Allievi, S: *La sfida dell'immigrazione*. Bologna, EMI, 1991.

--: Organizzazione e potere nel mondo musulmano: il caso della comunità di Milano. In: Waardenburg, J. et al (ed.): *I musulmani nella società europea*. Torino, Edizioni della Fondazione Agnelli, 1994.

--(ed.): *L'occidente di fronte all'islam*. Milano, Franco Angeli, 1995.

--: Données sociales et contexte culturel de l'implantation musulmane. In: Bistolfi, R. & F. Zabbal (eds.): *Islams d'Europe*. Paris, Editions de l'aube, 1995.

Allievi, S., A. Bastenier, A. Battegay, & A. Boubeker: *Médias et minorités ethniques. Le cas de la guerre du Golfe*. Louvain-la-Neuve, Academia-Sybidi, 1992.

Allievi, S. & F. Dassetto: *Il ritorno dell'islam. I musulmani in Italia*. Roma, Edizioni Lavoro, 1993.

Anderson, B: *Imagined Communities. Reflections on the Origin and Spread of Nationalism*. London & New York, Verso, 1991.

Appiah, K.A: Identity, Authenticity, Survival: Multicultural Societies and Social Reproduction. In: Gutmann, A. (ed.): *Multiculturalism. Examining the Politics of Recognition*. Princeton, Princeton University Press, 1994, 149-63.

Aragón, R: Análisis de la situación migratoria en España y perspectivas de futuro. In: Abumalham, M. (ed.): *Comunidades islámicas en Europa*. Madrid, ed. Trotta, 1995, 277ff.

Arbejdsmarkedsstyrelsen.- *At møde barrierer*. København, Arbejdsmarkedsstyrelsen, 1993.

Ayubi, N: *Political Islam. Religion and Politics in the Arab World*. London, Routledge, 1991.

Badrinath, C: *Dharma, India and the World Order*. London and Bonn, 1993.

Balic, S: *Das unbekannte Bosnien. Europa's Bruecke zur islamischen Welt*. Köln, Boeklau, 1992.

Ballard, R: New clothes for the Emperor? The Conceptual Nakedness of the Race Relations Industry in Britain. *New Community* 18:3 (1992), 481-492.

Bamba, A; *Introduction à la connaissance de l'islam et des musulmans dans le pays helvétique: le cas de Genève*. Diplôme de l'Institut Universitaire d'Etudes du Développement, Genève, 1992.

Barcelona Town Hall.- Immigració estrangera a Barcelona. Barcelona, 1993. *Boletín Oficial del Estado* 134(4 de Junio 1992), 18935.

Barth, F: *Ethnic Groups and Boundaries: The Social Organisation of Cultural*

Difference. Oslo, Universitetsforlaget, 1969.

Basset, J.C: Le croissant au pays de la croix fédérale. Musulmans et chrétiens en Suisse. *Islamochristiana* 15 (1989), 121-133.

Baumann, C.P. & C. Jäggi: *Muslime unter uns. Islam in der Schweiz.* Vorwort Hans Küng, Luzern, Rex Verlag, 1991.

Beck, H: De islam als zingevingssysteem voor de moslim in Nederland. In: Vedder, B. a.o. (eds.): *Zin tussen vraag en aanbod. Theologische en wijsgerige beschouwingen over zin.* Tilburg, Tilburg University Press, 1992, 226-239.

--: De islam: belemmering of stimulus voor het proces van eenwording van moslims in Nederland? *Theoretische Geschiedenis* 20:4 (1993), 385-401.

Bekendtgørelse 1972.- *Bekendtgørelse om seksualoplysning.* Bekendtgørelse 1972-06-15, nr. 313.

Bekendtgørelse 1986.- *Bekendtgørelse om slagtning af husdyr.* Bekendtgørelse 1986-03-26, nr. 200.

Belaid, L: Crise algérienne: la (non)réaction des Algériens vivant en France. *Etudes*, April 1995.

Beleidsnota "Minderheden in Gorinchem". Beleidsplan ter bevordering van een samenhangend minderhedenbeleid. Gorinchem, 1983.

Belluati, M., G. Grossi & E. Viglongo: *Mass media e società multietnica.* Milano, Anabasi, 1995.

Benhabib, S: Models of Public Space: Hannah Arendt, the Liberal Tradition and Jurgen Habermas. In: Calhoun, C. (ed.): *Habermas and the Public Sphere.* Cambridge, Massachusetts Institute of Technology Press, 1992.

Betænkning 1154.- *Dyreværnsudvalgets betænkning om dyreværn.* Betænkning 1154, 1988.

Blaise, P: Chemises brunes et fils de l'immigration au conseil communal. *Nouvelle Tribune* 5 December(1994), 6-9.

Blaise, P. & V. de Coorebyter: L'islam et l'école. Anatomie d'une polémique. *Courrier Hebdomadaire* no. 1270-1271, Bruxelles, CRISP, 1990.

Bloemberg, L. & D. Nijhuis: Hindoebasisscholen in Nederland. *Migrantenstudies* 3 (1993), 35-51.

Boer, I: De grens denken: een reflectie op de multiculturele maatschappij. *Krisis* 14 (1994), 25-29.

Bonner, G: *St Augustine of Hippo: Life and Controversies.* London, SCM Press, 1963.

Borrmans, M: Los matrimonios mixtos entre musulmanes y cristianos: perspectiva de pedagogía religiosa. *Encuentros* 32-33 (Nov.-Dec. 1974).

--: Presenza dell'Islam in Italia. In: Ianari, V. (ed.). *L'Islam fra noi. Conoscere una realtà vicina e lontana.* Leumann (To), Elledici, 1992.

Bourdieu, P: *Outline of a Theory of Practice.* Cambridge, Cambridge University Press, 1977.

Bæk Simonsen, J. et al. (eds.): *Islam i skolen.* København, DLH, Københavnerstudier 20 (1994).

Bowman, G: Christian ideology and the image of a holy land: the place of the Jerusalem pilgrimage in various Christianities. In: Eade, J. & M. Sallnow (eds.): *Contesting the Sacred.* London, Routledge, 1991.

Boyer, A: *Le droit des religions en France.* Paris, PUF, 1993.

Braudel, F: *A History of Civilizations.* London, 1994.

Calhoun, C: Introduction: Habermas and the Public Sphere. In: Calhoun, C. (ed.): *Habermas and the Public Sphere.* Cambridge, Massachusetts Institute of Technology Press, 1992.

Cardini, F: *Noi e l'islam*. Bari, Laterza, 1994.

Cáritas Española.- *Inmigrantes. Propuestas para su integración*. Madrid, Cáritas Española, January 1995.

Castro, F: L'islam e il diritto. Tra legge dello stato e legge di Dio. *Orientamenti* 4-5 (1993), 65-75.

CDA: *CDA-document stedelijk migrantenbeleid*. Opgesteld door de CDA-werkgroep Grote Steden in samenwerking met het Intercultureel Beraad. n.pl., 1992.

Celaya, C: La inmigración en el discurso esquivo de los partidos políticos. *Awraq* XIV (1993), 227-250.

Centlivres, P: *Devenir suisse. Adhésion et diversité culturelle des étrangers en Suisse*. Genève, Georg, 1990.

Cesari, J: *Etre musulman en France*. Paris, Karthala, 1994.

Cirkskr 1986-01-13.- *Cirkulæreskrivelse vedrørende indvandrerbørns deltagelse i idrætsundervisning*. Direktoratet for folkeskolen og seminarier m.v. 1986.

Cornelius, A. et al. (eds.): *Controlling Immigration. A Global Perspective*. Stanford University Press, 1994.

Cumper, P: Muslim schools: the implications of the Education Reform Act 1988. *New Community* 16/3(1990), 379-389.

Daniel, N: *The Arabs and Mediaeval Europe*. London, Longman, 1975.

Dassetto, F: Twintig jaar Islam in België. *Islamitische Nieuwsbrief* 2/8 (1990), 15-23.

--: *Musulmans de Belgique, appartenances et organisations*. UCL, Département des Sciences Politiques et sociales, Groupe d'Etudes des Migrations et des Relations Inter-ethniques, 1991.

--: Immigrazione e Islam europeo: superamento dell'etnicità e domande al pluralismo. In: Macioti, M.I. (ed.): *Per una societa multiculturale. L'immigrazione in Italia*. Napoli, Liguori, 1991.

--: *L'islam in Europa*. Edizioni della Fondazione Agnelli, Torino, 1994. Departament de Benestar Social.- Plan interdepartamental d'immigració. Barcelona, 1994.

Dassetto, F. & A. Bastenier: *The organisation of Islam in Belgium*. Research Papers Muslims in Europe 26, Birmingham, Centre for the Study of Islam and Christian-Muslim Relations, Selly Oak College, 1985.

--: *Media U Akbar, confrontations autour d'une manifestation*. CIACO, Louvain-la-Neuve, 1986, p. 106

--: *Europa: nuova frontiera dell'islam*. Roma, Edizioni Lavoro, 1991.

Departament de Treball de la Generalitat de Catalunya.- *Món Laboral*. Barcelona, 1991.

Derrett, J.D.M. et al. (eds.): *Beiträge zum indischem Rechtsdenken*. Wiesbaden, Franz Steiner, 1979.

Det Etiske Råd vedr. Husdyr.- *Udtalelse vedrørende rituelle slagtninger*. 1988.

Dew, F: *The difficult flowering of Surinam: ethnicity and politics in a plural society*. The Hague, Martinus Nijhoff, 1978.

Diop, A.M: Stéréotypes et Stratégies. In: Leveau, R. & G. Kepel (eds.): *Les Musulmans dans la société Française*. Paris, Presses de la Fondation Nationale des Sciences Politiques, 1988, 77-87.

--: Les musulmans négro-africains en France. *Migrations Société* Déc. (1989).

Donaldson, T. (ed.): *Britain's ethnic minorities: An analysis of the Labour Force Survey/ T. Jones*. London, Policy Studies Institute, 1993.

Doorn, J.A.A. van: Tolerantie als taktiek. *Intermediair* 51(1985).

--: Het miskende pluralisme: een herformulering van het minderhedenvraagstuk. In: Cain, G.G. a.o. (eds.): *Etnische minderheden, wetenschap en beleid*. Meppel etc., Boom, 1985[a], 67-96.

D'66: *In goede banen. Een analyse van het verschijnsel migratie.* Stichting Wetenschappelijk Bureau D66. SWB Cahier politiek & cultuur, 2(1993)nr.2.

Dwyer, C: Constructions of Muslim identity and the contesting of power: the debate over Muslim schools in the UK. In: Jackson P. & J. Penrose (eds.): *Constructions of Race, Place and Nation.* London, UCL Press, 1993, 143-159.

Eilschou Holm, N: *En sag for Menneskerettighetsdomstolen.* København, Juristforbundets Forlag, 1980.

Eley, G: Nations, Public and Political Cultures: Placing Habermas in the Nineteenth Century. In: Calhoun, C. (ed.): *Habermas and the Public Sphere.* Cambridge MIT Press, 1992.

Entzinger, H.B: Overheidsbeleid. In: H.B. Entzinger en P.J.J. Stijnen (eds.): *Etnische minderheden in Nederland.* Meppel (etc.), Open Universiteit, 1990, 244-264.

Esposito, J.L. (ed.): *Islam in Asia. Religion, politics, and society.* New York, Oxford University Press 1987.

Etienne, B: *La France et l'Islam.* Paris, Hachette, 1989.

Europarådet.- *De Europæiske Fængselsregler.* Vedtaget af Ministerkomiteen d. 12. februar 1987. Europarådet, 1987.

Felice, de R: *Il fascismo e l'oriente arabi, ebrei e indiani nella politica di Mussolini.* Bologna, Il Mulino, 1988.

Feirabend, J: *Islam in de lokale politiek. De politieke participatie van islamitische organisaties in Utrecht.* Nijmegen, Katholieke Universiteit Nijmegen, Instituut voor Rechtssociologie, 1993.

Fermin, A: Nederlandse politieke stromingen over de multiculturele samenleving. *Tijdschrift Vraagstelling* 2(1994), 49-64.

Ferrari, S. (ed.): *Lo statuto giuridico dell'islam in Europa. Quaderni di diritto e politica ecclesiastica* 1(1996).

Foblets, M.C: *De erkenning en de gelijkstelling van de islam in België: enkele actualiteitsvragen in de afwachting van een definitieve wettelijke regeling.* Recht van de Islam 8, Maastricht, RIMO, 1991.

Fortuyn, W.S.P: *Uw baan staat op de tocht!: de overlegeconomie voorbij.* Utrecht, Bruna, 1995.

Fraser, N: Rethinking the Public Sphere: a Contribution to the Critique of Actually Existing Democracy. In: Calhoun, C. (ed.): *Habermas and the Public Sphere.* Cambridge MIT Press, 1992.

Fundación Cánovas del Castillo.- *El fundamentalismo islámico.* Madrid, Fundación Cánovas del Castillo, 1992.

Gabrieli, F: Storia, cultura e civiltá degli Arabi in Italia. In: Gabrieli, F. & U. Scerrato a.o. (eds.): *Gli Arabi in Italia.* Milano, Garzanti-Scheiwiller, 1989.

Galston, W: *Liberal Purposes, goods, virtues, and diversity in the liberal state.* Cambridge, New York University Press, 1991.

García Hernando, J., J.Mª. Díez Fernández & O. Domínguez: *Los matrimonios mixtos en España.* Madrid, PPC, 1975.

Geisser, V: *Ethnicité et politique dans la France des années 1990.* Etude sur les élites politiques issues des migrations maghrébines. Thèse Institut d'Etudes Politiques d'Aix-en-Provence, 1995, T.2., p. 403-478.

Gemeente Rotterdam: *Nota Migranten in Rotterdam.* Rotterdam, Gemeente Rotterdam, 1978.

--: *Moskeeën.* Rotterdam, Gemeente Rotterdam, Bureau Migranten, 1981.

--: *Moskeegroepen als zelforganisaties.* Rotterdam, Gemeente Rotterdam, 1983.

Gemeentelijk inspraakbeleid voor minderheden. Een inventariserend onderzoek. Nota van de Vereniging van Nederlandse Gemeenten, Den Haag, 1982.

Gerholm, T. and Y.G. Lithman (eds.): *The New Islamic Presence in Western Europe.* London, Mansell, 1988.

Giddens, A: *The Nation-State and Violence.* Berkeley, University of California Press, 1987.

Goering, J: Reclothing the Emperor while Avoiding Ideological Polarisation. *New Community*, January (1993), 336-347.

Gokalp, A. (ed.): *La Turquie en transition: disparités, identités, pouvons.* Paris, Maisonneuve et Larose, 1986.

Gold, D: Organized Hinduism. From Vedic Truth to Hindu Nation. In: Marty, M. and S. Appleby (eds.): *Fundamentalisms Observed.* Chicago, 1991, 531-593.

Gordon, M.M: Toward a general theory of racial and ethnic group relations. In: Glazer, N. & D.P. Moynihan (eds.): *Ethnicity, theory and experience.* Cambridge Mass., 1978, 105-110.

Gowricharn, R.S: *Migranten en het arbeidsvraagstuk in Rotterdam.* Rotterdam, Stichting KROSBE, 1987.

--: Binnen de grenzen. In: Gowricharn, R.S. (red.): *Binnen de grenzen: immigratie, etniciteit en integratie in Nederland.* Utrecht, De Tijdstroom, 1993, 11-19.

Graaf, H. de: *Plaatselijke organisaties van Turken en Marokkanen: Een beschrijving en analyse van de funkties van Turkse en Marokkaanse organisaties in Rotterdam en de Turkse organisaties in zes Brabantse steden.* Den Haag, Nederlands Instituut voor Maatschappelijk Werk Onderzoek (NIMAWO), 1985.

Groenendijk, C.A: De openbare oproep tot gebed. Een voorbeeld van tolerantie van de overheid. *Cultuur en Migratie* 1(1994), 16-26.

Güler, O. & J. van der Heijden: De islamitische school in discussie. *Samenwijs* October (1990), 71-72.

Habermas, J: *Theorie des kommunikativen Handelns.* Frankfurt am Main, Suhrkamp, 1981.

--: *The structural transformation of the public sphere: an inquiry into a category of bourgeois society.* Cambridge Mass., M/T Press, 1989.

--: Struggles for Recognition in the Democratic Constitutional State. In: Taylor, C. a.o. (eds.): *Multiculturalism examining the politics of recognition.* Princeton N.Y. Princeton University Press, 1994.

Haenni, P: Dynamiques sociales et rapport à l'Etat. L'institutionnalisation de l'Islam en Suisse. *Revue Européenne des Migrations Internationales* 10 (1994), 183-198.

Halstead, M: *Education, justice and cultural diversity: an examination of Honeyford affair, 1984-85.* London, Falmer Press, 1988.

Hart, H.L.A: *The Concept of law.* Oxford, Clarendon Press, 1961.

Hira, S: *Er is meer tussen hemel en aarde dan werk en scholing: over emancipatie en etnische identiteit.* Rotterdam, SBWR, 1994.

Hobsbawm, E. and T. Ranger (eds.): *The invention of Tradition.* Cambridge, Cambridge University Press, 1983.

Horsman M. and A. Marshall: *After the Nation-State. Citizens, Tribalism and the New World Disorder.* London, Harper Collins, 1994.

Huntington, Samuel: The Clash of Civilizations? *Foreign Affairs*, Volume 72, No. 3, (1993), 22-49.

IQRA Trust: *Research on Public Attitudes to Islam.* Research Report No. 1. London, 1991.

Jackson, R. & E. Nesbitt: *Hindu Children in Britain.* Stoke-on Trent, Trentham, Books, 1993.

Jaeggi, C: *Türkische Muslime in der Schweiz. Probleme und Chancen der Kultur-begegnung.* Caritas Schweiz, Dokumentation 2/91. Luzern, Caritas, 1991.

Jeffrey, R: *What's Happening to India? Pimjab, ethnic conflict and the test for federalism.* Basingstoke, MacMillan 1994, 2nd edn.

Joly, D: *The Opinions of Mirpuri parents in Saltley, Birmingham, about their children's schooling.* Research Papers in Ethnic Relations (2). Warwick, Centre for Research in Ethnic Relations, University of Warwick, 1986.

--: *Britannia's Crescent: Making a Place for Muslims in British Society.* Aldershot, - Avebury, 1995, 139-162.

Kabbani, R: *Europe's Myths of the Orient: devise and rule.* Basingstoke, Macmillan, 1986.

--: *A Letter to Christendom.* London, Virago, 1989.

Kadernota Minderhedenbeleid Tilburg, Tilburg, 1994.

Karagül, A: *Islamitisch godsdienstonderwijs op de basisschool in Nederland. Theorie en praktijk in vergelijking met enkele Europese en Moslimse landen.* Amsterdam, Centrale Drukkerij UvA, 1994.

Kelsay, J: *Islam and War. A Study in Comparative Ethics.* Louisville/Kentucky etc., John Knox Press, 1993.

Kepel, G: *Les banlieues de l'Islam. Naissance d'une religion en France.* Paris, Editions du Seuil, 1987.

--: *A l'ouest d'Allah.* Paris, Editions du Seuil, 1994.

Kim, Y.-K: *Die Identitätsfrage der Muslime in der Diaspora.* Hildensheim etc., Georg Olms, 1994.

Klink, B. van: De identiteit van Nederland: eigen volk eerst? *Filosofies praktijk* 13, 2 juni (1992), 57-60.

Klop, C.J: De islam in Nederland: angst voor een nieuwe zuil? In: *Christen democratische verkenningen* 11(1982), 526-534.

Knight, K. & U. Hedegus: UK: Arguments for Voluntary-Aided Schools. *Dialogue*, August (1994)7.

Kofoed, J: *Midt i Normalen. Om minoriteter og den nationale idé.* København, DLH, Københavnerstudier i tosprogethed 24, 1994.

Koningsveld, P.S. van: Islam in Europe. In: Esposito, J. (ed.): *Oxford Encyclopedia of the Modern Islamic World.* Vol. 2, New York, 1995, 290-296.

Koninklijk Commissariaat voor het Migrantenbeleid: *Tekenen voor gelijkwaardigheid. Eindrapport van het Koninklijk Commissariaat voor het Migrantenbeleid.* Brussel, INBEL, 1993

Koolen, R: Provincie tikt gemeente op de vingers. Utrecht moet islamitische school toestaan. *Buitenlanders Bulletin* 3(1989), 11.

Kulke, H. and D. Rothermund: *Geschichte Indiens.* Stuttgart etc., Kohlhammer, 1982.

Kymlicka, W: *Liberalism, Community and Culture.* Oxford: Clarendon Press, 1989.

Lagendijk, J. & R. Suudi: Mythen ontrafelen en keuzen maken. De contouren van een progressief migratiebeleid. In: Bot, W., M. van der Linden & R. Went (eds.): *Kritiek. Jaarboek voor socialistische discussie en analyse,* 1993-1994. Utrecht, Stichting Toestanden, 1993, 23-36.

Landman, N: *Van Mat tot Minaret. De institutionalisering van de islam in Nederland.* Amsterdam, VU Uitgeverij, 1992.

Lapidus, I.M: *A History of Islamic Societies.* Cambridge (etc.), Cambridge University Press, 1988.

Leach, E: *Culture & Communication. The logic by which symbols are connected: an introduction to the use of structuralist analysis in social anthropology.*

Cambridge/New York: Cambridge University Press, 1976.

Leman, J: Ontmoeting op het terrein met moslims in België. In: J. Leman (ed.): *De integratie van de islam in België anno 1993*. Reeks Cultuur & Migratie 1992-2, Brussel, 1992, 7-24.

Leman, J., M. Renaerts & D. van den Bulck: *Islam en islamitisch recht in België*. Recht van de Islam 10, Maastricht, RIMO, 1992a.

--: De rechtspositie van de Islamitische Praxis in België. In: J. Leman (red.): *De integratie van de islam in België anno 1993*. Reeks Cultuur & Migratie 1992-2, Brussel, 1992b, 43-78.

Linhart, D: *L'établi*. Paris, Ed. Ouvrières, 1973.

List, G.A. van der: *Preadvies allochtonenbeleid*. Prof. Mr. B.M. Telderstichting, Den Haag, 1992.

Long, G: *Le confessioni religiose "diverse dalla cattolica"*. Bologna, Il Mulino, 1991.

López, B. & others: *Inmigración magrebí en España. El retorno de los moriscos*. Madrid, ed. MAPFRE 1993.

Lov om Folkeskolen 1993-06-30-L.509.

Luca Cavalli-Sforza, L., a.o: *The History and Geography of Human Genes*. Princeton University Press, 1994.

Lucrezio-Monticelli, G: L'appartenenza religiosa degli imigrati esteri in Italia. In: Di Liegro, L. & F. Pittau (eds.): *Per conoscere l'Islam. Cristiani e musulmani nel mondo di oggi*. Casale Monferrato, Piemme, 1991.

Lijphart, A: *The politics of accommodation: pluralism and democracy in The Netherlands*. Berkeley, University of California Press, 1968.

Maalouf, A: *The Crusades through Arab Eyes*. London, Al Saqi Books, 1984.

MacIntyre, A: Epistemological Crises, Dramatic Narrative and the Philosophy of Science. *The Monist* 60 (1977), 453-472.

--: *After Virtue. A study in moral theory*. London, Duckworth, 1981.

--: *Whose Justice? Which Rationality?* London, Duckworth, 1988.

--: A Partial Response to My Critics. In: Horton, J. & S. Mendus (eds.): *After MacIntyre. Critical perspectives on the work of Alasdain MacIntyre*. Cambridge etc., Polity Press, 1994.

Malcolm, N: *Bosnia*. London, MacMillan, 1994.

Mardones, J. Mª: *Las nuevas formas de la religión*. Estella, 1994.

Marletti, C. (ed.): *Televisione e islam. Immagini e stereotipi dell'islam nella comunicazione italiana*. Torino, Nuova Eri, 1995.

Martens, E.P. en J. Veenman: De positie van etnische minderheden in de Nederlandse samenleving: een statistisch overzicht: In: Smeets, H.M.A.G., E.P. Martens en J. Veenman, *Jaarboek Minderheden 1995*. Houten etc.: Bohn Stafleu Van Loghum, 1995, 43-92.

Martínez Montávez, P: *Al-Andalus, España, en la literatura árabe contemporánea*. Madrid, Etitorial MAPFRE, 1992.

--: *Pensando en la Historia de los Arabes*. Madrid, ed. Cantarabia, 1995.

Marty, M.E. and R. Scott Appleby (eds.): *Fundamentalisms Observed*. Chicago, The University of Chicago Press, 1991.

McCarthy, T: Practical Discourse: On the Relation of Morality to Politics. In: Calhoun, C. (ed.): *Habermas and the Public Sphere*. Cambridge Mass. MIT Press, 1992.

Mernissi, F: *Islam and Democracy*. London, Virago, 1993.

Middendorp, C.P: *Ontzuiling, politisering en restauratie in Nederland: progressiviteit en conservatisme in de jaren zestig en zeventig*. Meppel, Boom, 1979.

Middleton, G: *Lugbara Religion. Ritual and authority among an East African people*.

London: Oxford University Press, 1960.

Ministry of Justice.- *Acuerdos de Cooperación del Estado español con La Federación de Entidades Religiosas Evangélicas de España, La Federación de Comunidades Israelitas de España y La Comisión Islámica de España*. Madrid, Ministry of Justice, 1992.

Mira, E. & Racionero, L. & Trías, E: *El Mediterráneo, entre Europa y el Islam*. Valencia, 1991.

Modood, T: Establishment, Multiculturalism and British Citizenship. *Political Quarterly* 65:1(1994), 53-73.

Modood, T., S. Beishon & V. Satnam: *Changing Ethnic Identities*. London, Policy Studies Institute, 1994.

Mohr, V: Matrimonios mixtos. *Encuentros* 70(Feb. 1978).

Moore, S.F: Law and social change. The semi-autonomous social field as an appropriate subject of study. *Law and Society Review*, 7(1973), 719-746.

Mulder, L: Multiculturele samenleving: pluriforme ontvangstvrijheid. *Nederlands Juristenblad* 69, 8(25 febr.)(1994), 259-260.

Mungra, G: *Hindoestaanse gezinnen in Nederland*. Leiden, COMT, 1990.

--: Hindostanen in de lift. In: Gowricharn, R.S. (red.): *Binnen de grenzen: immigratie, etniciteit en integratie in Nederland*. Utrecht, De Tijdstroom, 1993, 113-125.

Mussolini, B: *Scritti e discorsi dal 1927 al 1928*. Milano, Hoepli, 1934.

--: *Scritti e discorsi dal Novembre 1936 al Maggio 1938*. Milano, Hoepli, 1938.

Nederlands Blok: *Islamieten in Nederland: Integratie of marginalisering?* Utrecht, 1994.

Nielsen, J.S: *Muslims in Western Europe*. Edinburgh, Edinburgh University Press, 1992.

Office fédéral de la statistique, - *Recensement fédéral de la population 1990*. Berne, Office Fédéral de la Statistique, Section de la structure de la population et des ménages (Feuilles 2.002-00.01 à 2.002-00.03).

Onderwijsraad: *Advies van de Onderwijsraad over de opleiding van islamitische geestelijken (imams) in relatie tot het voortgezet onderwijs*. Den Haag, 1994.

Oommen, T.K: Religious Nationalism and Democratic Polity. The Indian Case. *Sociology of Religion*. vol. 55, 4 (1994),pp. 455-472.

Paolucci, G: Bozza di Intesa tra la Repubblica Italiana e l'Unione delle Comunità ed Organizzazioni Islamiche in Italia. *Dimensioni dello sviluppo* 1(1993), 175-193.

Parekh, B: Britain and the Social Logic of Pluralism. *Britain: A Plural Society*. CRE Discussion Papers 3(990), 58-76.

--: Superior People: the Narrowness of Liberalism form Mill to Rawls. *Times Literary Supplement*, 25 February 1994.

Pedersen, L: Islam i Vesteuropa. Islams institutionalisering og synliggørelse. In: Dybbroe, S. et al (eds.): *Klaus Khân Bâbâ*. Aarhus, Aarhus Universitetsforlag, 1991, 113-32.

--: *Nyere islamiske bevægelser i Vesteuropa. - En analyse af det kulturelle nybrud som islamismen repræsenterer blandt de indvandrede muslimske minoriteter i Vesteeuropa*. Aarhus University, Dept. of Social Anthropology, 1993. (Under revision).

Penninx, R: *Naar een algemeen etnisch minderhedenbeleid? Schets van de sociale positie in Nederland van Molukkers, Surinaamse en Antilliaanse Nederlanders en mediterrane werknemers en een inventarisatie van het Nederlandse overheidsbeleid*. Voorstudie bij het WRR Rapport 17 (1979), *Etnische minderheden. Rapporten aan de regering*. Den Haag, 1979.

Plumwood, V: *Feminism and the Mastery of Nature*. London New York, Routledge 1993.

Poliakov, L: *The Aryan Myth: a history of racist and nationalist ideas in Europe*. London, Heinemann, for Sussex University Press, 1974.

Praag, C.S. van: Bolkestein tegen de rest. *Socialisme en Democratie* 49, 10(1992), 409-417.

Procee, H: *Over de grenzen van culturen. Voorbij universalisme en relativisme.* Meppel, 1991.

--: Pluralisme in (re)actie. *Comenius* 49(1993) 56-69.

Pronk, J: *De kritische grens. Beschouwingen over tweespalt en orde.* Amsterdam, Prometheus, 1994.

Pulsfort, E: *Was ist los in der indischen Welt.* Freiburg/Br., 1993.

Pulsfort, P: *Indien am Scheideweg zwischen Säkularismus und Fundamentalismus.* Würzburg etc., Oros-Verlag, 1991.

Pumares Fernández, P: *La inmigración magrebí en la Comunidad de Madrid.* (Ph.D. Diss.), Madrid, 1994.

PvdA: *Kansen geven en kansen grijpen. Migranten in de Nederlandse Samenleving. Standpunten van de PvdA.* Den Haag: Tweede kamerfractie PvdA, 1992.

PvdA-Verkenningen: *Immigratie: Waar ligt de grens?* Amsterdam, Partij van de Arbeid, 1993.

Ramadan, T: *Les musulmans dans la laïcité. Responsabilités et droits des musulmans dans les sociétés occidentales.* Lyon, Ed. Tawhid, 1994.

Ramsoedh, H. en L. Bloemberg: *The institutionalization of Hinduism in Suriname and Guyana.* Department of Human Geography, Amsterdam, University of Amsterdam; Paramaribo, Leo Victor, 1995.

Rath, J: Political action of immigrants in the Netherlands: class or ethnicity? *European Journal of Political Research* 16(1988), 623-644.

--: The ideological representation of migrant workers in Europe. A matter of racialisation only? In: Wrench, J. & J. Solomos (eds.): *Racism and migration in Western Europe.* Oxford/Providence, Berg, 1993, 215-232.

Rath, J., K. Groenendijk & R. Penninx: The recognition and institutionalisation of Islam in Belgium, Great Britain and the Netherlands. *New Community* 18/1(1991), 101-114.

--: Nederland en de islam. Een programma van onderzoek. *Migrantenstudies* 8 (1992), 18-37.

Rath, J. & A. Meyer: Ruimte voor islamitisch godsdienstonderwijs op openbare scholen. *Migrantenstudies* 10(1994), 33-53.

Rawls, J: *A Theory of Justice.* London, Oxford University Press, 1973.

--: *Political Liberalism.* New York, Columbia University Press, 1993.

Religieuze voorzieningen voor etnische minderheden in Nederland. Rapport tevens beleidsadvies van de niet-ambtelijke werkgroep ad hoc. (under the chairmanship of J.D.J. Waardenburg) Rijswijk, Ministerie van Welzijn, Volksgezondheid en Cultuur, 1983.

Reijnierse, W. (red.): *Almanak 1992/1993.* Rotterdam: SWBR 1992.

Riccardi, A: Il mondo musulmano in Italia. *Comunitá di Sant'Egidio: Cristianesimo e Islam. L'amicizia possibile.* Brescia, Morcelliana, 1989.

Roosblad, J: Het politieke discours rond de vestiging van een dependance van een islamitische basisschool in Amsterdam. In: Hampsink, R. & J. Roosblad (eds.): *Nederland en de islam.* Nijmegen. Katholieke Universiteit Nijmegen, Instituut voor Rechtssociologie, 1992, 53-126.

Roovers, W. & W. van Esch: *Islamitisch godsdienstonderwijs in Nederland, Engeland, Duitsland en België.* Nijmegen, ITS, 1987.

Ross, M.H: *The Management of Conflict.* New Haven (etc.) Yale University Press, 1993.

Sahgal, G. & N Yuval-Davis: Refusing Holy Orders. Women Against Fundamentalism.

Newsletter No. 1, November 1990, 2-3.
--: Fundamentalism, Multiculturalism and Women in Britain. In: G. Sahgal & N. Yuval-Davis (eds.): *Refusing Holy Orders. Women and fundamentalism in Britain.* London, Virago, 1992, 1-25.
--(eds.): *Refusing Holy Orders. Women and fundamentalism in Britain.* London, Virago, 1992.
Said, E.W: *Orientalism.* New York, Pantheon Books, 1978.
--: *Covering Islam. How the Media and the Experts Determine How We See the Rest of the World.* London, Routledge & Kegan Paul, 1981.
Salemink, T.A.M: Politieke partijen en de migranten. *Christen Democratische Verkenningen* 13, 12(1993), 488-498.
Samman, M.A. al-: *Mihnat al-aqalliyyât al-muslima fi al-'âlam.* Cairo, 1987.
Sarwar, G: *British Muslims and Schools.* London, Muslim Educational Trust, 1994.
Schacht, J: *An Introduction to Islamic Law.* Oxford, Clarendon Press 1964 (reprint 1974).
Schiffauer, W: Migration and Religiousness. In: Gerholm, T. & Y.G. Lithman (eds.): *The New Islamic Presence in Western Europe.* London etc. Mansell Publishing Ltd., 1988, 146-58.
Schlesinger, A.M. Jr: *The Disuniting of America. Reflections on a Multicultural Society.* New York, Norton, 1992.
Schmidt di Friedberg, O: *Islam, solidarietá e lavoro.* Torino, Edizioni della Fondazione Agnelli, 1994.
Schnapper, D: La citoyenneté à l'épreuve: les musulmans pendant la guerre du Golfe. *Revue Française de Science Politique,* vol. 43 n°2(1993).
Schwenke, H.J: Schoolstrijd in Den Haag: verandering in de religieuze cultuur van Surinaamse Hindoes in den Haag. *Migrantenstudies* 2(1994) 97-110.
Shadid, W.A.R. en P.S. Koningsveld: Integratie of verzuiling: Islamitisch godsdienstonderwijs of een eigen bijzondere school? *Samenwijs* febr. (1988), 2-3.
--: Bijzondere scholen voor etnische groepen in de locale politiek. *Samenwijs,* 9/5(1989), 155 & 169-170.
--: *Moslims in Nederland. Minderheden en religie in een multiculturele samenleving.* Alphen aan den Rijn, Samsom Stafleu, 1990.
--: *De mythe van het islamitische gevaar. Hindernissen bij integratie.* Kampen, Kok, 1992, 1995².
--: *Religious freedom and the position of islam in Western Europe. Opportunities and obstacles in the acquisition of equal rights.* Kampen, Kok Pharos, 1995.
Sharma, A. (ed.): *Our Religions.* San Francisco, 1993.
Shaw, A: *A Pakistani Community in Britain.* Oxford etc., Basil Blackwell, 1988.
Sikkes, R: Emancipatie of isolement. Buitenlanders stichten eigen school omdat bestaande onderwijs tekort schiet. *Het Schoolblad* 2(1989), 26-29.
Smeets, H.M.A.G: Beleidsontwikkelingen. In: *Jaarboek Minderheden 1995,* Houten etc., 1995, 11-42
Statistisch zakboek 1985 van het Centraal Bureau voor de Statistiek. 's-Gravenhage, 1985.
Struijs, A: Wie moet zich aanpassen aan wie? Over onderwijs, eigenheid en de vraag naar integratie in een multiculturele samenleving. *Filosofie & Praktijk* 14(1993) 5-18.
Stuurman, S: *Verzuiling, kapitalisme en patriarchaat: aspecten van de ontwikkeling van de moderne staat in Nederland.* Nijmegen, SUN, 1983.
Swaan, A. de: Sociale voorwaarden voor een multiculturele samenleving. *Jeugd en samenleving* 22:1, 1992, 15-24.
Tamarant, H. & Omar: Geschiedenis van de erkenning van de Islam in België: of hoe

men van alle markten thuiskomt. *Islamitische Nieuwsbrief* 2:5(1990), 3-8.

Taylor, C. & A. Gutmann (eds.): *The Politics of Recognition*. New York, Princeton University Press, 1991.

--: *Multiculturalism. Examining the politics of recognition*. Princeton N.Y, Princeton University Press, 1994.

Tennekes, J: Nederland een multiculturele samenleving? *Migrantenstudies* nr. 3(1986).

--: Cultuurrelativisme in een multiculturele samenleving. *Wijsgerig Perspectief* 27 (1986/7)-4.

Tennekes, J. & A.W. Musschenga: Minderheden: Dilemma's van een pluralistische samenleving. *Filosofie en Praktijk* 3(1984), 113-128.

Teunissen, J: Basisscholen op islamitische en hindoeïstische grondslag. *Migrantenstudies* 6/2(1990), 45-57.

Thurlings, J.M.G: *De wankele zuil: Nederlandse katholieken tussen assimilatie en pluralisme*. Nijmegen, Dekker & Van de Vegt, 1971.

Tibi, B: *Islam and the Cultural Accommodation of Social Change*. Boulder Colorado, Westview Press, 1990.

--: *Im Schatten Allahs. Der Islam und die Menschenrechte*. München, Piper, 1994[a].

--: Die Zerstörung des Religionsfriedens auf dem Balkan, in: *Universitas*. vol. 49,3, 1994[b], 205-215.

--: *Krieg der Zivilisationen. Politik und Religion zwischen Vernunft und Fundamentalismus*. Hamburg, Hoffmann und Campe, 1995[a].

--: Kein Modell für Europa. Das Beispiel Indien. *Die Politische Meinung*. Vol. 40, 312 (November 1995[b]), 79-85.

--: *Der religiöse Fundamentalismus*. Mannheim, 1995[c].

--: War and Peace in Islam. In: T. Nardin (ed.): *The Ethics of War and Peace*. Princeton University Press, Princeton N.Y., 1996 (forthcoming).

Tinnemans, W: 'Denkend aan Holland.....'. *Discussienota Groenlinks over migrantenbeleid*. Amsterdam, GroenLinks, 1993.

--: *Een gouden armband. Een geschiedenis van mediterrane immigranten in Nederland (1945-1994)*. Utrecht, Nederlands Centrum Buitenlanders, 1994.

Tornos, A. & R. Aparicio: *¿Quién es creyente en España hoy?* Madrid, 1995.

Tschannen, R; Islam in der Schweiz - ein geschichtlicher Rückblick. *Der Islam* 72 (1982), 12-19.

UKACIA (United Kingdom Action Committee on Islamic Affairs): *The Need for Reform: Muslims and the Law in Multi-Faith Britain*. London, 1993.

Valencia, R: Acerca de las comunidades musulmanas en Andalucía occidental. In: Abumalham, M. (ed.): *Comunidades islámicas en Europa*. Madrid, ed. Trotta, 1995, 175-188.

--: El cementerio musulmán de Sevilla. *'Ilu. Revista de Ciencias de las Religiones*, 0 (1995), 239.

Vega, C: Matrimonios mixtos en España. *Encuentro* 85(May 1979).

Verkiezingsprogramma's 1994. Verkiezingen voor de Tweede Kamer der Staten-Generaal, 3 mei 1994. Bijeengebracht door het Documentatiecentrum Nederlandse Politieke Partijen te Groningen en van een register voorzien door I. Lipschits. Groningen: Documentatiecentrum Nederlandse Politieke Partijen/'s-Gravenhage: SDU uitgeverij Koninginnegracht, 1994.

Vertovec, S. & C. Peach (eds.): *Islam in Europe. The Politics of Religion and Community*. London, University College London Press, 1995.

Voll, K: Chapter on India. In: T. Meyer (ed.): *Fundamentalismus in der modernen Welt. Die Internationale der Unvernunft*. Frankfurt/M, Suhrkamp 1989, 155-192.

Wagtendonk, K: Islamic schools and Islamic religious education. A comparison between Holland and other West European countries. In: Shadid, W.A.R. & P.S. van Koningsveld (eds.): *The integration of Islam and Hinduism in Western Europe*. Kampen, Kok Pharos, 1991, 154-173

Wardekker, W., S. Miedema & H. Baartman: Praktijken en theorieën van multi-culturaliteit. Introductie op het thema. *Canemus* 49(1993), 3-8.

Wassink, H: Leve de verzuiling. *Intermediair* 17 januari 1992.

Webster, R: *A Brief History of Blasphemy: Liberalism, Censorship and the "Satanic Verses"*. Southwold, Orwell Press,1990.

Weldon, F: *Sacred Cows*. London, Chatto and Windus, 1989.

Willemsen, G. & K. Nimako: Multiculturalisme, verzuilde samenleving en verzorgingsstaat. Naar een pluralistische democratie. In: Pas, G. (red.): *Achter de coulissen. Gedachten over de multi-etnische samenleving*. Amsterdam, Wetenschappelijk Bureau GroenLinks, 1993.

Wihtol de Wenden, C: Trade Unions, Islam and Immigration: Immigrants at work. *Economic and Industrial Democracy* 9 n°1(1988).

--: L'Islam en France. *Regards sur l'Actualité* n°158, Feb. 1990.

--: Les beurs et la guerre. *Esprit/Les Cahiers de l'Orient*, June 1991.

--: L'immigration maghrébine dans l'imaginaire politique français. In: Etienne, B: *L'Islam en France. Islam, état et société*. Paris, Presses du CNRS, 1991.

--: Discours sur l'Islam, Musulmans en terre d'Europe. Special issue, *Projet*, autumn 1992.

Wihtol de Wenden, C. & Z. Daoud: Banlieues: Intégration ou Exclusion? *Panoramiques* 4e trimestre 1993.

Yar, H: *Om de plaats van de Islam. Een studie naar de opstelling van de Belgische en de Nederlandse nationale overheden inzake de institutionalisering van de islam*. MA Thesis Political Sciences. Amsterdam, Vrije Universiteit Amsterdam, 1993.

Zahn, E: *Regenten, rebellen en reformatoren: een visie op Nederland en Nederlanders*. Amsterdam, Contact, 1991.